Bloomsbury CPD Library: Middle Leadership

By Paul K. Ainsworth

BLOOMSBURY

LONDON • OXFORD • NEW YORK • NEW DELHI • SYDNEY

Bloomsbury Education
An imprint of Bloomsbury Publishing Plc

50 Bedford Square
London
WC1B 3DP
UK

1385 Broadway
New York
NY 10018
USA

www.bloomsbury.com

Bloomsbury is a registered trademark of Bloomsbury Publishing Plc

First published 2016

British Library Cataloguing-in-Publication Data
A catalogue record for this book is available from the British Library.

ISBN: PB: 978-1-4729-1073-8
ePub: 978-1-4729-1075-2
ePDF: 978-1-4729-1074-5

Library of Congress Cataloging-in-Publication Data
A catalog record for this book is available from the Library of Congress.

10 9 8 7 6 5 4 3 2 1

Typeset by Integra Software Services Pvt. Ltd.
Printed and bound by CPI Group (UK) Ltd, Croydon, CR0 4YY

Contents

Acknowledgments

Writing a book is a journey, and this journey has been the longest and most challenging of my writing career.

I do not normally name people in my dedication, but on this occasion I wish to give my sincerest thanks to Mr Terry Allcott and Dr Martin Fussey for all of their support, without which this book would not be here.

As ever I thank my family, C, J and S for all you have done and your patience when the skies have been dark.

Thank you to J for all your generosity, sharing of ideas, writing help and the encouragement to keep going.

To H and all my other colleagues at Bloomsbury who have worked so hard in turning my manuscript into the final book.

Thank you to the series editor Sarah Findlater.

Finally to you as an aspiring middle leader, you really do make the difference in your school and for the children within it. I wish you well on your journey.

Introduction

In any school there are many types of leadership. You have bought this book because you want to become a middle leader or perhaps improve your middle leadership. Yet whether you are starting out as a middle leader, progressing to senior leadership or reaching executive leadership, there are always five stages of successful school leadership:

1. Prepare
2. Apply and obtain
3. First steps
4. Learn
5. Enjoy

The very best leaders will carefully work through these five stages so that they become a truly successful leader, reflecting on their progress. Wherever you are, on your middle leadership journey, these five steps will help you overcome the challenges and barriers that you may face.

Why become a middle leader?

Do you want to become the engine room of change in your school? Can you be the player manager who truly makes a difference to your team? These are both descriptions of being middle leaders and highlight that as a middle leader you can really move a school forwards. If you are looking for advice on becoming a middle leader or you want to be able to perform your current role even better, this is the book for you.

Where are you in your career at the moment? Have you been teaching for a few years, are looking for a fresh challenge and see the role of a middle leader as the next logical step in your career? Have you fallen into the role because a vacancy arose in your current school? Perhaps you wish to increase your salary, though you'll hear some voices in the staffroom say if this is your main motivation, you may quickly find that it is not enough. Or do you have a clear career plan which maps out the roles you wish to have, the length of time you wish to undertake them for leading to your long-term ambition. If you haven't, why not keep this in mind whilst you are reading.

What you must not forget though as you read this book is that the key to becoming a very effective middle leader is to ensure that you are the very best teacher that you can possibly be. Remember, just like the player manager, you are judged on your performance in the classroom as well as for leading your team.

Who are middle leaders?

A simple answer could be the people in your school who have leadership roles but are not members of the senior leadership team. Some middle leaders focus on the curriculum and are devoted to a certain subject or range of subjects. There are those such as heads of year who deal with pastoral issues and consider the behaviour and safety of pupils. There may also be co-ordinators of certain initiatives with roles that cross over curriculum and pastoral borders.

If you are the engine room of school improvement, what does this mean? Senior leaders may develop whole-school initiatives but it will be you, as a middle leader, who will translate the idea into practice by implementing it in your own classroom and those of the teachers you lead.

When I was a middle leader I preferred the 'player manager' analogy. I was always aware that I was responsible for leading a group of staff, improving their performance and deploying them in the most effective way, yet due to the number of lessons I delivered, I would still predominantly be judged on my performance in the classroom, whether this was on attainment, progress or the quality of my teaching and learning.

Undoubtedly the focus is now on leadership rather than management. You need to ask yourself: can you make a difference beyond your own classroom and are you gaining skills so that you have the ability to lead staff in improving the quality of teaching and learning in a particular area? If you are looking for the key difference between being a middle leader and a senior leader, it is as a middle leader you will be affecting change in one area of the school whereas senior leaders should be making improvements that stretch across the whole school, across a range of subject areas or year groups.

What will I get paid?

Middle leaders are also referred to as TLR holders. A TLR is a 'teaching and learning responsibility point' which is the additional sum of money you are paid for your leadership duties. A TLR can only be given for significant duties that you would not have to do as a classroom teacher. The guidelines for these are:

- they must be focused on teaching and learning
- they require a teacher to exercise their professional skill and judgement in leading, developing and improving the teaching practice of others
- the teacher must lead, manage and develop a subject or curriculum area or pupil development across the curriculum
- they should have an impact on the academic progress of pupils beyond that of teachers' own classes or groups of pupils.

Until September 2013 there were two bands of TLR payments: TLR1 and TLR2. TLR1 gives you a greater sum of money as a result of line-managing a significant number of people. You will find that each school will define this differently so in one school it could be line-managing more than five people and in another, ten. Schools can also set their own payment rates within these bands by dividing each TLR into three groups giving: TLR1a, TLR1b, TLR1c, TLR2a, TLR2b and TLR 2c. Nationally there is only an agreed minimum and maximum. When you are looking at roles in different schools, you need to check how much money they really mean. TLR3 was introduced in September 2013 for short-term or time-limited projects.

Example pay scale for year 2014–2015

Please note these figures are for example only.

Pay scale	Payment
TLR1 maximum	£12,643
TLR1 minimum	£7,471
TLR2 maximum	£6,322
TLR2 minimum	£2,587
TLR3 maximum (fixed term)	£2,551
TLR3 minimum (fixed term)	£511

End note

You may see middle leadership as a springboard to a future role, or you may find the role of middle leadership allows you to lead members of staff and also to continue with your first love of teaching your subject or a particular age range. You may find that your view alternates between these two positions. However, I hope that you find this book useful throughout – use it to scribble your thoughts in the margin, return to its pages throughout your middle leadership career and maybe even pass it onto another colleague to help them take their first steps in middle leadership.

How to use this book

The Bloomsbury CPD Library provides primary and secondary teachers with affordable, comprehensive and accessible 'do-it-yourself' continuing professional development. This book focuses on the first main step you'll take on the career development ladder – becoming a middle leader.

The book is split into two halves: Part 1 **Teach yourself** and Part 2 **Train others**.

Teach yourself

The first half of the book has been written so it can be read in different ways according to where you are on your journey towards middle leadership, your prior experience and the challenges that you face.

- You may be just considering becoming a middle leader and dip into the book to gain an idea of the different tasks that middle leaders may have to complete.
- You may have seen the job that you are looking for or you may be starting to apply for jobs and so choose to read this book in a linear fashion focusing on stages one, two and three; as a result you will build up a full and practical knowledge of how you can develop your application.
- You could be in the even better position of having an interview offer for next week and keen to concentrate on honing your interview technique or building your confidence by ensuring your knowledge of middle leadership is as thorough as possible.
- Perhaps you have accepted a middle leadership role and are reading this book in the school holidays prior to starting your role and will have a particular interest in first steps in middle leadership.
- You may be facing challenges in your middle leadership role and just need a boost to help you with these short-term difficulties.
- Finally, you may be enjoying your middle leadership and wonder if there is any fine-tuning you can give to your skills.

The first part of this book is divided into the five stages of your middle leadership career.

- Stage 1: Prepare – considers general advice in preparing for the role of a middle leader from considering the different types of roles to what your responsibilities might include. It starts with a self-evaluation questionnaire so that you can start the process by reflecting on what you already know and where your starting point is.
- Stage 2: Apply and obtain – explains the application process and gives advice on applying for a middle leadership role so you can prepare yourself thoroughly for the challenges you might face.
- Stage 3: First steps – provides help on those crucial first steps in your middle leader role, the period from appointment to those first few weeks in the school, so you can hit the ground running.
- Stage 4: Learn – is about learning the role, getting to know your school in more detail and focuses on the tasks you will be completing in that first year and how to ensure you make a strong impact in your school.
- Stage 5: Enjoy – considers how you can enjoy the role and fine-tune your middle leadership skills so you can be most effective in improving your area of the school. At this stage you may begin to consider what your next steps will be.

Most of the chapters in Part 1 have been divided into three sections:

- The basics
- The detail
- Final thoughts

If you would like to gain an overview of the chapter and briefly consider whether you need to study further, read 'the basics'. The set of basic questions at the end of this section will help you relate these initial paragraphs to your own situation and decide if you want/need to read 'the detail' or move straight onto the next chapter. Within 'the detail' you will find in-depth advice about the focus of the chapter. The 'final thoughts' section revisits what you need to know.

By using the description of the five stages above and 'the basics' at the start of each chapter you should quite quickly and easily be able to navigate your way round the book and focus on the sections that are relevant to your stage of the journey and experience. For further guidance there are also chapter summaries available to download from the online resources providing further overviews of what each chapter covers (see below for details of how to access the online resources). Wherever you are and whatever you want to learn however, it is recommended that you start off by filling in the self-evaluation questionnaire in chapter 1 to give yourself a chance to reflect and pinpoint where you are and what you want to achieve.

This comprehensive self-teach guide also includes teaching tips, to do lists at the end of each chapter and recommendations for how you can share your ideas and practice with other teachers in your school and beyond. A further reading recommendation or title to discuss in a CPD reading group is also included, as well as recommended blog posts in Blogger's corner.

Part 2: Train others

Once you have become an experienced middle leader it's time to help train other aspiring middle leaders or support new ones in areas you excel in. External training can be expensive and ineffective. In-house training, on the other hand, is hugely valuable as it can be made relevant to your training context – the teachers and children in your school. Whether it is one training session or a term's worth of training sessions, and whether you run them all yourself or get support from more senior colleagues, there is advice in this section to help you get started. This section includes:

- Advice for running good CPD
- A full set of training plans

Good luck with teaching yourself and training others! Keep us updated on your progress by tweeting using #BloomsCPD.

Online resources

For templates, questionnaires and PowerPoints from the book please visit: www.bloomsbury.com/CPD-library-middle-leadership

End note

Trying to find that elusive job is not always an easy process and you may need to be patient to find the right post. There will be times as a middle leader when you question whether you are in the right role. However, there will be other occasions when middle leadership will provide you with the perfect combination of classroom practice and leadership opportunity.

For many teachers, middle leadership is the beginning of a career journey which may see them reach the post of headteacher. You will look at other teachers who have stopped at various points from second in a department to Deputy Head. It is important to remember that, just as in teaching where the world never stops moving, you must also be continually trying to develop your own leadership skills so that you can lead your colleagues with confidence.

Part 1

Teach yourself

STAGE 1: PREPARE

1 Before you start: self-assessment questionnaire

This chapter is very different from the other chapters in the book as it is aimed to help you be honest with yourself about which skills you wish to develop. Being honest with yourself about how well you are performing in any particular area of your work is easier said than done. Often when looking at yourself it is hard to see things objectively. I find that it helps to think of the process of self-assessment as a safe place where you can be your most honest and open as no one else will be judging you but yourself.

How to complete the self-assessment questionnaire

Following this introduction there is a questionnaire which you can complete as a self-assessment tool. This will give you an opportunity to think about middle leadership and help you form a clear view on where you are now and what the next steps will be. There are many ways of approaching such a questionnaire depending on you as a person.

For some people, it is useful to go with your gut and listen to the first thing that comes into your mind – your instinctual answer – when you ask yourself the self-assessment questions. For others, it is better to spend a good amount of time really mulling over the questions slowly and in detail.

Quick response approach

If your preference for the self-assessment is to go with your gut only, then simply fill in the quick response section after each question with the first thing that comes into your mind when you ask yourself the question. Don't mull over the question for too long, simply read carefully and answer quickly. This approach will give you an overview of your current understanding and practice in middle leadership and will take relatively little time. Just make sure you are uninterrupted, in a quiet place and able to complete the questionnaire in one sitting with no distractions so that you get focused and honest answers.

Considered response approach

If you choose to take a more reflective and detailed approach, then you can leave the quick response section blank and go straight onto reading the further guidance section under each question. This guidance provides prompt questions and ideas to get you thinking in detail about each question and is designed to open up a wider scope in your answer. It will also enable you to look at your experience and pull examples into your answer to back up your statements. You may want to complete it a few questions at a time and take breaks, or you may be prepared to simply sit and work through all the questions in one sitting to ensure you remain focused. This approach does take longer, but you will gain much more from the process than the quick response approach alone.

Combined approach

A thorough approach, and one I recommend, would be to use both approaches together regardless of personal preference. There is clear value in both approaches being used together. This would involve you firstly answering the self-assessment quick response questions by briefly noting down your instinctual answers for all questions. The next step would be to return to the start of the self-assessment, read the further guidance and then answer the questions once more, slowly and in detail forming more of a narrative around each question and pulling in examples from your own experience. Following this you would need to read over both responses and form a comprehensive and honest summary in your mind of your answers and a final view of where you feel you stand at that point in time as a middle leader.

This is the longest of the three approaches to this questionnaire but will give you a comprehensive and full understanding of your current practice, thoughts and feelings in relation to middle leadership. You will be surprised at the difference you see between the quick response and the considered response answers to the same questions. It can be very illuminating.

- I have done this self-evaluation before.
- I only want a surface level overview of my current understanding and practice.
- I work better when I work at speed.
- I don't have much time.

Quick

- I have never done this self-evaluation before.
- I want a deeper evaluation of my current understanding and practice.
- I work better when I take my time and really think things over.
- I have some time to do this self-evaluation.

Considered

- I have never done this self-evaluation before.
- I have done this self-evaluation before.
- I want a comprehensive and full evaluation of my current understanding and practice and want to compare that to what I thought before taking the questionnaire.
- I have a decent amount of time to dedicate to completing this self-evaluation.

Combined

Fig. 1 How should I approach the self-assessment questionnaire?

Rate yourself

The final part of the self-assessment is to rate yourself. This section will ask you to rate your confidence and happiness in each of the areas that have been covered in the questionnaire with a view to working on these areas for improvement throughout the course of the book. The table below shows how the scale works: the higher the number you allocate yourself, the better you feel you are performing in that area.

Rating	Definition
1	Not at all. I don't. None at all. Not happy. Not confident at all.
2	Rarely. Barely. Very little. Very unconfident.
3	Not at all often. Not much. Quite unconfident.
4	Not particularly. Not really. Not a lot. Mildly unconfident.
5	Neutral. Unsure. Don't know. Indifferent.
6	Sometimes. At times. Moderately. A little bit. Mildly confident.
7	Quite often. A fair bit. Some. A little confident.
8	Most of the time. More often than not. Quite a lot. Quite confident.
9	The majority of the time. A lot. Very confident.
10	Completely. Very much so. A huge amount. Extremely happy. Extremely confident.

Fig. 2 Rate yourself definitions

Top tip

Self-assessment is a vital skill for self-reflection and progression in your professional life. It is important that we are honest, kind and constructive when it comes to self-assessing. It can be easy to be too harsh on yourself and allow your insecurities to cloud your judgement. Being objective and honest about yourself and your practice is hard and takes practice. Before you begin self-assessing, it is important to carefully consider the criteria you are using to assess yourself and focus on that at first without thinking about yourself. If you jump in and self-assess too early you may well have a clouded judgment and be unable to learn as much from the process. Don't rush it – it is too important.

Middle leadership self-assessment questionnaire

QUESTION 1: Do you enjoy leading people?

Quick response:

____

____

____

____

Questions for consideration

- What experience do you have of leadership?
- What did you particularly enjoy about leading?
- What did you find most challenging about leading?
- Could you describe your leadership style?

Considered response:

____

____

____

____

____

____

____

____

____

____

Rate yourself

QUESTION 1: How much do you enjoy leading people?

1 2 3 4 5 6 7 8 9 10

QUESTION 2: What makes a good leader?

Quick response:

____

____

____

____

Questions for consideration

- Is there a middle leader that you particularly admire?
- What is it about them or their style that makes you admire them?
- Are there middle leaders who you felt did not lead their team well?
- Why was that?

Considered response:

____

____

____

____

____

____

____

____

____

____

____

____

____

____

Rate yourself

QUESTION 2: How good a leader are you now?

1 2 3 4 5 6 7 8 9 10

QUESTION 3: Have you a vision of what you would like to achieve as a middle leader?

Quick response:

___

___

___

___

Questions for consideration

- Have you seen examples of subject or pastoral leaders who had a clear vision of what they were trying to achieve?
- How was the vision communicated to staff and pupils?
- How did this support the overall school vision?
- What is your vision of curriculum or pastoral leadership that you wish to work towards?
- Have you considered how this matches with the school's?
- Can you quickly explain your vision?

Considered response:

___

___

___

___

___

___

___

___

___

___

Rate yourself

QUESTION 3: How clear is your vision?

1 2 3 4 5 6 7 8 9 10

QUESTION 4: What is your general approach to building relationships with your stakeholders?

Quick response:

Questions for consideration

- Who do you see as your stakeholders now and in the future?
- How do you build relationships with other members of staff?
- How will you build relationships with other members of staff moving forward?
- How do you establish yourself with your pupils?
- Do you enjoy communicating with parents?
- What type of things do you think parents will want your opinion on?
- Are you likely to have to deal with governors?
- What do you think is the role of a governor?

Considered response:

Rate yourself

QUESTION 4: How confident are you in dealing with a range of stakeholders?

1 2 3 4 5 6 7 8 9 10

QUESTION 5: What methods of self-evaluation do you know about?

Quick response:

____

____

____

____

Questions for consideration

- Do you have any knowledge of different tools of self-evaluation?
- Which tools of self-evaluation have you used?
- Do you feel confident using self-evaluation tools?
- Which would you like to learn more about?
- Have you got examples of self-evaluation templates or systems that you can use?
- Have you had experience of feeding back self-evaluation findings?
- How do you use the evidence of self-evaluation?

Considered response:

____

____

____

____

____

____

____

____

____

Rate yourself

QUESTION 5: How confident are you with your knowledge of self-assessment?

1 2 3 4 5 6 7 8 9 10

QUESTION 6: What is your view on how appraisal can improve performance?

Quick response:

Questions for consideration

- Do you understand your school's appraisal policy?
- Are you clear on your school's appraisal cycle?
- What is the link between appraisal and your teacher's salary?
- Do you understand your role in incremental salary increases?
- How carefully or rigorously have you been appraised in the past?
- Were there aspects of your appraisal that you feel could have been improved?
- Are you confident in linking individual appraisal targets to whole-school targets?
- What do you consider are the important elements of appraisal interviews?

Considered response:

Rate yourself

QUESTION 6: How confident are you in leading the appraisal of your staff?

1 2 3 4 5 6 7 8 9 10

QUESTION 7: What do you think are the most important elements of productive staff meetings?

Quick response:

____

____

____

____

Questions for consideration

- Which leaders have led productive staff meetings?
- How did they structure the meetings to make them productive?
- What have been the worst staff meetings that you have attended?
- Why did you think that?
- What could have been done to make them more effective?
- What experience have you had of leading staff meetings?
- When have your meetings gone well?
- What did you do to achieve this?

Considered response:

____

____

____

____

____

____

____

____

____

Rate yourself

QUESTION 7: How confident are you in leading staff meetings?

1 2 3 4 5 6 7 8 9 10

QUESTION 8: How effective are you at managing your time?

Quick response:

Questions for consideration

- Have you developed your own systems for managing your time?
- Do you worry that you will not be able to fit in being a middle leader?
- Do you concentrate on one task at a time?
- Do you flit from one task to another?
- Are you always at school until late in the evening?
- Do you spend most of your weekend working?
- Are there colleagues who you admire who appear to be very productive?
- Have you discussed their tactics with them?

Considered response:

Rate yourself

QUESTION 8: How would your rate your time-management skills?

1 2 3 4 5 6 7 8 9 10

QUESTION 9: How would you use improvement planning to make yourself more effective?

Quick response:

Questions for consideration

- What do you feel are the key features of improvement planning?
- How does improvement planning link to appraisal?
- Have you observed strong improvement planning?
- What cycle was used?
- Are there templates or systems which you can duplicate?
- How would you involve your team in improvement planning?

Considered response:

Rate yourself

QUESTION 9: How confident are you in beginning improvement planning?

1 2 3 4 5 6 7 8 9 10

QUESTION 10: Is recruiting new staff something that you are looking forward to?

Quick response:

____

____

____

____

Questions for consideration

- How likely is it that you will be recruiting new staff this year?
- How difficult do you think it will be to make new appointments?
- What experience have you had in recruiting new staff?
- Have you a clear idea of the process of staff recruitment?
- What are the elements of staff recruitment?
- How confident do you feel in tackling these elements?
- How much autonomy do you feel you will have in making appointments?
- Who do you think you will work closely with when making appointments?

Considered response:

____

____

____

____

____

____

____

____

____

Rate yourself

QUESTION 10: How confident do you feel in finding strong new staff?

1 2 3 4 5 6 7 8 9 10

QUESTION 11: Are you looking forward to managing a budget?

Quick response:

Questions for consideration

- Do you know whether you will manage a budget?
- How big is the budget?
- Do you think this will be adequate for what you need?
- Have you seen budgets used effectively? Why was that?
- Have you seen budgets used ineffectively? Why was that?
- Have you been given clear advice on how a budget should be recorded?
- Have you seen the way budgets are recorded on account management software?
- Did you understand this?

Considered response:

Rate yourself

QUESTION 11: How confident do you feel in managing a budget?

1 2 3 4 5 6 7 8 9 10

The results

Take a look at how you rated your answers for each question in the questionnaire and compare your ratings with the chart below which will guide you to taking the next steps in your middle leadership role.

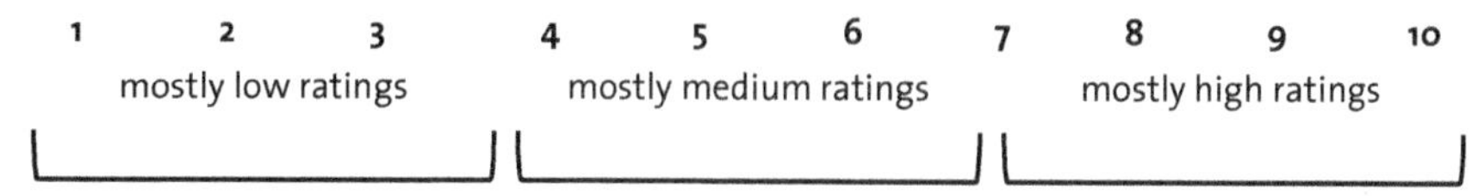

Fig. 3 How did you rate yourself?

Mostly low ratings

You have a way to go with your middle leadership but you are at the start of an exciting journey. You can choose which direction you wish your career to move in and the next few years will be an exciting time as you learn about middle leadership. If you haven't already got a middle leadership role, spend time observing other middle leaders in action and reflecting on how they work. You should also read Chapter 4 carefully which will give you important advice on how you can help prepare for middle leadership.

Mostly medium ratings

You have begun to think carefully about middle leadership and are definitely ready to become a middle leader if you are not one already. If you are supporting another middle leader perhaps now is the time for you to begin looking for a slightly more autonomous role. Focus on the aspects of middle leadership which you feel less confident about to round your skills.

Mostly high ratings

You have spent considerable time reflecting on you leadership and that of others and are developing strong skills as a middle leader. There are always things that you can improve on and you probably know what these are. You may be ready to coach or support other middle leaders in addition to those you line manage. We can learn a huge amount by teaching others as it often opens our eyes to new issues. We are all learners and we can always get better.

Now what?

The results are in. So now what? You have a self-assessment of your approach to being a middle leader and where your strengths and weaknesses lie and it is important that you now make the most of it. Take the time to action plan as a result of the answers you have given and the conclusions you have drawn. Don't make this simply another bit of paperwork you have completed. Use it to really open your eyes to how far you have come, where you are now and what you want to do next. Prioritise what you want to work on and get going on it.

TO DO LIST:

- ❑ Leave a little time after completing the questionnaire and then re-read your answers and really reflect on what they reveal.
- ❑ Consider any area that you would like to work on that has been highlighted by the questionnaire.
- ❑ Tweet the conclusion of anything you have realised or found interesting while doing the questionnaire and check out what others have said by using #BloomsCPD.
- ❑ Discuss the questionnaire questions as a team next time you meet together.
- ❑ Check out Zoe Elder's blog posts and consider how her views resonate with yours (see Takeaway box).
- ❑ Read *Who Moved my Cheese?* by Dr Spencer Johnson (see Takeaway box).

Chapter 1 takeaway

Teaching tip

Don't be too hard on yourself

As teachers we are often too critical of ourselves when we are self-assessing. We tend to focus on what we think we need to do better and don't give equal time to congratulating ourselves on what we do well. Think about the impacts you have made and make sure you keep making them and sharing them with others.

Pass it on

Sharing your ideas – Why it is good to share

Once you start reading about middle leadership and developing your technique it is likely that you will want to share your newly acquired skills. How you do this is a very individual choice. You may like to discuss things verbally in small groups or with one close confidant, or your may prefer to share ideas with strangers via social media. You will learn so much from doing this but it is also a little scary as once you open yourself up to others you may receive criticism so prepare yourself for this.

Support group

Why not have a discussion about the questions from the questionnaire with a colleague who you are close to and who is at a similar stage in their career. This may be someone in your school or a friend at another school. You may be surprised to find that they feel the same as you or you may even have complimentary skills so you can support each other in addressing areas for improvement.

Share and tweet

Share your views about what you have realised or found of interest while doing this questionnaire on Twitter using #BloomsCPD.

CPD Book club recommendation

Dr Spencer Johnson, *Who Moved My Cheese*?
(see Bibliography and further reading)

Bloggers' corner

Zoe Elder is a senior leader, a coach and author of *Full On Learning*. She blogs on a range of educational issues here. Visit her blog at: http://www.fullonlearning.com

2 What different types of middle leadership roles are there?

So you have decided you want to be a middle leader? You've read the introduction and being part of the engine room of change in a school is the challenge that you are looking for. You like working with other teachers and feel you would relish the opportunity to lead staff and develop their practice. The first stage in your journey is to consider the different types of leadership roles available and that is what this chapter will consider.

The basics

Broadly speaking middle leadership roles fall into two groups:

- curriculum/subject focus
- pastoral focus.

For each of these groups there will be different roles at varying points in the hierarchy. Obviously, in larger schools there will be a wider range of roles at more levels which can provide far more opportunities for internal promotions. In a smaller school there will be fewer hierarchical levels and hence fewer roles, but the upside is that if you really want to be a head of department you will be able to get there with fewer years of experience.

This chapter will help you consider curriculum and pastoral roles in more detail and help you decide which direction you want go in. It will also help you to be more aware of what the different level of roles mean and hence be more certain about whether to consider those jobs.

Basic questions

- Do you understand the difference between curriculum and pastoral middle leadership?
- Do you feel more suited to a curriculum or a pastoral role?
- Have you thought about what level of post you are now looking for?

The detail

Before we begin to delve into curriculum/subject and pastoral leadership in more detail, it is worth highlighting that there is less separation between the two than there was in the past. At its core, in both roles, you are trying to achieve the same thing and that is ensuring that the pupils make as much progress as possible.

Curriculum/subject leadership

In secondary schools, the majority of teachers have a real interest in the subject that they deliver and in some cases genuinely love or have a passion for it. This feeling is often the strongest at the beginning of your career. However, if you look around your staffroom you will see teachers coming to the end of their career who are still as interested in the actual subject as they have ever been. In primary schools, a teacher's passion is for the holistic development of the child as they are teaching them all subjects.

As a middle leader with a curriculum/subject specialism, your aim will be to ensure that the pupils studying this subject make as much progress as possible.

In a secondary school, you may be responsible for one subject and in some cases you may be the only teacher delivering that subject. If the school is bigger, or you are responsible for a core subject, you will have a team of teachers who you are leading. In some schools, subjects will be grouped together and you could be responsible for a group of subjects. You may have a team of subject specialists who each teach a particular subject or each teacher may work across the range of subjects.

In a primary school, curriculum leaders tend to co-ordinate a particular subject throughout the whole school – overseeing schemes of work, resources and developing teaching and learning throughout the school. So even in a small three-class rural primary school, you will be directly leading staff and have responsibility for other teachers.

Pastoral leadership

Pastoral leadership is the other side of the middle leadership coin. In pastoral leadership you will be looking at the well-being of a group of pupils. Whereas in curriculum leadership your initial prior experience is your teaching of the subject, in pastoral leadership your preparation for the role is likely to be through working as a form tutor in a secondary school or your role as a class teacher in a primary school.

A traditional pastoral role was based around three main elements: supporting teachers with pupils who were not behaving in a classroom situation; liaising with pupils' parents when they had particular concerns or complaints about an experience their child was having; finally and probably most common was supporting a pupil who had a particular difficulty in their lives. Difficulties could include emotional problems such as their parents splitting up, an illness which meant the child had issues around their attendance or financial problems if there is very little money in the household.

Recently, pastoral roles have begun to change with the emphasis now being on how a child may be supported so that they make good progress across the curriculum. A pastoral leader will still be supporting behaviour management issues, a pupil's access to learning or parental concerns but they need to keep in their mind what impact the actions have on improving a child's progress. The result is that the role of a pastoral leader is increasingly data driven mirroring that of a curriculum leader.

Until recently, pastoral leaders tended to be responsible for a certain age group of pupils. In smaller primary schools this could be a particular key stage or a different pupil grouping. In larger schools, pastoral leaders tended to manage year groups and have the title of 'head of year'. There has also been a trend to divide pupils into vertical groups so that a pastoral leader might be responsible for a section of each year group in the school. This is often described as a house system. Pupils would be placed within 'vertical tutor groups' so that each tutor group will have pupils of different ages within it. The pastoral leader is then described as a 'head of house'.

It is worth bearing in mind that in the independent sector and a small number of state schools there will also be pastoral leaders who care for those pupils who are boarders. Teams of staff will run boarding houses and take responsibility for pupils before and after school and also at the weekends.

More recently, whether schools have divided pupils into age group or vertical groups, the middle leadership role has been renamed as 'progress leader' or 'achievement manager'. This is highlighting the fact that the work of the pastoral leaders must impact on the progress of the child.

Leading teaching and learning

Whether a curriculum or a pastoral leader, you have to see yourself as having a role in leading teaching and learning. This is perhaps easier to directly understand if you are a curriculum leader. It is self-evident that as the person responsible for achievement in a particular subject area, the best way of improving this is to try and ensure the highest quality of teaching and learning in the subject. At the same time you will be line managing and leading your subject teachers.

The best curriculum leaders will look for opportunities to improve the teaching and learning in their subject area. This could range from carefully planning schemes of work so teachers have good resources to work from, to using meeting time as an opportunity for continuing professional development (CPD) so that you spend time training each other. This will be covered in more detail in chapters 14 and 20.

If you speak to pastoral leaders who have been doing their job for a period of time, they may not necessarily see themselves in the role of leading teaching and learning, commenting that they work with pupils. However the most effective pastoral leaders have begun to see that if they can impact on the teaching and learning that their pupils receive, and the standard of this rises, then the pupils will make more progress and in parallel, the behaviour of the pupils will also improve. A clear recognition of this is that in the job description of a middle leader you may see reference to 'quality assurance' with an expectation that you will help quality assure the provision that your pupils receive, perhaps by completing work scrutiny or pupil focus groups (see Chapter 12). You may also be expected to use your findings to help lead CPD on teaching and learning too.

Supporting staff

A second key aspect of being a middle leader is supporting the staff that you work with. You may think this is more obvious for pastoral leaders as it is likely that there may have been times when you have sought the help of a pastoral leader in dealing with a more recalcitrant pupil in one of your groups. Some inexperienced teachers can see this as almost magic, that the pupil they have been struggling to deal with can suddenly become more co-operative with the pastoral leader whose help they have sought. There is no mystique here; it is likely to be due to the level of respect and the relationship that the pastoral leader has built up over a period of time. You will also find, in the future, that dealing with a pupil on a one-to-one basis in supporting another colleague can be more straightforward than when you are working with that same pupil in a class situation.

Increasingly, curriculum leaders are also expected to support their staff in such situations, as pastoral leaders may only get involved when it is an issue across a number of subject areas. In addition, pastoral leaders cannot be expected to deal with all such situations. Those who try to do so can soon find that their role feels seemingly impossible. The best curriculum leaders will realise that everything

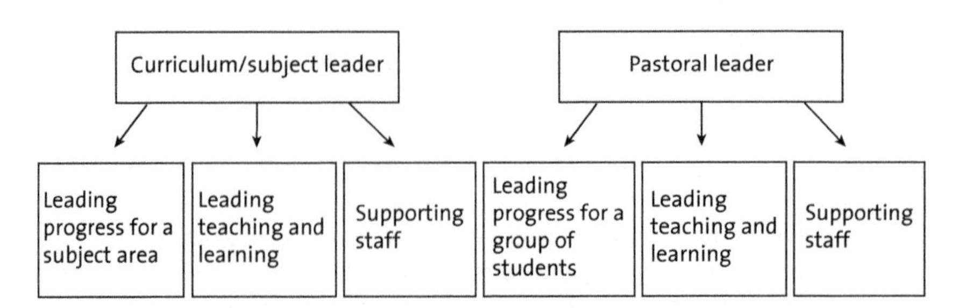

Fig. 4 Roles in middle leadership

that they can do to develop a positive climate for learning in their area can only be good for raising standards.

Final thoughts

It is likely that you will feel more of an affinity to either curriculum or pastoral leadership. However, hopefully you will also realise that the links between the two are much closer than they may have been in the past.

Another important consideration is what opportunities are likely to arise. Many teachers like to feel settled in a school for a period of time so that they can build relationships with children, staff and parents. You may be in this situation and cannot face the process of interview at a different school and all this entails. In such a circumstance, you will be likely to find that pastoral leadership positions do appear and may only be advertised internally in a school. The mere fact that in a secondary school there may be five heads of year posts (six or seven if there is a sixth form) compared to only one head of maths, means the probability is far higher that a pastoral leadership post may appear.

You may decide that in such circumstances you will be prepared to take on a pastoral leadership role to give you important middle leadership experience which may then be helpful for other roles, even if your preference is for a curriculum leadership role.

It is more likely that if your ambition is to be a curriculum leader that you will be faced with applying to other schools to gain such a position. However, you could also be lucky and find an opportunity arises at your own school. In larger schools, if you explain your ambitions to a supportive senior leader and are patient, you may find that a project is created for you – especially if you teach in a subject area which the schools has difficulties recruiting for or if your teaching is very highly rated.

TO DO LIST:

- ❑ Reflect on what you think is the difference between curriculum and pastoral middle leadership.
- ❑ Reflect on colleagues who you think are particularly skilled at middle leadership.
- ❑ Check out Laura McInernay's tweets on a range of educational issues: @Miss_McInernay (see Takeaway box).
- ❑ Read *The 7 Habits of Highly Effective People* by Stephen R. Covey (see Takeaway box).

Chapter 2 takeaway

Teaching tip

Pastoral or curriculum

Consider which staff you feel most comfortable in leading. Would you like to lead a group of staff in a subject-specific area where you will try to develop this subject amongst those staff? If so this shows a preference for curriculum leadership. If you would prefer to lead a group of staff who have a focus on the holistic progress of the child, this shows you are leaning more towards pastoral. When you are in a curriculum meeting or a pastoral meeting, try and to decide which one you'd be the most confident leading.

Pass it on

Sharing your ideas – discuss what works

Share your views on curriculum and pastoral leadership. Discuss with a colleague(s) what skills pastoral and curriculum leaders have. Think about those leaders who you perceive to be very effective in their roles. What do they do which seems to make a difference? Which of these actions and skills do you think you need to work on further?

Share and tweet

Share your ideas about what you think makes the best curriculum or pastoral leader using #BloomsCPD.

CPD book club recommendation

Stephen R. Covey, *The 7 Habits of Highly Effective People*
(see Bibliography and further reading)

Tweeters' corner

Laura McInernay is the editor of @academiesweek and tweets on wide range of educational issues on @Miss_McInernay that are well worth a read.

3

Which is the right school for you and your career?

If you search the *Times Educational Supplement (TES)* website between February and May, you will find thousands of teaching jobs. The majority of them will be main scale posts, but in any week there will be hundreds of middle leadership posts. How do you choose which one is right for you?

The basics

The first thing that you may consider is the location in which you would like to work. You may have a defined commuting distance, be clear on a certain area of the country, know whether rural or urban is right for you or be one of those rare colleagues who would consider anywhere in the country, or even the world.

Even after refining your search for your particular subject area and age range, you are likely to find that across the country there are a considerable number of jobs that you can apply for.

It is important to carefully consider the type of school that you are applying to. The following questions could help you:

- What type of school is it?
- How big is the school?
- What is the current Ofsted judgement of the school?
- What is the achievement like at the school?
- What is the student intake like?

You then need to look at the post and consider how the role will vary according to the type of school. You may consider questions including:

- Who will I be managed by?
- How many colleagues will I be responsible for?

If you want to be a better-prepared middle leader candidate you should consider these questions before you start looking so that you are aware of what your ideal post is. You need to be looking for a role in a school that you will be comfortable with and that fits with your previous experiences. What you cannot do is make the school fit you. The happier you feel at the school, the stronger you will be on interview day and this will follow through into you having the best chance of being successful in the role.

You may see this job as a stepping stone to another post, or you may feel that you wish to spend a considerable time in the role at the school. Either way, there is nothing worse than being offered a job where either the school or the role is not suitable and then find yourself looking for another job during your first academic year in the post.

This chapter will help you address the question: what type of school or role is right for you? It will also help you look at advertisements and help you narrow them down.

It is worth highlighting the fact that the more restrictions you place on the post, the fewer there are likely to be to apply for. Good advice could be to begin with quite a narrow criteria and then widen it over time if your job search is not proving successful.

BASIC QUESTIONS

- What location do you want to work in?
- Do you have a clear idea of the different types of schools you could work in?
- Do you have a strong idea of the type of school that you want to work in?
- What impact will the different type of school have on the job role?

The detail

Firstly, let us look at school locations and the different types of roles you could consider, and at the same time consider how this could impact on your role and the strengths that you may require.

Location

Have you got a specific idea for the location of the post? You may be tied to a particular area due to a house purchase or a partner's job, in which case your starting point may be the maximum duration of commute that you are prepared to do.

Remember, as a middle leader you may find the job takes longer than when you were a classroom teacher, so consider how much of your day you are prepared to spend travelling.

You may have very strong ideas as to whether you want to work in a rural school, an urban town school or one in a metropolitan city. There is no doubt that the pace of change is much faster in many schools in our larger cities and as a result opportunities for further promotion can be far quicker. However, you may feel unsuited to work in such an environment and yearn for a school in a rural location where the population of pupils and staff tends to be more static.

If you have no geographical constraints, then you will have a far larger number of jobs to apply for. But this can be overwhelming, so it is important that if this is you, you spend longer considering what type of school or role you are looking for.

You may start off with a narrow search area and widen it over time. If this is the case, why not plan this as this colleague has done. They have set themselves a target that they will get a leadership role in four years. Their current school has a 30-minute commute. In the first year of job hunting they will only apply for jobs where the commute is no longer than their current post. If they haven't got a job by the end of this year, they will widen their job search and also consider schools with a commute of up to 45 minutes providing they are in the same county. If they haven't got a job by the end of that year, they will widen their job search. If, after three years, they haven't got the middle leadership post they are looking for, they will consider moving house.

Year	Location
Current	Commute is 30 minutes
1	School in the same partnership of schools with no change in commute or shorter.
2	Consider a commute of up to 45 minutes. Stay in the same county.
3	Commute up to an hour with a view to moving house. Move county.
4	School in the same region but prepared to consider moving house.

Fig. 5 Career development plan

Type of school

There is a huge range of different types of schools in the UK that you could choose to work in, even more, if you are also looking at international schools. This section will concentrate on UK schools.

Age range

Whether you are a primary or secondary trained teacher, there are still decisions to make over the age range you wish to work with. Within the primary sector there are: nursery schools, primary schools and separate infant and junior schools. In the secondary sector there are FE, sixth form establishments and studio schools in addition to the more standard 11–16 or 11–18 schools. You could also consider those schools that merge primary and secondary, such as middle schools in the state sector and prep schools in the independent sector. These may give you the opportunity of leading across Key Stage 2 and Key Stage 3.

State or independent sector

You may have a strong opinion as to whether you wish to work in the state or independent sector, or you may be flexible. If you wish to be a middle leader in an independent school there are obviously fewer posts available – in which case you may have to widen your geographic search area. You may also find that independent schools have flatter leadership structures, i.e. there are fewer layers of leadership between the senior leadership team (SLT) and the classroom teacher, perhaps only one layer. This can mean that you are more autonomous but have a smaller team. Whilst some state schools have moved towards flatter structures, often to save money, there are still likely to be a wider range of middle leadership posts in state primary and secondary schools than in their independent counterparts.

Different types of state schools

Within the state sector there are a number of different types of school to consider. Firstly, there are church and non-church schools. In many parts of the country the majority of primary schools have a religious affiliation. If this is the case, this may not significantly impact upon your role. In secondary education there are fewer church schools, but again at a middle leadership level the role may not differ significantly to that in a non-church school.

Secondly, there are academy and non-academy schools. The majority of secondary schools have become academies either as a single school or as part of an academy chain. For primary schools the majority have remained as local authority schools. You may find that in certain academy chains there is less autonomy for middle leaders and you may be expected to operate certain schemes or structures. The plus side of this is that there may almost be an internal job market, and when you prove yourself successful, opportunities appear in other schools within the group.

Selective and non-selective

In the secondary sector in both state and independent schools there are still some selective or grammar schools which select pupils on academic ability. Obviously, the attainment of these schools is much higher than normal comprehensive schools. As a middle leader whether curriculum or pastoral focused, you will be likely to have different issues to tackle and have different demands placed on you. Equally, those schools that are non-selective but in a selective environment, may be quite different from other comprehensive schools as effectively the top third of the most able pupils have been 'creamed off'.

In primary or secondary schools all across the country, there are always those that have higher levels of attainment than other schools. This could purely be due to being an outstanding school. The reality is though, that the context of many schools presents an advantage or disadvantage to high achievement. You may wish to be a middle leader in a higher-attaining school or you may have no fixed opinion on this. When you are looking at the attainment of a certain school, it may be worth asking yourself the question: what are the factors that have aided this? Remember to also look at the progress the children are making from KS1 to KS2 or from KS2 to KS4. This may give you a different view on the school.

As a potential middle leader in a selective school, you must be very strong at teaching the more able pupils, whereas if you are working in a lower-attaining school, possibly with high progress, do your strengths lie in helping pupils who find learning difficult?

Mixed or single sex

There are still some single sex schools and this may appeal to you. There are also schools with an imbalance of genders often due to the impact of a single sex school in the locality.

Some teachers will comment that if you are a good teacher then the gender of the pupils does not matter. Yet equally, you may feel that you are particularly skilled in supporting the learning of boys or girls. In terms of middle leadership, one obvious impact of this can be the staff that you are leading. In a girls' school, for example, you may find that the staff are more female dominated.

Size of school

The final thing to consider is what size of school you want to work in. If you are a primary teacher wanting to work in a small rural school, you may find that paid middle leadership roles do not really exist – a subject co-ordinator may find that no remuneration is attached to the role. In larger primary schools there may be a wealth of middle leadership roles. Hence, some primary teachers may choose to work in a larger school to gain leadership experience before returning to a small school at a senior leadership level.

In secondary schools, no matter how small they are, there will be middle leadership posts. In the large secondary schools though there will be a huge range of middle leadership roles, even more if the school is arranged in a faculty model or if the pastoral model is based on vertical grouping.

The question for you to consider is: how much autonomy are you looking for at the beginning of your middle leadership journey? If in your first middle leadership role you want to have sole responsibility for a subject area, then you should be looking at a smaller school. However, if you want to work within a team, line managed by another middle leader, then a larger school is for you. If you do choose to work in a larger school, there are likely to be promotion opportunities arising which means that you may be able to build your career without moving schools. In a smaller school you may find that you need to move school to gain promotion.

Researching the school

Having looked at the different types of school that you could work in, your next stage is to begin looking at the specific job adverts and see what makes each school unique.

Application information and website

Your first step when looking at a school is studying the application information and the school website. You should find that the information falls into two sections: that which is generic to the school and would be given to all applicants, and that which is specific to the post such as the job description or information about the curriculum area or age range.

The school information should give you the factual information about the type of school. You may also find there is information about the ethos of the school and what it places importance on. You may see words such as 'academic', 'well-established', 'caring', 'dynamic' and 'pupil-centred' and you need to consider what you think this means to you. For example, a school which characterises itself as 'well-established' is less likely to be looking for innovative curriculum practice but may be more likely to be looking for middle leaders who can squeeze even more achievement from the systems in place. A 'dynamic' school may be open to a middle leader being prepared to trial new ideas but at the same time due to the pace of change, systems may be less embedded. These are obviously stereotypes and these could be things that you look at in more detail during the interview.

The information on the role should leave you clear as to the expectation which is placed upon you, the tasks that you are expected to complete and the people you will be responsible for. It is important to stress that job descriptions are not always complete and there may be other tasks that you will also be asked to complete. Equally, there may be items on the job description that you do not have sole responsibility for but which you may assist a senior leader in completing.

Ofsted judgement and achievement data

Schools will normally have a link to their most recent Ofsted report and a summary of their achievement data. It is important to be cautious when looking at Ofsted reports. Schools inspected on the most recent frameworks, i.e. after

September 2012 were inspected on a very different set of criteria to previously. There will be schools with an 'outstanding' judgement prior to this date with very similar achievement data to a school judged as 'requires improvement' on the new framework. Hence, it is dangerous to decide you only want to work in a 'good' or an 'outstanding' school. What is true, is that a school that is 'requiring improvement' or has been graded as a '4' by Ofsted, may have a different focus to one that was recently graded as '1' or '2' or one that has not been inspected for some considerable time. You will find that your focus as a middle leader is very different. Working in schools with lower Ofsted judgements can be an excellent opportunity to learn about leadership as there may be more change occurring. At the same time, a school which has a recent '1' or '2' judgement may give you an excellent knowledge of effective systems.

You should also look at the school data. The Department for Education (DfE) website has a host of information about a school's performance. For primary schools, you can look at KS2 test results and teacher assessments and study the performance of groups of pupils. For secondary schools, there is even more information. Not only can you look at the overall data on a school, but you can also look at the performance of groups of students and study the achievement within the EBacc subjects. If your curriculum area is not listed, you can compare any data given to you by the school with this information. If you are a pastoral leader, you may wish to look at the performance of groups of pupils and see if there are any obvious gaps.

News websites

It is also interesting to search the internet for news stories about a school you are applying to. First of all this can show whether there are issues that you may need to be aware of. However, some stories need to be taken with a pinch of salt. In addition, if there are lots of good news stories this can indicate a school that has strong community links and also if there are any particular strengths of the school.

Final thoughts

This chapter should give you an overview of the different factors you need to be aware of when looking at middle leadership in various schools. You need to think carefully about whether the information that you gather indicates that this is the school for you, or if this is the type of school that you want to apply for. It is not a question of just finding the right job, it is just as important to establish whether it is the right school too.

To do list:

- ❏ Reflect on what type of school you want to work in.
- ❏ Reflect on how you can plan your job search.
- ❏ Create a career plan.
- ❏ Check out Jill Berry's posts @JillBerry102 (see Takeaway box).
- ❏ Read *Teacher Toolkit: Helping You Survive Your First Five Years* by Ross Morrison McGill (see Takeaway box).

Chapter 3 takeaway

Teaching tip

Plan your career

Look at the table in figure 5. How would this look for your personal situation? What changes are you prepared to make to your lifestyle for the job that you really want. Could you also look ahead and think where you'd like to be in five years time and ten years time, so you create your own career path?

Pass it on

Sharing your ideas – career planning

Discuss the idea of career planning with a colleague who is a close friend. Have they got an idea of where they would like to be in certain periods of time? Can they think of people who have used these techniques in their careers? Ask leaders that you respect if they had a career plan or whether they left it to fate.

CPD book club recommendation

Ross Morrison McGill, *Teacher Toolkit: Helping You Survive Your First Five Years*
(see Bibliography and further reading)

Tweeters' corner

Jill Berry has been a leader in both state and independent schools and often tweets on career development issues @JillBerry102 – well worth a read.

4 How can you best prepare for the role?

It is important that your next step is to begin to try and gain the skills and experience that make you a strong candidate when applying for a post. It is much better to begin to think about this in advance rather than seeing a job you really like the sound of and then trying to think what experience you have gathered so far – though there are many successful candidates who have taken this second path.

The basics

If you are early in your career you may not have decided whether to take the curriculum or pastoral route and, in which case, you could try and build your skills and experience relevant to both types of posts. If you do this you will find that you become a stronger all-round teacher and potentially more employable.

By actively looking for opportunities to build your skills, you will also find that you enjoy your job more, as many teachers find that trying new things is what keeps us fresh and that it is the 'same old, same old' that leads to frustration and boredom.

It is very important though to keep a balance and ensure that you are still performing the core purpose of your current job well. Line managers and headteachers will not be impressed by the teacher who takes on lots of other projects but does not keep the basics of their current role up-to-date and moving forwards.

Basic questions

- Have you decided whether pastoral or curriculum leadership is for you?
- What skills and experiences do you think you need for the post(s)?
- How many of those do you think you already have and can demonstrate?
- Do you have ideas as to how you could bridge those gaps whilst performing your current role?

The detail

In this chapter we will look at some of the skills and experiences that you will need for different middle leadership posts and consider how you can use your current post to upskill yourself.

General preparation

No matter which type of middle leadership post you are aiming for, you will still spend the majority of your timetabled time teaching. Therefore the pre-requisite for most school leaders is that they expect their middle leaders to be strong teachers. This means that you need to develop your teaching to its strongest point.

Think about the performance management or quality assurance observations that you have had. Most school leaders will be expecting their middle leaders to be teaching 'good' lessons at a minimum, and some schools will say that they expect their curriculum leaders to be outstanding teachers.

You need to consider what areas for development have been suggested to you and attend to them. Look for opportunities to develop your teaching.

- Does your school have peer observation or coaching programmes that you could join? If not, could you ask teachers if you could observe their lessons and also would they give you their opinion on your lessons?
- Do you participate fully in the CPD programme in your school to make the most of this time? If you do this, it is more likely that your school will be more receptive to any requests you make for external CPD opportunities.
- Do not forget to consider the many books on classroom practice that you could read for ideas. Does your school have its own CPD library or could you ask for a certain book to be bought for you? Or you may just think it's quicker and easier to buy your own.
- Could you look at whether there are any local TeachMeets you could attend?
- Once you have developed your practice, why not ask for an additional observation from a senior leader or line manager so that you have an objective opinion to see if you are making the improvements that you believe you are.

Do not wait for someone else or for a school project to improve your practice – take control of this yourself! If it's something that you personally feel is important, you are more likely to work hard and be committed to it.

Leadership experience

One of the most common dilemmas for potential middle leaders is being caught in a catch 22 situation of requiring some leadership experience before you can get your first leadership role. This can seem one of the most frustrating elements of the application process and could be a hurdle to clear if you are aiming to move straight from being a classroom teacher to becoming head of a five-teacher faculty or department. If this is your concern, why not try using the tips in the next two chapters to see if you can get an interview. You may be pleasantly surprised! In some subject areas, such as maths and English, it can be the school's biggest concern will be recruiting a good teacher. It's always easier to develop a 'good' teacher's leadership skills than it is to move a teacher to being good.

In some ways, gaining leadership experience is of most use in helping you decide whether you wish to become a middle leader and also to give you confidence so that when you gain your middle leadership role you feel able to do the role.

There are several little tasks (see below) that you could perform which would give you some experience of leadership whilst you are a classroom teacher. They may also provide you with a wider interest. This can help your day-to-day motivation if you are starting to feel a little stale from the demands of a constant teaching timetable.

Developing schemes of work

One favourite task to gain experience is to offer to take responsibility for a certain element of the scheme of work. Perhaps there is a module that you could offer to develop for a middle leader. Most middle leaders will only be too pleased to share the load. Take care though that you are writing something that is suitable for other teachers and not just for you. You could start by asking your colleague's opinions and undertake some research of what other schools are doing – using Twitter or the *TES* website may be a good starting point.

Once you have collected ideas, is there an opportunity to trial some of the lessons? Even better, could you work with a colleague and complete some team teaching so you can see how the lessons work for you and someone else. Once this is done you need to write up the module. However tempting it may be to develop your own format, it is best to use those formats/templates already in place.

It is a good idea to discuss the project with the middle leader you are working for. They may have suggestions that you need to take on board, even if they seem frustrating. When you are a middle leader you will have to work within a school framework and this is the same thing. One of the most daunting parts of the process may be presenting it to the team of teachers you work with, but it is an important learning curve and will be excellent experience to draw on in the future.

Once the module has been used, do not forget to evaluate its effectiveness. Have the teachers found the module useful? Have the pupils enjoyed it and have the learning gains improved?

The last thing you must do is reflect on the overall experience – you will find this provides a good starting point for certain interview questions. You could base your reflections on these questions:

- What leadership experience have you gained?
- How did you encourage the teachers to work with you to design the module?
- How did you ensure that the teachers used the module?
- What methods did you use to evaluate its effectiveness?

Leading an event or activity

A second opportunity to gain leadership experience could be to co-ordinate an event or activity. This could be an event that is already running at the school and you offering to take it on. Such activities could include a school production, a trip or even a residential. To make it most useful for your career development you really need to ensure the event is linked to the role that you are aspiring to. For example, if you are looking to become a head of English, drama or performing arts, then directing a school production links closely to the role. Whereas if your aspiration is to become a head of science, whilst you will have gained good personal development the link is more tenuous to improving attainment and progress in science.

The same is true for trips or residential experiences. Developing a trip to a university for a set of science workshops could be used to highlight your commitment to raising aspirations of gifted and talented pupils. Or, as a future head of English, planning the 'Poetry Live' trip – especially if you can link this to the teaching that follows – is a good indication of how you will be prepared to be creative in raising attainment or improving progress. Whereas a trip to watch a sporting event or an end of term theme park outing shows a less direct link to improvement in teaching and learning.

If you are aspiring to become a pastoral middle leader these wider trips can have far more meaning, especially if you make the connections between such events and a rewards system or use them as examples of how you develop pupils' well-being and their commitment to the school.

The key thing is to consider not only how the event or activity can help you gain leadership experience but also how it could potentially develop the outcomes of the young people.

Whole school working

There may also be whole school opportunities that you could take advantage of which will give you a wider view of school improvement and provide good experience for you as a middle leader.

Some schools will operate working parties, led by a senior leader, to work on and develop polices within a school depending on the school's current needs. They may be general groups such as a teaching and learning group or a coaching group, where teachers from across the school share ideas on how to develop best practice. Joining such a group can be invaluable, as not only will you be developing your own teaching but you could also have the opportunity to work with another colleague to improve their practice or even share good practice across a wider group of staff.

You may work in a school where a very specific project is being worked upon. For example, there may be a working party to develop a policy across the school such as an assessment or behaviour policy. Joining such a group will give you greater experience for when you need to write such a policy for your own curriculum area or developing practice across a pastoral group.

Assemblies

There are often opportunities in schools to lead assemblies for a pastoral grouping (a house or a year) or even whole school assemblies. It is surprising how many teachers dread taking assemblies!

Leading assemblies can be very good experience for those wishing to become pastoral middle leaders as it is often a regular part of the role. Not only will you gain excellent practice at this but you will also start to build up a bank of material that can be used in another school. Many heads and deputies will have collections of assemblies going back to early in their careers which they may refer to when inspiration is lacking.

For an aspiring curriculum leader, the link from taking assemblies to their future role may seem more tenuous, but it does mark you out as a future leader in the eyes of senior leaders. This may be important for any internal opportunities that may arise but could also be drawn upon in any reference that they may write.

INSET and training

A key aspect in the work of many middle leaders is developing the staff that they work with. The best middle leaders will always make use of meeting time as an opportunity for sharing ideas to improving the quality of teaching.

You may find that there are opportunities to contribute to such sessions within your own curriculum area. You could be pro-active by approaching your middle leader to ask if they would be interested in you sharing an idea.

Some schools will also look for teachers to share ideas in whole school INSET sessions or may even look for a teacher/s to run a session on a particular idea. Leading such a session is not easy, but it can be a fantastic opportunity.

The concept of a 'TeachMeet' could also give you the opportunity to share ideas with colleagues from other schools too. Why not look and see if there are any in your locality which you could attend to see how such sessions work with the thought that you could contribute to future events.

Final thoughts

There are many ways in which you could develop your skills at a wider level as long as you are creative and open to different opportunities. Look around at other teachers in your school and see what they are involved in. Consider middle leaders who you admire and look at the different tasks that they are working on too.

All schools have their own cultures and as a result each school will have varying ways in which you can contribute to school improvement outside of your own classroom. These will give you good experience that you can use in your applications and also help you in the role once you have gained it.

It is worth giving a note of caution here. Do not forget your core role in school of being a teacher and form tutor. You must not let the basic elements of this function be compromised by other tasks you are working on. You must ensure that the quality of your teaching stays strong and progress/attainment remain high. And enjoy it! You may well miss it when you move up.

Finally, you must keep your future aim in your mind. There will be tasks that you could complete and which you may enjoy but which may not help you achieve your future ambition. This does not mean that you should not do them. So, if you love coaching a sports team or leading a choir, be aware this may not help you gain the middle leadership role you are looking for and do not expect this. However such holistic activities can add a lot of pleasure to your role in school and this positivity can lead to less direct benefits.

To do list:

- ❑ Plan and carry out a leadership task which is relevant to your career plan.
- ❑ Reflect on how effective the task was and how it can evidence your middle leadership skills.
- ❑ Check out Ross Morrison McGill's tweets and posts on @TeacherToolkit (see Takeaway box).
- ❑ Read *How to be an Outstanding Primary School Teacher* by David Dunn or *Pimp your Lesson!: Prepare, Innovate, Motivate, Perfect* by Isabella Wallace and Leah Kirkman (see Takeaway box).

Chapter 4 takeaway

Teaching tip

Plan a leadership task

Look at the ideas in this chapter, from writing a scheme of work to delivering an assembly. Think about which is the most pertinent for the role that you will be looking for. Speak to a middle or senior leader about whether they would support you in taking on this task.

Pass it on

Reflecting on a leadership task

Once you have planned and possibly completed the task, spend some time reflecting on how you can use the experience in your job search. Discuss your reflection with another colleague. Have they got any advice on things that you could have done differently that would have made the project even more effective?

CPD book club recommendation

David Dunn, *How to be an Outstanding Primary School Teacher* (primary)
Isabella Wallace and Leah Kirkman, *Pimp your Lesson!: Prepare, Innovate, Motivate, Perfect* (secondary)
(see Bibliography and further reading)

Bloggers' corner

Ross Morrison McGill is a deputy head teacher and the most followed teacher in the UK on Twitter: @TeacherToolkit and his blog is found at www.teachertoolkit.me – this is required reading for countless teachers.

5 Planning your application

You have now thought carefully about the type of middle leadership role you are looking for and the school you wish to work in. You have also completed and reflected on a leadership task. The next stage in the process is planning and writing your application.

The basics

Your written application is likely to be your opportunity to make that first impression so you need to make it count. You will not get a job based purely on a written application, but you can certainly lose one! For some middle leader posts there may be few applicants, possibly only you, and if you write a strong application they may still run the process with just you.

If there are more applications, most interviewers will have picked out one or two front runners prior to the interview – their natural instinct will be to will those candidates to perform well. We all know that the interview process is unnatural so some interviewers will overlook the odd error during the interview process if the application was very strong.

Many headteachers are recurrently surprised by the poor standard of so many written applications. There are occasions when mistakes are forgiven from main scale teachers, but for potential middle leaders more is expected, especially as there will be times when you are expected to write letters to parents. So do not waste your time by sending an application that you have not given your full attention to.

At the same time, a well-written application will increase your chance of being shortlisted for a middle leadership role which you lack experience for. There are many young middle leaders who have been given some leeway because their application was carefully considered and they followed this up at interview with a thoughtful performance.

Basic questions

- Have you completed a written application before?
- What advice have colleagues or peers given on your application?
- Did your application help you gain an interview?
- Have you any thoughts on the strengths or weaknesses of your application?
- What experiences do you have, both in a school and non-school setting, that will support your application?

The detail

The following sections give generic advice on how you can complete a strong written application. It begins by considering how you can prepare yourself to write your application before studying the three main elements of written applications: application forms, letters of application and CVs.

Preparation

When beginning to structure your written application you will be in one of two positions: the first is that you have seen an advertisement that you want to apply for; the second is that you have decided the type of post you want to apply for and are currently constructing a practice application whilst you have some spare time.

The first element of preparation is to consider why you are suited to the post. For a middle leadership post the school may provide an essential and desirables list. Use this to brainstorm, make bullet points or even write some initial paragraphs. These notes are the cornerstone on which you will be constructing your application. If such a list is not provided, why not use one from another advert for a similar job to help frame your thoughts.

The second element of the preparation is considering the type of school where the job is advertised. You will find it very different being a curriculum leader in an urban comprehensive with a 'requires improvement' judgement from Ofsted than if you were tackling the same role in a well-established independent school. You need to think carefully if this is the type of school you want to work in and, ideally, why this school specifically. Again jot down some notes as you can use these when you are constructing your application.

Make sure you also study the details of the application process. Do you have to contact the school for further details or is this all on the website? Many schools have their application form permanently on the website. Check the closing date for applications. You may find it is different on the school website compared to on a website like the *TES*, so it will do no harm to double check this with the school.

Application form

Application forms should be one of the most straightforward elements in the job hunt. Most schools have an electronic version of their application form – in which case you should complete it electronically too. Schools expect a level of ICT competence from a middle leader whether it is for using an interactive whiteboard during a lesson, writing pupil reports online or using the school's tracking system. If you have completed an application form online you are immediately showing a school that you have these skills.

Much of an application form is factual information and you need to make sure that you enter this correctly. Many candidates make errors on the dates of their qualifications. If you have had different roles in your current school, make sure this is clear and that the dates marry up.

Do not forget to double check that you have completed all the boxes, paying particular attention to items like your DfE number and the criminal convictions question. You do not want the employer to be left worrying you have something to hide!

The three sections of the form where you can begin to strengthen your application are in the sections on employment history, INSET and further details. If you have only had one or two roles of employment, check to see whether there is space on the form to add bullet points about certain tasks that you have undertaken. For example, if you have improved or written a scheme of work you may be able to include this.

Many teachers mistakenly believe that INSET only counts if it is a day course that's been paid for. But what about those staff meetings when you have been trained on tracking, target setting or assessment and feedback. You can include these in this section. If you find you have a big list why not refer back to the essentials and desirable section of the job details to see which are most relevant. If you have led any INSET at your school you may be able to list it in this section too by using the subheading: 'INSET delivered'. You could also include TeachMeets, other educational events and subject specific events here too.

You need to check the application information to see how the further details section is expected to be used. Some schools will use this rather than a letter of application – in which case, refer to the next section on letters of application (see below) to help you fill this in. If a school permits you to write a letter of application, you can use the further details section to get your message across. For example, you could go through the essential and desirable sections of the job information and highlight those tasks you have already completed and those skills that you possess. You could use this space to highlight what you have done and achieved in your current post and previous posts. This can be communicated in bullet points rather than continuous prose. You can then use your letter of application to relate the most important of these to the role that you are applying for with your justification. Using this system ensures that your letter will always be less than two sides of A4.

Golden rules for completing the application form

- Always try to word-process your application form.
- Ensure there is something in every box.

- Double-check that the dates in your employment history and education are correct.
- Ensure the further information section dovetails with your letter of application.
- Include information from your letter and other additional information.
- Be prepared to have to explain any gaps in service.

Letter of application

There is a growing trend for candidates not to write a formal letter of application but instead to send a brief email with their attached application form. Your letter of application is the key selling point in your armoury and I would always encourage you to spend time writing this properly.

The best letters of application show a coherent structure and, in the words of one of my former principals, 'tell a story'. Most strong candidates use the same structure for the opening and ending paragraphs of their letter. There is a greater variation in the middle paragraphs of the letter. The following suggestions could be used to organise your letter with appropriate paragraph content. There is an example for a curriculum leader application and a pastoral leader application and there then follows examples of written paragraphs for each type of letter.

Paragraph		**Content**
1	Opening paragraph	• What is the post that you are applying for? • Where have you seen it advertised?
2	Second paragraph	• Why are you attracted to this school and post? • What is your current post?
3	Curriculum paragraph	• What is your vision for your subject? • How do you think pupils learn best in your subject?
4	Teaching paragraph	• Why are you a good teacher? • What evidence do you have for this? • What observation gradings and attainment data do you have?
5	Management paragraph	• What is your management/leadership style? • How would you work with your team? • Give examples of specific projects that you have led. • How have they made a difference in terms of school improvement?
6	Pastoral paragraph	• What type of relationships do you form with pupils? • What type of behavioural management techniques do you favour? • What pastoral experience do you have, e.g. form tutor? • Have you delivered assemblies? • How do you support staff with behaviour issues?

Paragraph		Content
7	Wider skills paragraph	• What are your wider skills? • What extra-curricular activities have you led?
8	Closing paragraph	• Summary of your personal attributes. • Remind the reader why you can help this school progress. • Thank the reader for considering your application.

Fig. 6 Paragraph content for a curriculum leader application

Paragraph		Content
1	Opening paragraph	• What is the post that you are applying for? • Where have you seen it advertised?
2	Second paragraph	• Why are you attracted to this school and post? • What is your current post?
3	Pastoral leadership paragraph	• What is your vision for effective pastoral leadership? • How do you think this improves pupil performance?
4	Pastoral paragraph	• What type of relationships do you form with pupils? • What type of behavioural management techniques do you favour? • What pastoral experience do you have, e.g. form tutor? • Have you delivered assemblies? • How do you support staff with behaviour issues?
5	Management paragraph	• What is your management/leadership style? • How would you work with your team? • Give examples of specific projects that you have led. • How have they made a difference in terms of school improvement?
6	Curriculum paragraph	• What is your subject specialism? • How do you believe pupils learn best in this subject?
7	Teaching paragraph	• Why are you a good teacher? • What evidence do you have for this? • What observation gradings and attainment data do you have?
8	Wider skills paragraph	• What are your wider skills? • What extra-curricular activities have you led?
9	Closing paragraph	• Summary of your personal attributes. • Remind the reader why you can help this school progress. • Thank the reader for considering your application.

Fig. 7 Paragraph content for a pastoral leader application

This is just one suggestion for how you can tackle writing your application letter. You could also write chronologically what you have achieved over time. A further alternative would be to consider the headings within the job profile and ensure that each paragraph tackles those headings. Whichever method you choose, take care not to write solely about what you have done. To take your letter to the next level you are also aiming to write about what you have learnt from these experiences and how this will mean you can hit the ground running when the school offers you the job.

You must be careful in how you use acronyms, project titles or job roles as all schools will have their own terminology. With any acronyms always write them in full the first time, and with project titles, try and give a brief explanation. It may be worth checking with a colleague in a different school to see whether their understanding of the terms you use is the same. There are some acronyms that do have universal usage, such as AfL – meaning Assessment for Learning – but even then, the first time you refer to the topic you should write it in full.

Opening paragraph

The first paragraph of your letter should be short, covering no more than the job you are applying for and where you have seen it advertised.

I am very excited to apply for the post of Head of English at Highfields School currently advertised in the Times Educational Supplement.

If you are very short of space in the rest of your letter, some candidates will instead use a reference, e.g.

Ref: Head of English advertised in the Times Educational Supplement, 7th January.

Second paragraph

The second paragraph should briefly explain why you are applying for the job. It is likely that this will be related to your current post and your main skills and attributes. It is important that you comment on why you want to work at this particular school so that the reader is not concerned that you are submitting a similar letter for a multitude of jobs. Personalising your letter to the school early on should help you make a connection with the reader so that they are more open to the rest of your letter.

Extract from a numeracy co-ordinator applicant

I have been teaching the year 5/6 class at Oak Primary School for the last three years. I have developed a strong range of teaching skills in this time and have a particular interest in developing maths in Key Stage 2. The Hawthorns has an excellent reputation amongst local educationalists as a child-centred school and I have studied your recent Ofsted report with interest. One of the issues that Ofsted commented upon was the development you have made in your maths teaching and learning. I would relish the opportunity to become your maths co-ordinator and build upon these improvements/build upon the progress you have made since your Ofsted.

Curriculum paragraph

For a curriculum leadership role, the following paragraph would come next. If you are applying for a pastoral leadership role, this is the type of information which you may include a little further down in your letter (see Paragraph content for a pastoral leader application, below).

Example of a curriculum paragraph

This example is by a science teacher who describes their vision for science before then briefly introducing the idea of curriculum design to support achievement.

I firmly believe that when teaching science we should seek to inspire the pupils by asking questions of the world around us. I would encourage my teachers to use a practical-based teaching approach wherever possible. Science should be about pupils creating their own hypothesis and then considering how they can best test these. Pupils can then develop their theoretical knowledge to underpin this approach. Alongside this, it is important to find the right courses for the pupils so that they achieve at the highest level, whether this is a carefully differentiated Key Stage 3 scheme of work or well-chosen pathways at Key Stage 4 which, for the most able, build towards an appropriate A-level syllabus.

Pastoral leadership paragraph

In the third paragraph of a pastoral leader's letter, you may begin to develop your vision of effective pastoral leadership and how you think this improves pupil performance.

Extract from a head of year applicant

The key to the most effective pastoral leadership is how it positively impacts on pupil performance. Whilst it is important as head of year to work to improve the behaviour of those pupils who find classrooms difficult and to support those teachers who are being challenged, it is also crucial to look at the wider spread of pupils within the year. There are likely to be pupils who are not reaching their targets but are not causing disciplinary issues. These pupils need to be identified and then appropriate intervention strategies introduced early enough so that they make expected progress.

Pastoral paragraph

If as a pastoral leader you do choose to write about your teaching later in the letter, then in paragraph 4 you need to explain in a little bit more detail how you will work with the children and your experiences so far. If you are applying for a curriculum leader role you may write a similar paragraph later in your letter (suggested as paragraph 6 in the paragraph content for a curriculum leader application, above).

Extract from a year leader applicant

Positive relations between teachers and pupils are vital in schools but are the mainstay for pastoral leaders. As both a teacher and a tutor, I have always sought to try and find out more about the pupils. I find that it is the little questions that you ask children about their lives in and out of school that help build the best relations. I am always looking for opportunities for positive interactions and such knowledge can greatly help. If children recognise that you care about them as a whole person, they are more prepared to listen when you are having the more difficult conversations. As a form tutor I like to be proactive in contacting parents both to share the positives and discuss any difficulties. Assemblies are also important in communicating your message to the wider group of children and I regularly support my current head of year by leading assemblies as an individual or by directing form assemblies. This year I have acted as a mentor for a PGCE student during their second practice and one of their targets was to develop classroom management techniques. The student observed me working with difficult pupils, co-taught lessons with me and we have analysed video recording of her lessons focusing on behaviour management. Such experiences would all ensure that I would be well-prepared for being an effective head of year at your school.

Teaching paragraph

It has already been highlighted that school leaders will be looking to appoint middle leaders who are strong classroom practitioners. In the fourth paragraph of a curriculum leader's letter you should be looking to address this point. As a pastoral leader you must not forget this point either. In the letter plan already suggested you may use this in paragraph 7 of your letter (see above) or you may choose to place it earlier. In this paragraph you should be looking to explain why you are a good teacher and what evidence you have of this.

Extract from a numeracy co-ordinator applicant

To lead the development of maths in a primary school, it is important to be able to teach at a high standard so that your colleagues are confident in your capability. In my performance management observations this year, my maths lesson was graded as outstanding and my English lesson was graded as good with outstanding features. In a recent Ofsted inspection, my year 5 maths lesson was described as excellent within the published report. In terms of progress, the target at my school is that pupils make 0.75 levels per year and we also measure the pupils who make 0.5 levels in a year. Last year the progress in the children I taught for both maths and English was described by performance managers as highly effective and above national expectations.

Leadership paragraph

For both curriculum leaders and pastoral leaders it is important for you to give the reader an opportunity to consider how you would lead a team. This is best shown by giving an example of a project that you have led. This is even stronger if there was a tangible improvement in either achievement or behaviour.

Extract from a candidate for a head of maths position

An effective head of maths must be able to identify areas where achievement can be improved and then work with the other members of the department to implement any changes. I like to work in a collaborative and inclusive style so that my colleagues are involved. I have recently rewritten sections of the year 9 scheme of work to address the changes in the new National Curriculum. I firstly identified the new skills that needed teaching and discussed with my colleagues whether they should be included in current modules or whether new modules needed writing. I shared the amended modules and new modules with my colleagues for feedback before trialling them with another colleague. The completed scheme of work is now ready for September and my colleagues are more confident in addressing the demands of the new curriculum.

Wider skills paragraph

Towards the end of the letter it is likely that you will discuss any wider skills or experiences you have which may benefit the school, such as extra-curricular work that you have been involved in. A hint here is to be careful about including activities that are particularly offbeat as some interviewers will use this to pigeon hole you rather than focusing on leadership skills or leadership potential! Also do not write too much in this section as you are applying for a middle leader post and senior leaders will wish your major focus to be on improving a particular area of the school.

Example of a wider skills paragraph

Involvement in extra-curricular activities can be particularly useful in building relationships with a range of pupils. I have a strong interest in sport and this year I have managed the netball team for my tutor group's year group. Each year I have also run a mixed netball competition for the year group, which has culminated in a staff/pupil match to raise money for the year group's charity initiative. This year I also organised a trip to watch our local super league netball team, which was particularly inspiring for some of the pupils.

Closing paragraph

The last paragraph should succinctly highlight in no more than two or three sentences why you are the perfect candidate for the post. You should also include the niceties of thanking the reader for considering your application and hoping that you have the opportunity to meet them at interview. The following extract could be written by a senior leader applicant, but there are also phrases that could be drawn on by any applicant.

Example of a Key Stage 2 co-ordinator's final paragraph

I have a core belief that all children should have the opportunity to learn in a safe and secure environment so that their skills can be nurtured. Key Stage 2 should be an exciting time in a child's education that prepares them well for the challenges of the future. I would bring energy and passion to your school whilst remaining sensitive to the needs of your staff, enabling me to become a vital member of your team. I would like to thank you for considering my application and I hope that I have the opportunity to meet you at interview.

You may be fortunate to have one unique selling point that other candidates don't have. This may be the reason you get interviewed even when there are more experienced teachers applying. You may have had an academic paper published, played sport at a high level or be very skilled in the arts. The important thing about such a talent is not to devote your whole letter to this point but instead when you do mention it, highlight the positives of this to the reader.

Presentation of your letter

Finally, take care over the presentation of your letter. The advertisement may direct you to sending your application to an administrator within the school but it is worthwhile finding out the headteacher's name and addressing your letter to them. Always use the business letter layout conventions. If you are short of space there is no reason why you should not shorten the school address to the person, post and the school's name.

Now is not the time to use fancy fonts, instead be conservative and use Arial, Calibri or Times New Roman with a minimum of point size 12. Your letter must not exceed two pages although you can change the margins on your letter to give you some space.

> Remember, you can use your CV or the further information on the application form to include additional experience that you have, rather than writing more than two pages.

Finally, make sure the application arrives on time with the correct postage. A belt and braces approach is to both email and post your application pack. In an ideal world, an emailed application should arrive at least a day before the closing date.

Golden rules for your letter of application

- You must word-process your letter.
- It is always a good idea to ask someone to proofread your letter.
- Always personalise your letter to the school that you are applying to.
- Always use a standard business letter layout including where the addresses are located on the page.
- Use prose not bullet points.

- Check who the letter should be addressed to.
- The minimum font size you should use is point 12.
- Keep your letter to less than two pages.

Your CV

Increasingly schools are not necessarily asking for CVs. One of the major reasons for this is that in the state sector the application form will be part of the school's response to the safeguarding agenda and will enable a school to ensure that they have all the information about a candidate that they require. You must never send a CV instead of a completed application form. Some schools will immediately discard such applications.

CVs may be requested by independent schools and in the state sector by recruitment agencies. They may also be asked for by overseas schools.

You should try and keep your CV to two sides of A4 paper. One way of achieving this is to carefully consider the layout and ensuring you use bullet points for many of your statements. The main text should not be less than font size 11. You might choose to use font size 12 for important statements such as the name of the school that you work in. Finally, you might increase the size of text to 14 for titles such as 'Employment history' or 'Qualifications'. Never use more than one font in your CV; standard choices are Arial, Calibri or Times New Roman. Rather than using a different font for more individuality, use italics or bold. However even with these guidelines you need to be careful that your CV does not start to look messy.

There are two types of CV:

- chronological CV – based around recording your employment history in date order
- functional CV – emphasises your skills and expertise.

Chronological CV

A chronological CV is a very factual document and the major part of such a CV is your employment history. Typically, a chronological CV will begin with your personal details, then employment history, education, interests before finishing with your references.

If you are making steady progress in your school and have obviously made good choices in your career pathway, this type of CV will demonstrate your career progression well. Perhaps you are looking at an assistant headship position in a secondary school and have moved from teacher, to head of department to head of faculty to a whole school project. This type of CV will immediately highlight this information in an easily understandable way for a recruiter. If you do not have many major key achievements but have focused on performing your job very competently, a chronological CV is a strong choice.

Example: chronological CV employment history section

This example shows how a candidate for Head of English may structure their employment history in a chronological CV..

Employment history

2011–Present:	Forest Academy (11–19 co-ed comprehensive, 1,450 nor) Co-ordinator of Key Stage 5 English (TLR2b) Responsible for A-level English language and English literature Over the last three years the student performance has risen by half a grade
2008–2011:	Forest Academy (11-19 co-ed comprehensive, 1,450 number on roll (nor)) Teacher of English and Year 12 Form tutor
2006–2008:	Beach College of Technology (11–16 co-ed comprehensive, 600 nor) Teacher of English

Fig. 8 Chronological CV employment history section

Functional CVs

Whereas a chronological CV begins with your employment history, a functional CV begins with your key achievements and you only give a brief description of each post you have held in the employment history.

Functional CVs are ideal if you have followed a less traditional career structure or if you are eager for promotion. If you are currently a main scale teacher but you are looking to become a head of faculty, a functional CV will allow you to show the different experiences that you have had. You can use the key achievements section to highlight the different projects you have led as a classroom teacher, INSET sessions you have delivered or academic research you have conducted.

If you have moved around a variety of different posts or have left the profession at different times, a functional CV can be ideal as you can use it to highlight what you have achieved in those different posts rather than the range of different posts you have held.

If you have lots of achievements and you struggle to fit them all into your letter of application, a functional CV can be ideal to ensure that the recruiter can see them. If you are a more mature candidate and looking to make a significant promotion for the first time, a functional CV takes the spotlight away from how long you have been in any one post or any one school and instead highlights what you have achieved as a teacher.

If you are looking to gain a middle leadership post in a different sector than you currently work in, a functional CV will enable you to focus on the transferrable skills and experiences that you have had.

Example: functional CV key achievements section

This example shows how a teacher looking to become Head of Key Stage 2 in a primary school may structure the experiences gathered as a classroom teacher in a small primary school in a functional CV key achievements section.

Key achievements:

- Led the implementation of the Values Education programme across Key Stage 2
- Implemented a PSHE programme for Key Stage 2
- Delivered weekly assemblies to Key Stage 2 pupils addressing the 'mindsets' agenda
- Level 1 hockey coach

Fig. 9 Functional CV key achievements section – below

Personal profiles

If you look at CVs prepared by employment agencies there is often a personal profile. This consists of two or three sentences which describe yourself and the type of role you are looking for. It is a fascinating process to try and summarise your experiences and aspirations in such a short number of words and one that is worth refining for interview preparation as well as for a CV.

Example: functional CV personal profile

Notice how this example is written in the first person and summarises key elements of the candidate's job application.

> **Personal profile:**
>
> I am looking to become the maths co-ordinator in a large primary school drawing upon my outstanding classroom teaching (Ofsted 2011), further professional studies with the Open University and my mentoring of Initial Teacher Training students.

Fig. 10 Functional CV personal profile – below

Golden rules for CVs

- Think carefully as to whether a functional or chronological CV is right for you.
- Never send a CV instead of an application form if one is asked for. A form is often used for safeguarding purposes to collect very specific and consistent information.
- Only use one font in a CV.
- Be consistent in your font size; one size for titles, another for key points and slightly smaller for longer points.

Final thoughts

Your written application is crucial to you getting an interview. There is no excuse for not ensuring this is done properly. It is a good idea to begin thinking and planning your application before posts appear by keeping a good record of your career and some notes on why different experiences useful. It can be worthwhile asking to read other people's applications and also to look at the examples in this book, but never copy another application. You may also find there are people who are prepared to help you improve your letter, such as a trusted colleague or friend.

To do list:

- ❑ Reflect on how you think you would structure a letter of application.
- ❑ Reflect on the skills and attributes that you would describe in your application.
- ❑ Update and improve your CV.
- ❑ Have a go at writing a letter of application.
- ❑ Check out Tom Bennett's tweets @TomBennett7 (see Takeaway box).
- ❑ Read *Get That Teaching Job!* by Paul K Ainsworth (see Takeaway box).

Chapter 5 takeaway

Teaching tip

A mock application

If you have some time, why not look for a job which might appeal to you in the future and obtain the details. Compare yourself against the job description and then jot down some notes as to how you would begin to present yourself in a letter of application.

Pass it on

Sharing ideas – mock application

Discuss with a close colleague what you think the requirements are for a middle leadership position and compare this with the job description that you have obtained. Highlight the skills and attributes which you think would make your colleague suited for the post and ask them to do the same for you.

CPD book club recommendation

Paul K. Ainsworth, *Get That Teaching Job!*
(see Bibliography and further reading)

Bloggers' corner

Tom Bennett has some great tweets from his experience as a teacher, writer and researcher that are well worth a read. Follow him on Twitter @TomBennett7 and check out his blog: behaviourguru.blogspot.co.uk

6 Preparing for your interview

The next stage towards becoming a middle leader will be your first interview.

The basics

In some subject areas there can be a real shortage of middle leadership applicants and you could even find yourself in the position of being the only person selected for interview. Do not think that you have the job in the bag though, as you might find that a school may still be reluctant to offer a sole candidate the permanent post. They may be tempted to offer a different position, so you still need to convince them that you are the right person.

For other roles in popular schools you could find there are six interview candidates and the headteacher explaining that not all candidates will be interviewed but instead some will be 'cut' at varying points in the process.

It is highly likely you will already have had a teaching interview for the position you currently hold, though there is also the chance that you have been appointed following a successful supply position. Middle leadership interviews tend to build on those that schools use for main scale posts. In some schools, they may use the identical process but just change questions in the interview. In other schools, they may add a variety of tasks and assessments and the process can almost mirror a senior leadership process.

In addition to determining whether you are a good teacher, the school will be trying to consider whether you have the skills to lead other staff and sometimes, just as importantly, whether your style of leadership will fit with that of the school.

Basic questions

- Have you been for a middle leadership interview before?
- What tasks did you find challenging on that occasion?
- What feedback did you receive?
- Have you been offered a middle leadership interview?
- Have they informed you of the tasks of the day?

The detail

In this following section we will briefly look at how you can present yourself for an interview, some of the different tasks that a school may ask you to tackle and an example of the interview questions that you could receive for a middle leadership post.

Presenting yourself

You will be aware that the moment that you arrive at the school for interview, everyone is trying to assess whether you should be appointed. If this was the case for a teaching post, it is even more so for a middle leadership post as a whole range of individuals will be trying to decide whether you can lead that curriculum area or year group.

In both curriculum and pastoral leadership roles you will be leading staff and presenting the school to stakeholders such as parents far more than you would as a classroom teacher, so you need to consider how your appearance and demeanour portrays your ability to do this. As a result, you may choose to dress a little more professionally than you would normally. Try not be too cluttered with bags and folders when you arrive at the school as anything which can fluster you needs to be avoided. You want to immediately give the impression of being a professionally capable individual who can lead staff, and not be remembered for other reasons.

The important thing to remember is that as soon as you arrive in the car park you are in interview mode at all times and you are being watched.

Tasks

The majority of middle leadership interviews last one day. There is the potential for a two-day interview process, but this is unlikely. A school will select a variety of tasks for you to undertake but you will be limited by time.

- Delivering a lesson (p.63) – most schools ask teachers to deliver a lesson and then have a formal interview, so you would expect to do these.

Other tasks which may be included are the following:

- giving a presentation (p.64)
- in-tray exercise (p.64)
- pupil panel or pupil interview (p.65)
- professional discussion (p.66)
- data task (p.66)
- lesson observation (p.66).

It is unlikely that you will be asked to do all of these as that would be moving into the realms of a senior leader interview process. You may also find that some tasks lend themselves to certain positions, so an in-tray exercise or a pupil panel may be more directly suited to a pastoral leader interview process, whereas presentations, professional discussions, data tasks or lesson observations may be used more frequently for curriculum leader interview processes.

Delivering a lesson

Teaching a lesson is one of the make or break moments in the interview process. The bottom line is that schools need good teachers. Equally, if you do not appear a confident practitioner, a school will be concerned as to whether you can lead staff whether in a curriculum leader or a pastoral leader role.

There are whole books written on teaching perfect or outstanding lessons but this is probably not the time to move completely out of your comfort zone and deliver something in a completely different style. It is hard enough to deliver an outstanding lesson in your own school with classes that you know never mind in a new school with pupils that you do not know. So your aim should be to deliver a solid good lesson.

You want the observer to see you take control of the class and communicate strongly with them. Whereas independent learning is a good thing, you want the observer to have the opportunity to see you do some teaching, so that they can recognise that you have ability to model a process for the pupils. For schools that are obsessed with the Ofsted agenda, you need them to easily see that the pupils have made progress by making good use of plenary moments during the lesson, not just at the end. For this to work, there needs to be opportunities for pupils to show that they have achieved something. In written subjects, pupils must write something down; in maths they need to have tackled problems, and in a practical subject you need to bring in some practical work so that the observer can see that you can manage the health and safety aspects of your subject.

You need to show differentiation whether the group is an ability set or mixed ability. All schools will have certain agendas – whether it's stretching the most able or improving the performance of a certain group of pupils. If you can identify this in advance it can help your lesson planning.

Lesson timings will always be difficult with pupils that you do not know, so always include an extra task to draw upon and have a strategy ready for if the pupils take a long time over one of your tasks. Include these in your planning so that the observer can see that you have considered possibilities.

If you are being interviewed for a curriculum leader position, it would be a strength to show how the lesson would be included within a scheme of work and what the end of module assessment may look like.

Finally, at the end of the lesson ensure you quickly reflect on how the lesson went and make some notes, as it is likely that this will be asked about during the interview.

Giving a presentation

Presentations are probably the most popular task to give a potential middle leader as it gives the interviewer the opportunity to assess how the candidate approaches a problem, relates it to their potential role and then communicates this to other people.

Most presentation tasks tend to be about ten minutes – mainly to give the panel a chance to see all the candidates and also to ask a few questions. This means you probably do not require any more material than you could write on two sides of A4 paper.

Popular topics often fall into three groups:

1. How do you see your role in this school?
2. How would you approach a particular development task in the school?
3. Your opinion on a current educational issue.

However, in effect whichever of these groups your title falls into you also need to cover the other two groups so that the panel is clear that you recognise what your role is, you understand current educational issues and that you can relate these to a particular area of school improvement and the impact this will have on the pupils.

Presentations also give you an opportunity to show that you have ICT competence. Most candidates will use a PowerPoint but you could, if you have the skills, show some variety by using a 'Prezi' (free presentation software, see www.prezi.com). Remember though, the panel are interested in what you say you would do rather than being entertained by the graphics of your presentation. You want to be seen to be professional and competent in terms of the visual display. So do not spend hours on this aspect of your presentation.

In tray exercise

In-tray exercises are a great way for interviewers to assess how a candidate will cope with a range of problems given to them. An in-tray exercise is when you have to sift through a list of tasks or problems and decide on the order in which they should be done and who should do them. Sometimes you will also be expected to solve the problem, for example you might have to write a letter or an email. This is particularly pertinent for pastoral leader candidates who may find every lunchtime becomes a prioritisation exercise.

When you are doing an in-tray exercise you need to read each item carefully. You will have to decide what order you should do the items in and what you need to do. Possible errors are:

- trying to do everything yourself – senior leaders will be checking that you pass the right issues on to them and delegate others. (If you find that you are referring every issue to SLT then you may have gone a bit far!)
- read the instructions carefully to see whether you need to actually do the task during the exercise, e.g. write a letter/email to a parent in response to an issue. Do not just write when you would do this. The interviewer is likely to be including this task to see how well you can write such a response.

Often the best practice for such a task is talking to someone who is currently in this role about what issues they have faced in the preceding week and then consider how you would approach them yourself. Lastly, remember that if it is anything to do with pupil safety, it has a very high priority!

Pupil panels or pupil interview

Pupil panels or pupil interview can be one of the most random moments in any interview process. You never really know how they have been set up by the school and how formal they will be.

Pupil panels can be very structured events – these are the ones that have been carefully planned by a school council under the watchful eye of a senior leader. The pupils have carefully considered questions and know the order in which they are being asked. Sometimes they are chaired by one of the pupils. There can be occasions when one or more members of staff are observing the pupil panel. Such pupil panels are very similar to a formal interview and you have to treat their questions with the same seriousness you would from the headteacher – after all, you are not really sure who is giving the feedback to the headteacher, the pupils or those staff watching.

There are also pupil panels which can owe more to a Jonathan Ross interview – these are the ones where the school has left the pupils to their own devices; no one is observing the panel and you can receive questions like:

- What's your favourite joke?
- Can you do an impression?
- If you were a biscuit, what would you be?

This type of interview can seem very tiresome but the best advice is to participate with good grace whilst retaining your dignity.

Professional discussion

Professional discussion may be used to ascertain your specialist subject knowledge, particularly if there is no one on the formal interview panel who possesses this expertise. For a language teacher, the discussion may take place in the target language. A scientist may be asked for their thoughts on a particular element of the curriculum. An English teacher may be engaged in a discussion on an aspect of literature. Sitting on the other side of the fence, this is the one occasion when I may ask the departing post-holder to participate in the interview beyond providing information for candidates.

Data tasks

For a potential curriculum leader, a data task should be seen as a very positive opportunity to analyse current data on the area that they will be leading. You may be given current data on the school which would give you a chance to delve into the performance of the subject area. A potential pastoral leader could be asked to look at a piece of tracking on a year group. Generally you will be asked for strengths in the data, weaknesses and then action that you could take to address any issues.

If you are a curriculum leader and you know this task is on the programme, it may be worth finding out a few pieces of national information about your subject area. If you are a maths or English teacher, be aware of expected progress for pupils of different starting points. For other subject areas, take a look at the GCSE grade C pass rate for pupils of different prior attainment. These can all be found in 'Raise online' (www.raiseonline.org).

A pastoral leader would be looking to see if there are groups of pupils who are underperforming. You could do this by identifying and listing the individual pupils who are not progressing as they should The next stage would be to see if you see any trends according to pupil groups such as gender, pupil premium, prior attainment etc.

Lesson observation

A curriculum leader could be asked to observe part of a lesson whether in the flesh or a video clip and then give their comments. As a potential curriculum leader, whilst it is useful if you can indicate how this could relate to an Ofsted grade for teaching over time, this is not as vital as it would be for a senior leader. Instead, a school is likely to be more interested whether you can assess the strengths and weaknesses of a lesson and then if you can suggest the feedback you would give to the member of staff.

They may also want to know what development needs you have identified in the member of staff. After all, as a curriculum leader one of your key tasks will be developing the quality of teaching and learning in your curriculum area and one way of achieving this is by correctly identifying areas for improvement and appropriate actions you would take.

Formal interview

The final part of the selection process will be the formal interview. Expect to be interviewed by at least three members of staff, perhaps the headteacher, another senior leader and a governor.

Many interviews will follow a similar pattern.

- They often begin with questions which allow a candidate to introduce themselves and perhaps give their view on a part of the process already such as the lesson they have taught.
- Then there will more detailed questions about the role and how you will tackle it. Some of these will be questions about your style of leadership and others will be more specific to the role that you are being interviewed for. There tends to be around five or six questions in here.
- The final set of questions will be more procedural in nature and you may find them in any interview.

The following table gives some suggestions of the type of questions you may be asked at either a pastoral or curriculum leader interview with some hints for what you may wish to include in your answers.

Questions	Notes for your possible answers
Tell us a little bit about yourself and what inspired you to apply for a job at this school.	This should be an open goal question and one that you have considered. Describe your career over the last few years and why this has prepared you to become a curriculum leader. Try and weave in something specific about the school and why you wish to work there.
You have just taught your lesson: what went particularly well and if you were to repeat the lesson, what would you do differently?	The common error here is to focus on either all the positives or all the negatives. Try and give a balance of things that went well as well as those you would improve on next time.
Can you describe your leadership style and how this has contributed to the success of the department you currently work in?	Some candidates will have a theoretical model which they use to describe their leadership, but this is not essential. Instead the interviewers will be looking for you to give examples of when you've been a creative thinker, led colleagues, developed a project and worked within a team to raise standards. Your ideal answer would describe a project that you have led. It does not have to be a major improvement but could be as simple as a module that you have written and other colleagues have used.
What do you think your personal strengths and weaknesses are as a middle leader?	This is another common question. You should be looking for a strength that is linked to the middle leadership role. In terms of weaknesses, you should be thinking of something that you wish to develop. It could be a technical issue such as conducting lesson observations or a leadership skill. A commonly-used answer is taking on too much.
What do you feel will be the main challenges for this curriculum area over the next three to four years? How will you prioritise these?	You are trying to show in your answer that you are aware of the national agenda for education as a whole and for your subject area. Education moves so quickly that such issues are constantly changing. Linking the issue to in-house CPD within your department can strengthen the answer.

Questions	Notes for your possible answers
What sort of support do you think teachers would need for the development of...?	This is a second opportunity to discuss how you deliver CPD in your curriculum area. Interviewers will be most impressed with in-house solutions such as coaching, mentoring, action research, collaborative planning and peer observation – although you can suggest a colleague attending an external course and then sharing the information.
How would you support a team member who was struggling with classroom discipline?	Firstly the interviewers are looking for empathy. Most colleagues can struggle with a certain group. In such situations you are looking for strategies where both you and the curriculum area can support the colleague. This could include moving children or delivering sanctions as a team. If the colleague is having lots of difficulties, it could be there is a training issue where you need to coach and mentor the colleague. It is worth highlighting that in some situations the difficulties may be so entrenched that senior leadership support is required.
How would you know if your department was a successful one?	This could be an opportunity for you to highlight self-assessment and you could discuss data, lesson observations and pupil views. You could also discuss pupil take-up of the subject at option points or pupil involvement in extra-curricular activities.
How can ICT aid teaching and learning?	In this question you are looking to strike the balance between your knowledge as a teacher and as a middle leader. You could use examples from your teaching to show an understanding of emerging technologies within the classroom and throughout the school. You could then strengthen your answer by suggesting how you would develop this across your curriculum area including how you would encourage and empower those colleagues who are less confident with ICT.
A Year 7 girl comes to see you in tears claiming that her mother and stepfather have been arguing lots and she is refusing to go home that evening. What would you do?	This question is checking your understanding of child protection issues and that in serious situations you would liaise with senior leaders. Such a situation probably needs to involve the designated senior person as, if it can't be resolved, it needs to involve a referral to social services which a middle leader would not usually be expected to do.

Questions	Notes for your possible answers
How do you see your role in contributing to the extra-curricular provision at this school?	You are looking to give examples that show your willingness to engage with the wider teaching role and contribution to the whole school. As a middle leader you might also suggest ways in which you could lead activities that support your curriculum area's profile and the pupil's achievement.
Is there anything else you would like to ask us or is there anything else that you would like to add which would support your application that has not been previously covered?	Try and limit yourself to one or two questions. If you still have concerns over salary or non-contact time, you are better to ask these after you have been offered the job! If you haven't any questions, you could use this moment to reiterate why you would like the job.
Are you a firm candidate?	Hopefully the answer to this is yes. If you still have concerns, again maybe the time to raise these is when the job is offered to you. However, if during the interview you have decided you definitely do not want the job, you should say so at this point.

Fig. 11 Interview questions: curriculum leader

Questions	Notes
What experiences have you had in the past in dealing with other agencies that make you think you will be an effective head of Year 7?	So much of a pastoral leader's role is built on understanding the importance of a multi-agency approach and the head of year's role in liaison. You may have only had one experience of working with an outside agency and you should be looking to reflect on how effective this was and what you would do differently next time. Then you can move onto other outside agencies who you believe a pastoral leader may need to work with, from the local police to medical services.
Can you describe a difficult conversation you have had to have with a parent and how you resolved the situation?	It would be easy to describe a situation where a parent has been unhappy with a teaching decision you have made but this may give rise to a doubt in your ability. Instead, a stronger answer could be to describe an occasion when you have communicated on behalf of the school, such as being proactive as a tutor and dealing with a behaviour issue in other lessons. All interviewers will have sympathy with you if the parent was difficult and would not expect the resolution to lead to delighted parents. So describing a situation where parents were just accepting of the school action is realistic.

Questions	Notes
A parent complains that their quiet, well-behaved son is not making much progress because of more disruptive students in many of his classes. What do you do?	This is often a difficult situation and the first thing that you need to highlight is that you would arrange a meeting with the parent, listen to what they have to say and research the issue further. In such circumstances you may need to work with the appropriate curriculum leader; if there is a major issue you will need to share it with senior leaders. You may have an example as a tutor when you have dealt with the problem before.
How important do you think using data is to being an effective head of year?	The role of data for pastoral leaders has hugely increased. You need to explain how pastoral leaders need to have access to tracking data so that they can intervene when pupils are underperforming in a number of subjects. You must also be able to see if there is underperformance in groups of pupils within your area.
How would you support a team member who was struggling with delivering tutor time sessions with their form?	Firstly the interviewers are looking for empathy. Most colleagues can have a struggle with a certain group. In such situations you are looking for strategies where both you and the curriculum area can support the colleague. This could include moving children or delivering sanctions as a team. If the colleague is having lots of difficulties, it could be that there is a training issue where you need to coach and mentor the colleague. It is worth highlighting that in some situations the difficulties may be so entrenched that senior leadership support is required.
How would you know if you were doing a good job?	Success for a pastoral leader can be difficult to judge. The most obvious is the academic progress the pupils are making in comparison to their starting points. Yet at the same time there is the intangible ethos that a group of pupils may have around their attitude to learning and the school in general.
How do you see your role in contributing to the extra-curricular provision at this school?	You are looking to give examples that show your willingness to engage with the wider teaching role and contribution to the whole school. As a pastoral leader, you might also suggest ways in which you could lead activities that also support building the ethos for your group of pupils. This may involve running in-school competitions and challenges and organising trips and visits.
Is there anything else you would like to ask us or is there anything else that you would like to add which would support your application that has not been previously covered?	Try and limit yourself to one or two questions. If you still have concerns over salary or non-contact time, you are better to ask these after you have been offered the job! If you haven't any questions, you could use this moment to reiterate why you would like the job.

Fig. 12 Interview questions: pastoral leader

Final thoughts

Interview processes are emotionally exhausting for all those who participate in them. You may be very fortunate and get the job you are looking for at your first interview, but for many aspirant middle leaders this will not be the case and you will have to pick yourself up and apply for another role.

From each interview process, whether you are successful or not, there will be things that you can learn and areas that you wish to gain more knowledge of. You may be offered some feedback from the school but other schools will refuse to do this. If you receive feedback just write down what you are told. When your emotions are more balanced, it is always worth spending some time reflecting on the process, the feedback you received and what you feel you would like to do differently next time.

Finally, remember that the interview process is not just about a particular school finding the person with the best technical skills; it is also the more abstract idea of finding the 'right' person for that school in that circumstance. However painful it may be if you are unsuccessful, if you want to be a middle leader you will get there.

TO DO LIST:

- ❑ Reflect on your interview experiences so far.
- ❑ Reflect on the discussions you have had with colleagues on interview.
- ❑ Create some interview question and answer flash cards.
- ❑ Tweet some challenging interview questions.
- ❑ Check out Mary Myatt's blog posts on her adviser experiences (see Takeaway box).
- ❑ Read *Get that Teaching Job!* by Paul K. Ainsworth (see Takeaway box).

Chapter 6 takeaway

Teaching tip

Preparing for interviews

A useful task is to work your way through the interview questions that appear earlier on in this chapter and make notes as to how you would answer the questions (without looking at the examples provided of course!). You could build up set of postcards as students do for examinations and every time you hear of a different interview question, write it on a card with notes on how you would answer it. When you are asked to interview, take these cards with you.

Pass it on

Practise an interview

Some people will suggest asking a senior leader at your school to give you a mock interview but this can also feel awkward if you are explaining why you would like a job at a different school. So instead why not work with a trusted colleague, discussing interview questions and how you could each answer them from the skills and experiences that you have. Sometimes it is easier for somebody else to remind you of things that you have done well, which you can take for granted.

Share and tweet

Have you heard of or been at the end of any difficult or out of the ordinary interview questions? Share them using #BloomsCPD – also, if you were the interviewee tell us how you answered them!

CPD book club recommendation

Paul K. Ainsworth, *Get That Teaching Job!*

(see Bibliography and further reading)

Bloggers' corner

Mary Myatt has some great posts from her experience as a school adviser. Visit her blog at: marymyatt.com/blog or follow her on Twitter: @MaryMyatt

STAGE 3: FIRST STEPS

7 Visiting your school

Once the interview day is over and you have been offered the job, it can sometimes feel a little unreal as the next day you return to your current post and resume your role. The date from being interviewed to the 1st September (or new term) can often feel a long time and your mind is likely to be filled with hopes and perhaps some worries about your new role.

The basics

Most schools will release you to spend a day in your new school, but for a middle leadership role your school is likely to be reluctant to give you more than one day as they will have to cover your classes when you are out. If your new school specifically requests you to spend more than one day with them, you may need to ask the senior leader to negotiate with your current school, and they may have to pay the cost of the supply cover for such days.

If you do only have one day, you need to make sure that this day is as effective as possible. You need to gain all the facts so that you are fully prepared for starting the post on the 1st September (or in the new term). In summary, the information is likely to be on your middle leadership responsibilities and your teaching responsibilities. It can be tempting to forget about the latter through your excitement at becoming a middle leader, but remember that getting it right in the classroom is crucial so do not skimp on this information. You may have visited previous new schools as a classroom teacher: try and think back to what useful knowledge you gathered and what you wish, in hindsight, that you had found out.

BASIC QUESTIONS

- Have you had other visits to schools after a successful interview?
- What went well and what do you wish you had done differently?
- Do you know who is the best person to contact?
- When are you thinking of visiting?
- Who would you like to meet?
- What information are you aiming to gather?

The detail

This following section will help you consider the planning needed to gain the most from this visit to your new school. It will look at who to liaise with, when is the best time to visit and who you need to see on the day. Then it ensures that you have everything you need for those first weeks of term as a new middle leader and also as a new classroom teacher.

Who to contact

As a new middle leader it is not always obvious who is the best person to contact about arranging a visit to your new school. In an ideal world when you were offered the job, you may have been told but amidst your excitement, even if you were told, it is quite normal to forget such a piece of information.

It may be worth thinking back to the interview panel and who was on it. It is likely that the headteacher led the interview and the senior leader who will line manage you in your new middle leadership role also participated.

If you can remember that person's name, they may be the most appropriate to contact. If you have forgotten, which is quite understandable, I would suggest contacting the head's personal assistant (PA), especially if it is a big school. They may have been involved in planning the interview day and you may have met them. If you explain your query, it is likely that they will know who the best person to speak to is. In a small school, you may find that the headteacher is also your line manager and in this circumstance, you will need to speak to them. Before you do pick up the phone though, read on first so that you make best use of your time.

When to visit

It is often very tempting to arrange a visit so that you attend soon after the interview. It is human nature to wish to do this, as this second visit can make your appointment seem more real. Yet if you visit too soon, you may find that the school does not have the information you really require for September. If you live locally to your new school, you could call in one afternoon to complete paperwork such as your DBS check and in doing this you may have the opportunity to say hello to your new colleagues.

If you have gained a middle leadership role in a secondary school, you really need to wait until the timetable is compiled before you go and visit as otherwise you will not know which classes you are teaching and hence which resources you need to obtain.

In a primary school, the key thing is knowing which year group you will be teaching. It is likely that this will be confirmed immediately after the summer resignation date, but it may be determined sooner.

In all situations, you have to be sensitive to your new school. Remember they are still working on the current school year, whereas your mind is firmly focused on next year. You have to be guided by your new school's wishes even if that means you have to be a little more patient than you really wish to be.

Who to see

To a certain extent, this will depend on what is happening in school on the day of your visit. Many new middle leaders will wish to see the headteacher to begin to build a relationship with them away from the pressure of an interview. This should give you an opportunity to discover more about their vision for their school and the section that you are responsible for. You can ask more questions at this point than you may have felt able to at interview.

It is important to spend some time with the colleague who will be line managing you, often another member of the senior leadership team. If they have been in this role for a year or longer, they should be able to explain the strengths and weaknesses of the curriculum or pastoral area that you will be leading. They should also be able to tell you if there are any immediate priorities that need addressing and also give you pen portraits of the individuals you will be leading.

You may not have had the opportunity to speak to the current postholder during the interview process, so this may give you a good opportunity to talk to them. You may find it interesting to compare their views with your future line manager's, but it is also important to be aware that they may give you a jaundiced view of the role, even if they are not intending to. It is natural that the previous postholder will begin to detach themselves from the school and role and hence they may give you a less positive view than is the reality.

Hopefully, you will also be able to talk to the colleagues that you will be line managing. However, do not expect to spend too much time with them as they will be working hard on completing the year and may not really want to think about the next school year before they have even had their summer holiday! You could also be starting in a school at Christmas or Easter and again you need to be sensitive to the pressures that they are under.

Finally, do not forget other middle leaders who may be leading you. If you are taking on the role of a pastoral leader, ensure you talk to your new curriculum leader about your teaching requirements – especially if they have not been too involved in your appointment. They may even feel a little resentful to have this happen to them. If you are a curriculum leader it is a nicety to spend a little time with your pastoral leader. This is something that many new curriculum leaders forget but pastoral leaders can be important new allies.

What information to gather

Your first aim should be to refamiliarise yourself with the vision of the school and the whole school priorities which are being worked towards. You may be going to a school that is preparing for an inspection and they may have a number of key issues which they are seeking to address to achieve their goal. In addition there may be some staff changes, both departures and arrivals that you need to be brought up to speed on. You could find that that your area is not fully staffed and temporary solutions are being sought. In terms of staffing, there may be issues that you were not made aware of at interview such as competency, disciplinary or personal issues and it is also important to ask what you need to address immediately, things that are proving barriers to or even stopping progress in your area.

You need to ask what procedural things you will be expected to do during your first few days in post. For example, you may be expected to conduct performance management/appraisal of your team. In which case, it is worth asking for copies of the policy and the targets that your team have been working towards. You may be expected to lead a team meeting in your first few days. All this information should be included in a plan of the INSET day.

If you are a curriculum leader, you will be responsible for schemes of work so you will wish to take these away to look at. It is not always a good idea to radically rewrite these before you start as you may find the pupils work quite differently than in your previous schools. You need to know which groups you will be teaching and what their academic profile is so that you can best prepare for those initial lessons. You may even work with a senior leader to allocate groups to your team, or you may find this has already been done by the previous postholder. In such circumstances, you may not find the timetable is kind to you! Ensure you take away the resources that your groups will be working through, especially if the curriculum area uses a commercial scheme of work.

There are some policies that are worth collecting, such as: teaching and learning, marking and behaviour management – though these may be covered in an induction process and some schools will take all their staff through these key policies during INSET days.

You may like to ask about the opening arrangements for the school over the holiday period as you may want to spend time organising your new classroom. You need to be sensitive though and do this after the previous postholder has cleared their things. One tricky point for many new postholders is ICT access. You will probably want your new school laptop if there is one, access to the school network and your new email address. However, many schools are reluctant to do this before you begin employment. It is also likely that any hardware you will be given needs to be collected from the current postholder.

Lastly, it is worth asking for key dates for the diary.

> Remember schools often have different holidays and you don't want to end up booking something over the holidays and then find it's during term time for your new school.

Issue	Who to ask	Information required
Whole school vision and priorities	Headteacher or line manager	• How do you contribute? • Are there issues you need to tackle in your area?
First Days	Line manager	• Timetable for an upcoming INSET day (if there is to be one) • Appraisal policies
Staffing	Line manager	• Allocation of teachers to groups • Staffing shortages • Disciplinary/competency issues • Personal issues
Teaching	Current postholder/ teachers in your area	• Schemes of work • Resources • Class lists • Pupil data • Policies (teaching and learning, marking, behaviour)
Miscellaneous	Line manager	• School opening times • Important diary dates

Fig. 13 Gathering information during your school visit

Final thoughts

It is likely that prior to beginning your new post you will feel a combination of excitement and anxiety. You need to use your school visit to try and assuage your anxieties and one of the best ways of doing this is to ensure that you are properly prepared for your first week in your new school.

After you have read this chapter, spend some time planning what you think you need to get out of your visit to your new school. Think carefully about what information you really need in order to be able to hit the ground running. At the same time, you need to be sensitive to your new colleagues. Remember there will be other new teachers starting who will also want support and that your new colleagues need to say their farewells to the departing colleagues. You do not want to get in the way of this by being too demanding.

To do list:

- ☐ Reflect on how you would organise a school visit prior to taking up a post.
- ☐ Reflect on colleagues' opinions of how you can make the best impression.
- ☐ Check out John Tomsett's blog posts on johntomsett.com (see Takeaway box).
- ☐ Read *Teacher* by Tom Bennett (see Takeaway box).

Chapter 7 takeaway

Teaching tip

Plan a visit

If you were a new middle leader starting at your school, think about which people you would want to talk to and also what information you would like to take away with you.

Pass it on

Share your ideas – visits to your school

Discuss with colleagues the occasions when new starters have visited your school. How did they present themselves? How was the visit received by other colleagues? Consider what you could learn from this. Also ask your colleagues what experience they have had of visiting other schools prior to starting a post. What would they do differently?

CPD book club recommendation

Tom Bennett, *Teacher*
(see Bibliography and further reading)

Bloggers' corner

John Tomsett has some great posts on a vast range of educational issues that are well worth a read. Visit his blog at: johntomsett.com or follow him on Twitter: @johntomsett

8 Your first days with the staff

It is possible that you will have one day with the staff before the children arrive in school. If you start in September, there will possibly be two full days before lessons are under way. If you start at Easter this may not be the case, and you may go straight into lessons, in which case the advice in this chapter may feed into moments within your first week.

The basics

The first days with the staff are important, and every new middle leader will have a range of priorities which could include:

- getting to know your team
- building your profile amongst the wider staff
- recognising the development needs of your area
- beginning to bring about improvement.

You are looking to use the opportunities within these INSET days to build your foundations within the school so that you can achieve such priorities quickly and smoothly.

When you visited your new school prior to start date, you should have organised to receive a copy of the plan for the INSET days, and it is likely that there will be occasions when you are expected to lead elements of the day with your new colleagues. If you are a curriculum leader you will probably have a curriculum meeting to plan, and if you are a pastoral leader there is likely to be a meeting for your team of tutors. Depending on how tightly your school has planned these days, there may or may not be working time for your teachers to organise themselves in preparation for their first lessons. If there is, this gives you some informal time to begin to understand the workings of your area.

There will be also be time when you are together as a whole staff. There will be a mixture of information given by senior leaders and also some training where you will be expected to work with different staff members on given tasks. There are likely to be occasions when you are in a meeting led by other middle leaders, either team or curriculum meetings. There may be social gatherings too, possibly a meet and greet for new staff or a whole staff lunch. Finally, there will be the informal moments too, such as that first coffee in the staffroom before the organised activities begin. If you start at Christmas or Easter there may not be an INSET day prior to starting and you will have to work harder at finding out key information to help you in your first weeks.

Basic questions

- Have you got the school plan for the first few days?
- What activities will you be leading?
- What other activities do you need to attend?
- Which staff do you already know?
- What would you like to achieve during these days?

The detail

The aim of the following sections is to give you the confidence to tackle these first few days so that you can begin to establish yourself with your team and the wider staff and to ensure your first interactions with the pupils are as smooth as possible.

Planning your first meeting

Along with teaching your first lessons, running your first meeting is likely to fill you with the most excitement and anxiety. Just as you will be carefully planning your first lessons with your new groups, you should aim to spend the same amount of time planning your first meeting.

Questions you could consider are:

- How long have you got for the meeting?
- How long do you need for the meeting?
- How many people will be at the meeting?
- Are there any other new colleagues?
- What administration do you need to cover?
- Is there an opportunity for teaching and learning or other skills?
- Which colleagues are involved in each agenda item?

Your first element of planning may be to brainstorm the issues that you think you need to cover in the meeting. It is easy to get carried away with establishing yourself as a leader and thinking too deeply about your philosophy and your principles. One of the strengths of a good leader is thinking of one's team and what they wish to get out of such a meeting. For the first curriculum meeting of the year, your staff will be likely to be anxious about making sure they have set lists and the appropriate resources for the first few weeks of term. In the first pastoral meeting, tutors will wish to know if there are any tutor group changes, whether any pastoral issues have occurred since school was last in session and what the programme is for the first few pastoral meetings. These may not sound the most exciting tasks in your leadership career but they are important to get right, and in doing so you begin to form your foundation as a competent middle leader.

If you are a curriculum leader, it is important to remember that not every colleague in your meeting will have an interest in each item. I can remember sitting in a new head of maths first departmental meeting as a senior leader. We started with Year 7 and worked our way chronologically upwards. It took an hour before we reached Year 11 and the first group that I taught. I looked around the meeting and there was another colleague in the same situation. By the time we reached the classes that he would be teaching he was far less receptive than he may have been earlier. You may also have members of staff who teach in more than one curriculum area, and if so you may need to co-ordinate with the leader of that curriculum area.

Whether curriculum or pastoral leader, you may decide that in your first meeting you would like to do some joint planning to try and help form your team. Time will be against you so do not be too ambitious. As a pastoral leader, it could be sharing resources for the first tutor time. As a curriculum leader, you could work on the first lessons for the newest year group, if this isn't already planned. Don't worry if you do not do any work on development as it is likely you will have another meeting quite soon and by then you should have more ideas for suitable improvement projects.

	Agenda item	Notes	Colleagues
1.	Opening remarks	• Thank people for attending the meeting and that you look forward to working with them. • If you have other new colleagues, this is a good opportunity for everyone to introduce themselves and say what roles they have.	All colleagues
2.	Priorities for the term	• You may use this as an opportunity for linking your area's priorities to those given by the headteacher (possibly stated at the beginning of the day). • You could also ask your team what they believe the priorities are for this term. • This could also give you an opportunity to briefly comment on your subject philosophy.	All colleagues

	Agenda item	Notes	Colleagues
3.	Look through each year group	• Check everyone has class lists and share any pupil concerns at this point. • Check schemes of work are available and highlight any key assessment dates. • Check appropriate resources have been shared. • Are there any other issues about this year group that people wish to raise?	Organise your order for discussing individual year groups according to which colleagues are involved.
4.	The first project	• Choosing a small project can help form your team. It is best if it is something that you have confident knowledge of. • Any materials you can offer can emphasise your organisational capability but take care not to overface people or for it to be seen as a fait accompli.	This does not have to involve everybody, especially if you have a colleague who teaches mostly in another curriculum area.
5.	Rest of the day	• Check that your team knows the plan for the rest of the day. • Agree your next meeting, even if this is when to meet for coffee or lunch if you now have some working time.	

Fig. 14 Example agenda for a first curriculum meeting

In a pastoral meeting, your notes should apply to all colleagues so there isn't an additional column. However if you are working in a vertical arrangement (vertical tutoring is where you have pupils from each year group in one tutor group) and to there are specific items for Year 6 or Year 11 teachers, then you may wish consider how you arrange your meeting.

	Agenda item	Notes
1.	Opening remarks	• Thank people for attending the meeting and say you look forward to working with them. • If you have other new colleagues, this is a good opportunity for everyone to introduce themselves and say what roles they have. In pastoral teams, this gives colleagues from different curriculum areas the opportunity to meet.

	Agenda item	Notes
2.	Priorities for the term	• You may use this as an opportunity for linking your area's priorities to those given by the headteacher (possibly stated at the beginning of the day). • You could also ask your team what they believe the priorities are for this term. • This could also give you an opportunity for you to briefly comment on your pastoral philosophy and what you hope to achieve.
3.	Pupil issues	• Check everyone has their group list. • Share any pupil concerns which may have occurred since school was last in session. • For new tutors, ask existing tutors to share any key information that they feel is appropriate. This could range from difficult parents to children who need to be separated from others
4.	Calendar dates	• Share specific calendar dates that are pertinent to the year group. • This could range from open days for secondary school or post-16 establishments, to exam weeks and option processes.
5.	Pastoral programme	• Check pastoral scheme of work is available and highlight key dates. • Check appropriate resources have been shared. • Ask tutors to share any activities which proved successful last year.
	The first project	• Is there an activity which the group could work towards such as a competition, a charity project or a group of assemblies?
	Next meeting	• Highlight the date of the next meeting.

Fig. 15 Example agenda for a first pastoral meeting

Whole staff meeting

It is always nerve-wracking to attend your first whole school staff meeting in a new school. This is the moment when reality can really hit home and you are truly a member of staff in this school. Your previous meeting will have been the formal interview process during which it is very difficult to really understand the culture of the school. Hopefully you will have also visited for a day, but this can also be a somewhat unreal experience.

It is only natural to have a few doubts when the headteacher and other senior leaders take the floor on an INSET day or they make their first announcements in briefing, as to whether this is the right place for you. Part of this will be due to the anxiety of leading your team meeting later in the day and also your concerns of teaching your first lessons over the next few days.

My best advice is to let the morning wash over you, as otherwise you can worry over the odd turn of phrase or sentence. What you do need to pay attention to is any whole school priorities which are being described. Will these apply in your role as a classroom teacher or will they be initiatives that you need to move forwards as a middle leader?

You may have lots of questions which you feel need clarifying, things you are unsure of or ideas from your previous school that you would like to suggest. Sometimes anxiety can encourage us to make more interjections than we would normally. So on this first morning, why not play 'meeting poker' and only allow yourself one chip (one question/point) in this whole staff session. You can ask your line manager any other questions or points you wish to raise on a one-to-one basis at another time of the day. Take particular care if members of your team encourage you to ask questions in whole staff sessions – you do not know their motivations yet. What can seem an innocent question to a new person could open a hornet's nest from last term!

Informal meetings

There will be lots of informal moments during these first few days. You may be one of those individuals who relish such opportunities to meet a range of new people, or you may be at the other end of the spectrum and be initially quite shy in such circumstances.

As well as spending time with your team, it is a good idea to try and build relationships with other colleagues in the school. Often other new members of staff can be a good starting point as then you can share questions with them and see whether it is something that they are also unsure of. Other new members of staff might also feel a little lost and they may be glad of another friendly new person.

You should also try and build relationships with other middle leaders at the same level in the hierarchy as you. If you are the head of English, you might find the head of maths or science very helpful over your first few weeks as you try and establish which school routines need following. This will be equally true for a range of other postholders. A good and useful conversational starting point is to ask how they are using these days. There are two notes of caution when listening to their reply: do not feel the need to unpick all your planning if your preliminary thoughts have been different and also, just as important, be sensitive as this is not necessarily the best time to give a long monologue of what you are planning to do.

Finally, there may be opportunities for discussions with school senior leaders. It would be only natural for them to want to find out how one of their new middle leaders is settling in to their school. If you do have doubts, now is not the time to share them; instead remain positive and use the conversation to clarify a couple of queries that you may have. You want senior leaders to see you as a safe pair of hands who they can rely on as soon as possible.

Final thoughts

Your first proper day in a new school is always going to be nerve-wracking and there will be times when you feel a little lonely without the safety net you have built up in your previous school. In addition, a wide range of staff will be watching how you carry yourself and express your opinions.

Ensure you prepare properly for the parts of the day that you have control over, such as any meetings that you need to lead. Be sensitive to the thoughts of others, both those in your team and other members of staff. Most importantly, it can be a good idea to be patient before expressing your opinions too openly. Try to begin to form relationships with a range of staff.

To do list:

- ❑ Reflect on how you would organise your first meeting with staff.
- ❑ Reflect on the views of your colleagues as to what makes such a meeting a success.
- ❑ Check out Rachel Orr's blog posts on education and high-heels (see Takeaway box).
- ❑ Read *Fish* by Lundin, Paul and Christensen (see Takeaway box).

Chapter 8 takeaway

Teaching tip

Planning your first meeting

See if you can find agendas for meetings that occurred at the beginning of terms. Brainstorm what else you think should go in such a meeting. Think about how meetings are arranged at your school and what constraints there are such as colleagues having to be at more than one meeting. How would you deal with these issues?

Pass it on

Share your ideas – feelings about meetings

Discuss with a trusted colleague about how you both feel in meetings at the beginning of a term. What makes you anxious and nervous? What makes you positive and feel encouraged for the start of term? How would you arrange the meetings so that colleagues felt enthused for the challenges that lie ahead?

CPD book club recommendation

Stephen C. Lundin, Harry Paul, and John Christensen, *Fish*
(see Bibliography and further reading)

Bloggers' corner

Rachel Orr has some 'orrsome' posts from her experience as a headteacher mixed with her unique collection of high-heels that are well worth a read. Visit her blog at: highheelsandhighnotes.wordpress.com or follow her on Twitter: @RachelOrr

9 Your first days with the pupils

It does not matter how many years you have been teaching, meeting classes of pupils for the first time in a new schools is always nerve-wracking. You never know how the pupils will respond to you and we all recognise that pupils in any school are likely to try and test out their new teachers. You will also usually find that the pupils will behave differently from the way they did during interview lessons, the pupil panel or when they gave you a tour of the school.

The basics

As a new middle leader you will undoubtedly feel additional pressure to prove yourself in the first few weeks. You will not want to be seen as someone who has difficulties with the pupils; instead you will want to try and build a good reputation from day one.

What you should not expect is that the pupils will behave any differently towards you because you are now a head of department or head of year. I have heard inexperienced middle leaders say to me, 'But I'm head of English: if they won't behave for me which English teacher will they behave for?', often remembering the relationship that their former head of department had with the children in their previous school. They will only have seen that particular colleague in that role and hence not have observed the time and effort they put in to building that relationship.

That is not to say that pupils are not interested in hierarchy. They often are, and as a result you may find that pupils who are not in your classes will be intrigued to know what the new head of Year 10, for example, will be like and such pupils may appear at your door and ask you seemingly random questions.

It is also true that the manner in which the pupils respond to you can relate to the previous postholder. Taking over from a well-loved teacher can be a double-edged sword in that the children may have developed a good attitude towards the subject yet they will honestly tell you that the previous incumbent was better than you for whatever reason. If you are taking over from a colleague who was having difficulties, the pupils will often be pleased to have a more effective teacher but they will also have been used to behaving in a certain way in that classroom which you will then have to change.

Basic questions

- How would you characterise the expected behaviour of the pupils at the school?
- Do the pupils appear to behave in a similar manner in your area as in other classrooms in the school?
- Are you aware of any difficulties that the pupils may have had with the previous postholder?
- Are there other colleagues who you lead that you believe you will have to support at the start of the year?

The detail

This following section will help you consider the different roles that you may have to take with the pupils in your first week, such as building a relationship with your classes and supporting other members of staff with the pupils that you teach.

Your class/es

There is obviously a significant difference in the relationship with your class or classes if you are in a primary or a secondary school. In a primary school, it is likely that you will have one class, as you did before you became a middle leader, so in many ways this section is less important to you. What you need to concentrate on telling yourself is that you were a good teacher in your previous school and will be the same in your new school. Just take your time and begin to develop the good habits that you formed with the children that you used to teach.

In a secondary setting it is obviously very different, as you will meet many different groups of pupils depending on the subject that you teach and the number of lessons on the timetable for your subject. In addition, if you are a curriculum leader it is also likely that you will have a tutor group to manage too.

Tutor groups

As a curriculum leader you may be tempted to skip over this section and be surprised that it is so early in this chapter, thinking surely teaching groups are more important. This is the mistake that many curriculum leaders make because they are so committed to their subject. Remember that you may see your tutor group twice a day, every day and you may have them for a number of years.

You may not have a tutor group but instead be expected to lead intervention sessions in this time or oversee other tutor groups. Whatever the situation you need to ensure that you approach these sessions as diligently as any lesson you teach.

If you quickly form a positive relationship with your tutor group, this will give you some breathing space at the beginning of each day, rather than possibly starting each day with confrontation.

As a new middle leader you may find that you are not given the most straightforward tutor group. Often schools will look at their new staff and try and give newly qualified and inexperienced teachers the tutor groups that seemingly have the fewest problems, whereas you may have been given the tutor group that has had three different tutors in a relatively short space of time!

Often on the first day you may have an expanded period of time with your tutor group. You need to ensure that you are well versed in all the administrative procedures that need completing during this time as you will want the pupils to see you as someone who gets things right. In addition, just as you wouldn't go into one of your first lessons without planning, do the same with this tutor time. Always make sure that you have a couple of activities up your sleeve so that time is not spent with your tutees just sitting around. It is a good idea to play to your strengths here, so if you are an English teacher you may do a speaking and listening exercise, or if you are a PE teacher you may organise some kind of challenge. I have often used ideas like a picture quiz in groups as it can be a relatively straightforward task to run.

The best tutors are often those who have good routines, whether they are how the children enter the room, expectation during registration, how administration is organised or activities on certain days. Your first week with your tutor group is the time to build these routines, so think about teachers in your current school who are effective, consider what has worked well for you before and try to use these ideas in your new school.

Teaching groups

It is likely that on your first day you will also meet some of your teaching groups for the first time and, just as you did with your tutor group, you need to begin to introduce the routines that you expect them to follow for you.

It is relatively common practice for teachers to initially seat pupils using an assertive seating plan, but as you do not know the pupils, it is inevitable that there will be mistakes and children end up being placed in bad combinations. However, what it does do is signify to the pupils that the classroom is your space.

There is a likelihood that you may not have the ideal classes. You may find that the previous curriculum leader had the trickier groups in order to support their staff and the routine has continued. It may also be likely that you have a higher proportion of examination groups, including those that are halfway through a GCSE or an A-level course so you will want to make a strong impression with these groups.

Some people will advise you to play it safe with your groups in these first few days and that you should not try anything too radical with the children as it could go wrong because they are not used to your methods. My suggestion would be to do what seems natural. Starting a new school is not necessarily the best time to try and re-invent your teaching and try to be somebody else. Instead, ensure your lessons are well-planned and do not be afraid to use some of your favourite lessons from the past. However, remember that the pupils may respond to your ideas and style very differently from pupils at your previous school; that is all to do with the relationship that you had built up with the children over time, so do not be despondent if this is the case.

The best teachers are likely to have some difficulties with managing the behaviour of pupils in a new school, so do not be surprised if this happens to you. If it does, try to use the systems that are currently in place in your new school as well as your own tried and tested methods. I can always remember working with an experienced teacher who was struggling in a new school and I observed her lesson. She was trying to manage the children's behaviour using just her own methods and the pupils were confused, which did not help their behaviour. I discussed it with her and suggested that she use the school systems. This was not failure on her behalf it was what the systems were there for. Once she began to do this, the behaviour of the pupils greatly improved. As a middle leader you need to think of yourself as modelling school practice and supporting the school systems. One of the clearest ways of doing this is to use them yourself.

Assemblies

As a pastoral leader it is likely that you will have to deliver an assembly in your first few days. This is the moment when you have the opportunity to introduce yourself to all the pupils and give an indication of how you expect things to operate in the year ahead. Your team of tutors will be watching closely and this audience is almost as important as the pupils.

As a subject leader you might well have the opportunity to be involved in assemblies but it will rarely be asked of you in the early days. If you feel this is a particular strength of yours, you may choose to seek out the opportunity as a way of establishing yourself with the pupils.

Everyone has their own style of delivering assemblies and if you are new to this task, then you might not have found your style yet. Some teachers just have the assembly 'gift' and can stand up without any notes and inspire the pupils, or that may be what it looks like to you! The reality is that their skills have been developed over a long period of time or considerable effort has been spent planning the assembly but this is all behind the scenes.

You need to find out some basics about leading an assembly at your new school, such as whether there is a projector. What about a sound system? I tend to find that the best assemblies will have some images, often displayed in PowerPoint, which gives the pupils a visual stimulus. In my first assembly – until I knew the reliability of the ICT system – I would shy away from using sound or videos from the Internet.

Supporting your colleagues with managing the pupils

One of your roles will be to support your colleagues with managing pupils. One of the difficulties with being a new member of staff is that you will not know who the more difficult pupils are; nor will you have been involved in organising the groups so are likely to be unaware of what challenging combinations of pupils there are.

You will also have a range of colleagues to support. There may be some who are new to the school and they will have the same teething problems with their classes that any new member of staff might have, including you. There will also be those longer serving colleagues who may have on-going difficulties with certain pupils.

Creating the climate

For many lessons, the manner in which the pupils arrive in the building or enter the classrooms makes a significant difference to the learning environment. In many schools there will be a system for how pupils should make their way to the classroom. They may wait in form groups outside the building or line up outside the classroom. You need to find out what the school system is and discuss with your colleagues how you can make it most effective. Taking a leading role in ensuring the pupils follow the system and supporting your colleagues immediately begins to build your profile. Yet there is a balance between doing this and still ensuring the beginning of your own lesson is as purposeful as possible.

Discipline issues in other classrooms

Hopefully this will not be an issue in your first week, but it could be. As a middle leader you will be expected to help your colleagues with low-level disciplinary issues. For pastoral leaders there can be a danger that you immediately get called to deal with members of your year group if they are causing a problem. However, this can mean that you are regularly called away from your own classes. This is even worse when you are new to post as you are also trying to build relationships with your classes. In many schools such matters are initially dealt with in curriculum areas or, if more serious, there will a member of staff 'on call', or a 'pupil exit' system managed on a rota basis.

In addition, one of the central tenets of behaviour management is that teachers, wherever possible, need to manage their own sanctions. So in a bid to be helpful, try not to take on managing detentions for other teachers.

For a curriculum leader, it is likely that you will be first port of call in helping your teachers. In many schools, a period of time out with the curriculum leader is part of the sanctions ladder. You need to manage these with the minimum disruption to your own teaching. It may even be worth considering how you arrange your classroom so that there is a space for you to take such a pupil for a few moments without interrupting your teaching too much.

In many schools, curriculum areas will manage their own detention systems and will share this out so each member of staff is not running their own set of detentions every day. It may be tempting to offer to take all of these for your colleagues but whilst such an action is kind, it is unlikely to be sustainable in the long term. Instead your role may be to be available in case there are problems.

You may quickly notice that there seems to be a problem with a colleague and one pupil. The temptation can be to look for a quick win and to offer to take that pupil into your class. However, at this stage you may not know the rationale for how the groups were organised. I can remember one curriculum leader taking this action in their first week at a new school without knowing that the previous postholder had taken a number of difficult children into their group already to support colleagues. The addition of this further pupil just made the group unteachable. Unfortunately, once you have made this decision it can be difficult to reverse. So it is often worth not making such a decision in haste.

Final thoughts

The first few days and weeks with the pupils are important. You may find that you have a honeymoon period to begin with and everything goes very smoothly, or you could be unlucky and the pupils might seek to test you from very early on. It could be that your colleagues are the ones having difficulties and you have to support them.

It is never easy and there may be occasions when you feel that you have not got it right, and in such circumstances you may have to regroup and think how you can tackle the difficulty more successfully.

The most important thing is that you plan what you can, whether that's your first assembly or your first tutor session. Also make sure that you have contingencies for if things don't go according to plan for both you and your colleagues.

TO DO LIST:

- ❑ Reflect on how you could build strong relations with pupils.
- ❑ Reflect on colleagues who have joined your school and how they have managed that process.
- ❑ Check out Alice Hoyle's blog posts on PSHE (see Takeaway box).
- ❑ Read *Getting the Buggers to Behave* by Sue Cowley (see Takeaway box).

Chapter 9 takeaway

Teaching tip

Plan an assembly

Plan your first assembly. You may already deliver assemblies, so could look through your 'back catalogue' and think which assembly you'd use as your first one in your new school. How could you improve it further? If you don't deliver assemblies, then plan one and see if there is an opportunity for you to deliver it in your current school.

Pass it on

Share your ideas – building relationships

Discuss with a close colleague how you go about building good relationships with new classes. Think about colleagues who have recently started at your school; what have they done that has been effective? Also consider what mistakes you think they may have made and what you would do to avoid them.

CPD book club recommendation

Sue Cowley, *Getting the Buggers to Behave*
(see Bibliography and further reading)

Bloggers' corner

Alice Hoyle has some great posts on PSHE. Visit her blog at: sexedukation.wordpress.com or follow her on Twitter: @AliceHoylePSHE

10 Your vision

During your first few days of middle leadership you will have already begun to work towards something. You will have some idea of what you are trying to achieve. This is your vision. You may consider vision is too grand a term for your aims but vision is what it is, even if you don't explicitly use the word.

The basics

There are likely to be three aspects to your vision which you will need to consider. Firstly your vision for leadership, secondly the school vision and finally your vision for your curriculum area or school area.

1. **Vision for leadership:** Before starting the role, you will have thought about how you want work with your team. You may have thought of other middle leaders who you feel were effective in their roles and whose style you admired. This is your vision for leadership.
2. **School vision:** Finally, from the interview process, your visits to the school and your first days in post you will have listened to the headteacher and other senior leaders explain what they are trying to achieve. Even though all schools are beginning from the same starting point, which is to ensure that all children achieve, all schools will work in different ways and have their own thoughts on how pupil achievement will be promoted.
3. **Vision for your curriculum or school area:** Of equal importance is your view on how your subject area or school area will support the pupils: what they will learn, how they will be developed and also the style in which the teachers will operate. This is your vision for your curriculum area or school area.

Basic questions

- How do you want to work with staff and pupils?
- Can you think of an effective middle leader who you admired?
- How can your role within the school support the pupils?
- What is the vision of the school in terms of pupil achievement and discipline?

The detail

The aim of the following sections is to give you an opportunity to examine these three components of vision and allow you to develop your own vision whilst ensuring that you are working in harmony with the overarching school vision.

Your vision for leadership

There will be some middle leaders who have completed some further study into educational leadership and may have begun or even completed their master's degree and as a result will have a firm grounding in educational leadership. There will be other leaders who may have picked up and read some of the popular works on leadership. You may not have done either of these things but you will have watched and listened to a range of educational leaders as they have dealt with you, other colleagues and pupils. There is no doubt that through all of these, you will have considered how you would like to lead staff.

Educational management and leadership

Educational management and leadership is sometimes defined as working with other adults to achieve a positive outcome for the pupils in a school. Some people will debate the difference between management and leadership, and in school we tend to talk about leadership rather than management (hence the title of this book is 'Middle Leadership'). In a nutshell:

- Leadership is about knowing where you are trying to get to and what you are trying to achieve.
- Management tends to be thought of as the steps or systems which are used along the way to help you reach your target.

One of the interesting things about middle leadership is that even though you have your team, you do not have the same power as a headteacher or other senior leaders to insist that things are done. Sometimes the role of middle leader can feel a little ambiguous. You are trying to encourage other teachers to embrace your plans. They may not share your enthusiasm for developing the provision and this can be even more personally trying if they are more senior to you in the school hierarchy.

Leadership theory

One way of dealing with this ambiguity in roles and seniority could be to consider researching leadership styles. There is a lot that can be learnt from looking at leadership theory, which can be used to both improve your own practice and also as a method of trying to understand why others behave in the way they do.

The following few paragraphs give you an opportunity to read an introduction to some leadership theories without wading through the tens of thousands of entries on 'leadership' on the Amazon website or from an academic perspective looking at more than 65 different classifications of leadership which have been developed in the last 60 years. It does, however, include some academic references that you may need if you decide to return to this chapter for further studies.

Due to this complexity, sometimes leadership terms can be used in school documents without people being aware of their true definition. One example of this has been the increasing use of the term 'transformational leadership' – many senior leaders are unclear of its precise meaning.

It was suggested that there is a leadership continuum from transformational leadership to laissez-faire leadership (Yammarino, 1993). I have amended this slightly with the inclusion of heroic leadership.

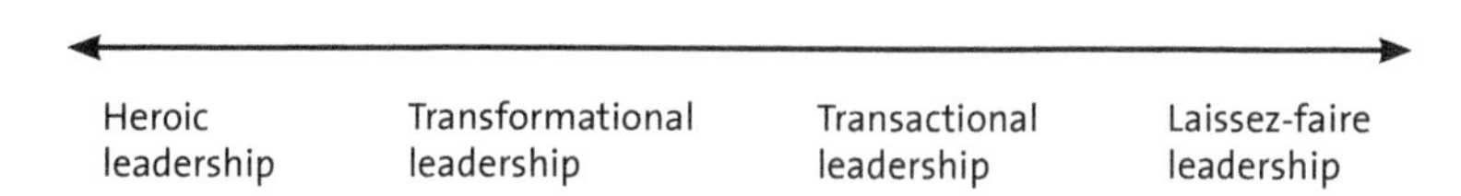

Fig. 16 Leadership continuum

Many people have an instinctive definition of heroic leadership and laissez-faire leadership. However, it is likely we may be less clear on the middle styles. The heroic leader leads by charismatic example whereas the laissez-faire leader, as the French phrase signifies, takes a 'hands-off, let things ride' approach. 'Transformational leadership is described as a process that changes and transforms people' whereas transactional leaders 'exchange things of value... to advance their own aims and agendas' (Northouse, 2012).

The leadership continuum shows the leader taking a more assertive role as we move from right to left. It was suggested that as you move from laissez-faire through transactional leadership to transformational leadership the leader's effectiveness peaks (Bass and Avolio, 1990a). It is very tempting for a school leader, in a sudden urge to implement a project, to slip into a heroic leadership mode and as a result it would then be assumed that the effectiveness of the leadership reduces.

Leadership styles in practice

To gain a better understanding of the effectiveness of these leadership styles in practice it is worth comparing them against actions that you have either seen or taken yourself and then consider what the response has been to them.

Heroic leadership

Heroic leadership is immediately recognisable and we may well have worked with people who display these traits. This is the leader who rules by the authority of their hierarchical position or as once vividly written, the heroic leader 'roaring in, soliciting approval like a colonel'. We tend to think of these characters as the headteacher. There can be a temptation after you have attended a middle leaders' meeting and have the backing of the senior leadership team to announce to staff that (a certain course of action) is what we are going to take – an example of heroic leadership. You may have analysed the situation perfectly and conducted reading on the situation. The solution may even be the best one on offer, but when delivered in such a style it is unlikely to work to its full potential.

You may become instantly aware of this, if your teachers mutiny against one of your proposals. You may have had SLT support at the beginning of the process, but this can disappear at such a point. This can be particularly frustrating if you have observed other colleagues present initiatives in a similar style where these conflicts have not arisen. However, as the experienced Vice Principal, Jo Smith observed:

'Heroic leaders are memorable but hard to emulate as any teacher knows who has tried to copy the classroom management style of a revered colleague and failed miserably only to experience success in an independent way' (J. Smith, 2008).

You may be luckier and be working with a member of staff similar to those of one colleague who famously said, 'Just tell us what to do and we'll do it!' However in the long term, such initiatives are unlikely to survive in this climate especially if you move roles.

Laissez-faire leadership

If you do get your fingers burnt when introducing a proposal, you may receive the feedback that the solution is to consult staff. You therefore take on the advice, consult and find there is no apparent consensus. In such circumstances it is easy to take a laissez-faire attitude and just allow colleagues to get on with their own thing. Perhaps as a curriculum leader or pastoral leader you are looking to introduce additional enrichment sessions for the pupils. However, as a committed middle leader who wants to do the best for your pupils, it is easy to compensate for this lack of a co-ordinated approach and replace it with activities that you organise yourself. Whilst you are providing opportunities for the children, this is only through your own personal efforts and is likely to be unsustainable in the long term.

Transactional leadership

Another solution is to look for a reward that you may be able to use to persuade your colleagues to help you. However as a middle leader, often the only rewards you can give are your thanks. If a member of staff is running an activity for you, it is unlikely that you could give them that time back via non-contact time. The reality is though, that any reward you could give is likely to be small and hence will not persuade your more recalcitrant colleagues to support you. In addition, those who do work with you would have been likely to have done so anyway.

Transformational leadership

The transformational style of leadership has received much positive praise in recent years. People who exhibit this leadership style often have a strong set of values and ideals and use these to motivate people to work with them. As a middle leader you are likely to have such beliefs with the central aim that all pupils reach their full potential. What makes transformational leadership more accessible is that it can be broken into four groups (Bass and Avolio, 1990a), sometimes known as the four Is and you may find that one of these fits with your personality more closely than the others.

- **Idealised influence** – leaders who use their charisma to act as strong role models so that others wish to follow them. You may be one of those legendary teachers with excellent pupil discipline and it might be these characteristics that your colleagues recognise and so then want to become a part of your success.
- **Inspirational motivation** – a leader communicates his/her own high expectations to others. Perhaps you are the teacher who can deliver really high-quality training sessions to staff which inspire them.
- **Intellectual stimulation** – the leader uses creative and innovative ideas to challenge the beliefs of others. It may be that your greatest strength is your ability to research proposals and then develop a logical process of improvement. If this is the case, don't rush to tell your colleagues the proposals but instead take your time to explain why they have been developed and what evidence you have found which indicates they will be a success.
- **Individualised consideration** – this describes the leader who provides a supportive climate and listens carefully to those they are trying to lead. You may recognise that your best method of developing projects is by working with individual staff or with small groups. Don't rush to develop things across all your staff, but instead chip away at individuals with the aim of reaching a critical mass of advocates which then creates a tipping point for a change of whole school ethos and culture.

What leadership styles should you develop?

Hopefully these leadership pen portraits give you some idea as to the leadership style you may wish to develop. You can see your middle leadership role as a real opportunity to try out different leadership styles and hopefully find the one that is the most appropriate for any particular occasion. It is this trial and reflection process that will really develop your leadership skills.

All leaders will develop their own style for working and generally as long as it is effective, you can lead in your own way. Obviously if your leadership style is at an extreme from most of the other leaders in the school it will be less effective. An obvious example of this is if you are a highly assertive leader, this manner of working may be frowned upon in very caring collegiate settings.

It is far more important though that the vision for your team is in keeping with whole school vision as otherwise the value of your team's efforts may not add to the school's. In fact, in the more extreme cases it can damage a school's overall effort. The obvious example is the long-serving and powerful curriculum leader who thinks only of their subject and whilst ensuring their own results are high, they can act as barrier for the development of other curriculum areas and hence stop improvement in whole school performance.

Your school's vision

Your first step is trying to capture in your own mind what your new school's vision really is. A starting point would be to read again the vision which should be on your school's website. Try and think about what it really means to you in practice. How does this impact on your curriculum area or responsibility? Unfortunately many a school's vision is very generic and you could find two very different schools with a set of very similar bullet points for their vision.

Your next piece of research is to think about what the headteacher and other senior leaders have said on interview day, INSET days or even in individual conversations. The particular areas of development that may have been suggested to you will be the vision in practice. Schools and their vision are often on a continuum and thinking about these simple ideas may also help you.

For example in terms of attainment, at one end of the spectrum are those that are highly academic. This could be primary schools that are preparing children for particular schools and under the old Key Stage 2 levels, 100% of the pupils would regularly receive level 5 in both English and Maths. There may be a very selective secondary school and have a very traditional curriculum. Their continual vision is competing to gain the highest attainment scores with the aim of appearing in national newspapers' top 100 (or higher) league tables. This type of school will be dominated by the pursuit of A/A* grades whether at GCSE or at A-level. Such a school will have a very different vision from those schools whose intake consists of a large number of pupils with low prior attainment. This type of school may be looking at different pathways with lots of different qualifications as they try and capture the achievement of their children. Obviously the vision of a curriculum or pastoral middle leader will have to be very different in these two types of school – even though at their core, they may share the same aim of every child achieving their potential.

You could also look at the vision of a school and how it manages the overall pupil experience. There are some schools that have very rigid systems. There is no wriggle room for pupils or even a teacher in how issues are managed. This is the type of school where if a pupil makes a minor infraction, a forgotten tie or missed homework, a sanction is immediately given. There are no grey areas and no looking at the individual circumstance – the same sanction is given. In one school I worked in of this nature, there was almost a competition between staff as to who could give the most sanctions. In other schools there will be a more personalised response. If children make errors the individual needs of the child will be looked at and there will be a conversation about how best the children can be supported. Both of these systems can be highly effective and again they share the same focus of trying to ensure that the behaviour of pupils is positive.

Finally, it is interesting to look at how schools are working on teaching and learning. There are some schools who are constantly researching new practice and are trying to move forwards in their teaching and learning. They will have strong systems for sharing this and a culture of openness where members of staff are encouraged to enter each others' classrooms and have discussions over pedagogy. Senior leaders may take the view that they will accept innovations that do not prove immediately effective as long they know about them and there is a rationale behind their implementation. There will be other schools who are not in a hurry to move forwards, instead they take a more patient viewpoint by looking at what other schools are doing and once the method is proven they will then seek to consider whether this is something which can be implemented in their school. This is the type of school that expects everything to work the first time and hence by its nature is more conservative. Both types of school are still looking at strong teaching and learning but have different routes towards this.

The interesting thing about each of these pen portraits is that the same school may be at a different point on these continuums at varying points in time. Also interestingly, the point on the continuum can be heavily influenced by the nature of the headteacher, and a change at the top can quickly change the culture of the school.

Your vision for your curriculum or school area

Once you have unpicked the vision of your school, you then need to think about how this impacts upon the vision for your team. What are the things that you are really passionate about? For some curriculum leaders this can be a love of their subject or for pastoral leaders it can be a passion for inter-group competition. These two areas would fit into any school whatever their vision, and there are things as an individual that you can introduce which will make a difference to the pupils. Obviously it is all the more effective if you have other colleagues supporting you and helping move these forwards with you.

If you are looking at the strengths and weaknesses of your area, it may be best to consider this in three sections; the achievement of the pupils, the behaviour of the pupils and the quality of teaching and learning. Obviously if one of these is a particular strength, the sensible action might be to keep the systems going. However, if you feel one or more of these is not good then you need to begin to think about how it can be improved. This leads on to a second question which is: what are your views on how a particular weakness is best supported? Some school leaders ask themselves, 'What does a good one look like?' For example you could ask yourself what good behaviour would look like in your area. What would you see in classrooms? How would pupils be relating to teachers? How would this be evidenced from pupils' work?

At this stage in your career, you may have strong opinions on each of these but you may also take a more pragmatic view. However, you still need to begin to think and talk to your colleagues about these issues, collecting ideas and advice about how things can be moved forwards. If you do have a very strong vision it may be pragmatic not to expound on this too passionately as you may make sweeping judgements which, over time may prove to be less accurate than you initially thought and in the course of this you could risk alienating your colleagues.

However well thought out your vision is for your area, the only way it will prove effective is if it is shared and then worked towards by other members of your team.

Final thoughts

Research has shown there is a continuum of middle leaders. At one end, there are those for whom the most important thing is their subject area or the pastoral care of the children they are responsible for. At the other end are those individuals who are really passionate about the concept of leadership. For these colleagues the fascination is in building a team and a vision and the strategies that can be used to move forwards. You may find at varying points in your career that you are in different places on this continuum. This could be due to your time in post, the precise nature of your role or the stage that your school is at in its development cycle.

Perhaps the key to being a highly-effective middle leader is recognising this in yourself and carefully considering what you want to achieve next. You must remember though that you are a leader and to help your school move forwards you need to bring out the best in the people in your team, and that is the real art of leadership.

To do list:

- ❑ Reflect on what your leadership style is.
- ❑ Reflect on an appropriate vision for your area.
- ❑ Write out your leadership vision.
- ❑ Check out Geoff Barton's tweets on leadership (see Takeaway box).
- ❑ Read *8 Qualities of Successful School Leaders: The Desert Island Challenge* by Jeremy Sutcliffe (see Takeaway box).

Chapter 10 takeaway

Teaching tip

What is your vision?

Spend some time thinking about what your vision is for leadership. How would you lead your colleagues in your area? What would your expectations be and how would you encourage and motivate your colleagues to meet these expectations? Also consider the leadership experiences that you have had in the past. What went well and what didn't? If you were in the same situation in the future what would you do differently next time?

Pass it on

Share your ideas – swapping visions

Have a discussion with a close colleague about what you consider would be an effective vision of learning in your curriculum area or school area. Think about how close your current area is to meeting that. Look at the school vision and consider how closely your vision for an area supports this. If it is very different why is this the case?

CPD book club recommendation

Jeremy Sutcliffe, *8 Qualities of Successful School Leaders: The Desert Island Challenge*
(see Bibliography and further reading)

Tweeters' corner

Geoff Barton is an experienced headteacher and is always well worth a read. Follow him on Twitter @RealGeoffBarton

11 Building relations with stakeholders

In your first few days as a middle leader, you will have begun to build relations with the pupils and the colleagues that you lead. Over your first term you will meet a range of stakeholders, including the full range of staff, parents, governors and other members of local communities.

This chapter gives you guidance on:

- presenting yourself to stakeholders
- forming relations and solving problems.

The basics

Your initial focus will quite rightly have been on getting to know the pupils that you teach and a range of staff in the school. However. you will quickly find that for various reasons you will begin to meet a wider range of people who are often referred to as 'stakeholders'.

- **Support staff:** In chapter 8 we focused on supporting fellow teachers and in chapter 6 we looked at meeting a range of teachers. It is also important, particularly in big schools, to get to know the wider range of support staff as they can help make your life much easier.
- **Parents and carers:** This will be the most obvious external group but it will depend on the type and culture of the school you work in and the role you have as to how quickly you meet them. There can be issues which hang over from before you started in the role which would mean that parent contact is more intense than may otherwise be expected, so it is important that you create a good impression.
- **Governors:** Governors are the second group that you may begin to come into contact with. In some schools, governors are in almost every day and in others they may rarely visit except to participate in interviews. Those colleagues who are driven towards a very clear career path may consider building relations with governors as a very important requisite and there may be occasions when governors are involved in self-review or they may even hold a sum of development money and you will want them to look kindly upon you.
- Finally there is a huge range of other **members of the community** who you may come into contact with, from faith leader or voluntary groups such as the Rotary, to services from the police to healthcare professionals. Every school will differ as to whether middle leaders interact with such individuals or not.

Basic questions

- Which support staff have you met and been introduced to?
- Are there any planned parent meetings in the first weeks?
- Have there been any parental issues so far which have required resolving?
- How frequently do governors visit the school and meet with teachers?
- Do you have a role in working with wider stakeholder groups?

The detail

In the following sections we will look at how, as a middle leader, you may interact with these stakeholders and what you could do to make things run more smoothly.

Support staff

The first few days in your post can seem like a whirr of activity and in a big school you can easily become lost in a sea of faces and names. Often it is members of the support staff that you can overlook or of whose roles you may be unaware.

In a small school, it is likely that the division between teaching staff and support staff is less evident. If there are between ten and fifteen members of staff or fewer, often the whole group will meet together and it is much easier to get to know everyone's name and role. However in these schools, what you will find is that everyone does a multitude of tasks and lines of responsibility may be less clear. If you have worked in a larger school with a bigger support staff team, you may have been accustomed to delegating more so you should be aware of any new expectations placed upon you.

In a large school there will be a whole range of support staff divided into their own teams, such as site, administration, finance, student support and catering. It can be very difficult to remember every team leader's name, let alone each of the staff members. However for your long-term success at the school, it is vital to get to know these individuals. You may also find that many of them live in the local community and have children at the school. As such, they have one of the biggest investments in the school.

There will be some teachers who barely give these colleagues a second glance or only speak to them when they need something, hardly the way of encouraging them to go the extra mile for you. Take the time to try and greet everyone. Many support staff will be swamped at the beginning of term – often their busiest time – so long conversations may not be welcomed at this point. One useful tip is to ask your line manager to take you on a tour of the school a couple of weeks into term and re-introduce you to the support staff with the aim of each of them explaining their roles to you and what they will be able to help you with. I have personally found that the site team and catering staff can help you the most. You never know when you'll need a premises officer's help, whether through losing a key or even to help change a flat tyre! In my first school I always chatted with the catering staff and after a couple of weeks they would try and give me Tupperware containers of food for my tea!

Parents and carers

One of the big changes in becoming a middle leader can be the increased time you need to spend in dealing with parent and carer concerns. You may notice this most if you are promoted to a middle leader role in your existing school as you can make the best comparison. If you currently work in a culture where teachers are regularly expected to contact parents, you may be more used to dealing with parents.

In primary schools, the access for parents to teachers is much more open. It is normal for parents to collect their children and to expect regular informal contact with teachers. Some schools will make extra efforts to facilitate this by asking classroom teachers to take the children onto the playground at the end of the day and then to be available for those quick conversations.

In a secondary school, there often isn't that culture and hence parents and carers will tend to contact the school when they feel there is something important that is worrying their child or troubling them.

Formal meetings

In the first few weeks of term, especially if you have a class that is new to the school, there may be a settling in evening for parents to meet key teachers. If you are a class teacher you must be prepared for this evening. Firstly ensure that if there are any groups of children you teach who you need specific information about such as SEND, more able or G&T ensure that you have noted this down, so that if parents or carers do ask, you are ready. This was important when you were a class teacher, but as a middle leader you need to get such things right. In the same way, you need to be organised and have information to hand on how the pupils are settling in, the starting point you believe they are at and if they are making progress.

What is always difficult is when parents and carers ask you about pupils that are not in your classes. It is good practice to always make sure you have some kind of spreadsheet established for such an eventuality. You may have very little information on it at the moment, just data such as starting points and SEND status and it is always useful for the children to have taken some kind of assessment. If a parent of a child not in one of your classes asks you how they are settling in, you can show them this information and if the table also had additional columns of data that will be collected you can explain this to parents. Such obvious forward planning can help ease parental concerns.

Email, phone, letter or in person

One of the changes in being a middle leader is that you will get more queries than before and that they will come in many different forms. Just as when you were a classroom teacher you will receive emails, telephone calls, letters and, depending on your school, parents or carers arriving in person.

It is often good advice to respond to the parents and carers in the way that they have contacted you. So if you receive an email, reply by email. You may choose to ask the school office to send the reply for you so the parent does not have your individual school email address but again this depends on the school. The same principle can be used for letters or phone calls. There are some colleagues who are very adept at making telephone calls and may always choose to respond in this way.

If you are a pastoral leader you may find that parents and carers will descend on the school, particularly for welfare issues. Senior leaders will not expect you to miss lessons to deal with such emergencies and in many cases, if you are teaching, will pick these up for you and then pass the message onto you. There may be situations when a senior leader does decide your lesson needs covering so that you can speak to the parent or carer yourself.

Advice is never see a parent or carer on your own, always have somebody with you to take notes and to be able to vouch for your behaviour. As a male teacher, I never see a female parent on my own unless I know them very well – in this situation I ask a female colleague to join me. I am also usually accompanied if I am meeting with a lone male too. For certain telephone calls, I place the call on speakerphone and ask a colleague to make notes, this is particularly the case if I know the parent or carer to have a volatile personality or is a frequent complainant.

Dealing with concerns

Unfortunately, as a middle leader you will receive a range of concerns. The following tables give you some of the more frequent ones.

Topic	Issue
Homework	• Too much • Too little • Never set • Not marked
Progress	• Not enough made • Going backwards • Won't reach a certain grade
Discipline	• Overall behaviour in a class is not good enough • One or two pupils disrupting
Assessment	• Rarely marked • Never marked
Teacher manner	• Had made an inappropriate comment • Is too sarcastic • Doesn't answer the pupils' questions
SEN	• Teacher did not seem to know the child was on the SEN register • Pupils have to copy from the board • Little differentiation
More able	• Work is too easy • Pupil is bored • Pupils in other schools are doing much more challenging tasks

Fig. 17 Examples of parental concerns for a curriculum leader

A pastoral leader will often receive all the same concerns that as a curriculum leader does. Part of the skill of being an effective pastoral leader is determining which of these are subject specific and so can be dealt with by the relevant curriculum leader.

Topic	Issue
Bullying	• Comments to child • Threats towards child • Violence towards child
Friendship issues	• Children falling out • Children struggling to make friends
Social media	• Could overlap with bullying and friendship issues and include 'sexting'
Welfare	• Eating issues • Self-harm • Mental health issues

Fig. 18 Examples of parental concerns for a pastoral leader

You will often find that parents and carers are very emotional when bringing such issues to your attention. The emotion may be apparent through them being upset, blaming the school or being aggressive. In such circumstances, there may be little that you can practically do to help such parents. What you need to do is listen to their concerns and then investigate the issue. This may involve you talking to the particular child, other children and teachers. Through doing this, hopefully you will reach a plan of action in how to move forwards.

There will be occasions when parents or carers have a direct request that you cannot agree to, such as change a child's teaching group. These are difficult conversations and you have to be polite and hold your line but try and give a future opportunity where this to happen.

Always make notes of any meetings with parents and carers. Some staff will use their diary for this or put their records on an electronic diary. Your school may even have a specific pro forma for this.

It is now very common that if parents and carers don't receive the response they want, they will move up the chain with their concern. You must not worry about this, it is just part of modern life. Your notes at this stage are useful as you can then explain to the senior leader what actions you have taken. There will be occasions when a senior leader has to make a different decision. This does not mean that your actions were wrong, but sometimes a senior leader will do this as they believe the possible ramifications from the parent or carer are too great and a pragmatic decision is required.

The most important things in dealing with parent and carer concerns are:

- Make sure that you are professional.
- Make sure that you have accurate information and you research carefully.
- Try to be polite – having another member of staff with you can help.
- Don't take it personally, however frustrating or upsetting you may find it.

Governors

When you were being appointed, it is likely that a governor was involved in the interview process. In some schools that may be the last you see of the governors, but in others they may be frequent visitors to the school. This may range from the chair of governors having weekly (or even more regular) meeting with the headteacher, to governors being attached to certain curriculum or pastoral areas and expecting updates from the middle leaders involved.

It is a good idea to have a list of governors and particularly highlight those who have children at the school. Whilst governors are not supposed to put the needs of their child first, they often do and frequently they will also have the ear of the headteacher. So if you receive concerns from a governor about their child, it is a good idea to share them with a senior leader.

Governors come from a wide range of backgrounds, often not education. Before meeting a governor it is worth finding out if they do have background in education. If you do meet with them just check what the agenda is before hand as you may quickly find out it is about their child rather than governor business.

Some schools give curriculum areas the opportunity to bid to the governors for funds for development. Such an opportunity can help raise your profile and that of your area. So make sure that any bids are well-written, reasonably concise and focus upon what the pupils will gain from the investment.

Other stakeholders

Increasingly, there is a huge range of other stakeholders that you may have to work with, often delegated to you by senior leaders. So as a head of year, for example, you may find that you are hosting a community religious leader as they are taking an assembly with your year group. As a head of technology, you may be asked to work with the Rotary for a 'Junior Masterchef' competition.

There may be occasions when you would like help from an outside agency such as the police or social services for one of your pupils. In such circumstances you need to be careful, as it will be senior leaders not the middle leaders who take responsibility for such situations for a whole host of reasons. There is no reason why you could not suggest such an intervention to a senior leader though. You might also be asked by a senior leader to liaise with such an individual, and different sizes of school will have their own protocol for such matters. However, you should ensure that you take proper notes of such meetings and share them with the relevant senior leader.

Final thoughts

As a middle leader you are likely to meet with and work with a wider circle of people than you did as a classroom teacher. At times you will find this a very challenging aspect of the role, and at other times it may be the most interesting.

In all your dealings with adults you are looking to show a professional manner and be seen as someone who knows what they are doing. There will be occasions when it does not seem to matter what you do or have done, it is not working. Remember this happens to everyone at some time. So always make careful notes and share your thoughts with other middle leaders and senior leaders whilst working within reasonable limits of confidentiality.

TO DO LIST:

- ❑ Reflect on the role of governors.
- ❑ Reflect on how you would deal with parental issues.
- ❑ Check out Shena Lewington's website on governance (see Takeaway box).
- ❑ Read *Ahead of the Class* by Marie Stubbs (see Takeaway box).

Chapter 11 takeaway

Teaching tip

What do you know about governance?

You may have had little contact with governors and may not know what their role is in school. Spend some time researching who the governors in your school are. What different groups do they represent? Think about how often they are seen in school and what tasks they complete. Why not ask a senior leader if they would be prepared to give their thoughts on governers and how they support them.

Pass it on

Share your ideas–parents

Ask the middle leaders in your school discuss the most common queries they receive from parents over the course of a term and their strategies for dealing with them. Have there been any that have been particularly difficult to deal with and what advice would they give you?

CPD book club recommendation

Marie Stubbs, *Ahead of the Class*
(see Bibliography and further reading)

Bloggers' corner

Shena Lewington is a passionate blogger-governor: www.clerktogovernors.co.uk and you can follow her on Twitter: @ClerkToGovernor

12 How to conduct your own self-evaluation

From the moment you first thought about applying for this job, researched the school and walked into the building you will have been conducting your own self-evaluation. It will have been informal, but you will have been making judgements on how effective you consider the overall school is and also the curriculum area or pastoral area which you are now leading. It is likely that you have looked at the current Ofsted report and performance data on the school. You may feel that these are in tune with your thoughts or it may be that you feel there is a gap between the reality of what you are seeing and external judgements.

The basics

One of your key tasks as a middle leader is to consider how you can improve the provision that you lead. The only way that you can really do this is to conduct your own self-evaluation. You may find that in your school there is a self-evaluation schedule run by senior leaders and which does not involve you, or you may be a significant part of process. It does not matter which of these reflects your position, or if your self-evaluation is formal or informal, you still need to be looking at what is going on around you to see how you can make changes.

Self-evaluation normally involves a range of tools which will look at the outcomes the children achieve, the teaching the children receive, the assessment that is given to them and increasingly frequently, the views the pupils have themselves of their education.

Basic questions

- What judgements have you already made on your area's effectiveness?
- What evidence did you use to form these views?
- Is there a whole school self-evaluation schedule that covers your area?
- Do you know what involvement you have in this?
- Have you used any self-evaluation tools in the past?
- Which self-evaluation area would you like to develop skills in?

The detail

This following section will give you an overview of self-evaluation including a brief consideration of whole school self-evaluation. It will then give you an introduction to the tools of self-evaluation from a middle leader's perspective and will also look at how you can use them most effectively.

Self-evaluation

In some schools, self-evaluation may be felt to be the preserve of senior leaders and Ofsted. You may even have had less than positive experiences of department mini-Ofsteds led by senior leaders. Increasingly though, schools are trying to move away from situations where self-evaluation is done to teachers by senior leaders to a process that instead involves a range of middle leaders. After all, the likelihood is, that as a middle leader, you would not wait for senior leaders to conduct their self-evaluation and tell you what needs improving in your area. Instead you would have already had your own thoughts and be developing your own plans to do this.

Self-evaluation conducted by senior leaders and Ofsted is very formal in nature in that self-evaluation tools are used in a precise manner. The tools that they are likely to use are:

- data analysis
- lesson observations
- work scrutiny
- pupil focus groups.

Pro formas will be used so that what is seen is carefully recorded, strengths and weaknesses are noted and then judgements are made. Good self-evaluation should then draw this evidence together through a process called triangulation to make overall judgements. These should not be made from just one source of evidence but instead a judgement should only be recorded if it can be triangulated, i.e. the same thing, good or bad, is seen in a number of different places.

As a middle leader you may be asked to take part in a formal self-evaluation of your area and use the tools in this manner. In your role, you may only be asked to take responsibility for one or two of the tools, perhaps a lesson observation for performance management/appraisal purposes or a work scrutiny. You may also decide to think about which tools you could use with your team to help you decide what does need improving.

Self-evaluation tools

Data analysis

You will probably have already done some data analysis at this point, even if this was just studying the attainment data on the Department for Education (DfE) or the BBC website.

In conducting data analysis you are looking to see whether the pupils within your area are performing as they should be. This could be comparing the results for your curriculum area to those across the school or to national figures relevant to your area. You are also looking to see if different groups of pupils gain similar results. For example, compare the results of boys and girls, SEN children to those without SEN, children with low prior attainment with those with high prior attainment or those pupils who do gain the pupil premium with those who do not. You will also be looking to compare the results of different teachers and classes to see whether they are consistent. You obviously need to be sure to take into account the nature of different groups, particularly if ability setting is used very differently.

One of the most significant changes in data analysis is the focus on progress for all pupils. Schools are moving away from just looking at attainment data such as the proportion of pupils who achieve a level 4 in Key Stage 2 or those pupils that achieve an A*–C grade.

Currently in primary schools, as it has been for a number of years, the emphasis has been on the progress that children make from their Key Stage 1 assessments to their Key Stage 2 tests. The expectation has been that pupils make two levels of progress during Key Stage 2 or half a level a year. However, in the new measures, there is a change to baseline testing in reception and then to measure the progress the pupil makes by the end of KS2. In secondary schools, the expectation in English and maths has been that the pupils make three levels of progress from Key Stage 2 to Key Stage 4.

The use of the Progress 8 measure in secondary schools ensures progress is important for all subjects. The results that pupils gained in primary school will be used to make a prediction as to the grade that pupils should achieve in all their different subjects.

Subject leaders in both primary and secondary schools will be concentrating on current and past data. They will look at what percentage of pupils made the expected progress in the previous year. They will compare different groups of children to see how the progress compared. They will also be looking at the current pupils and seeing who is on track to make expected progress and if they are not, deciding what can be done about it.

The following simple table could be used to summarise progress in your curriculum area.

Class/Teacher	1	2	3	4	5
Percentage of pupils on target					
Percentage of boys on target					
Percentage of girls on target					
Percentage of low prior attainment on target					
Percentage of medium prior attainment on target					
Percentage of high prior attainment on target					
Percentage of SEND on target					
Percentage of non-SEND on target					
Percentage of pupil premium on target					
Percentage of non-pupil premium on target					

Fig. 19 Table to show progress of different pupil groups

Pastoral leaders will be looking at their current pupils and checking which pupils are on track to make progress in all their subjects, most subjects, a few subjects or none of their subjects. They should be studying these pupils in the final groups to see what can be done to support them.

Lesson observations

Most teachers will first think of lesson observation when asked to consider self-evaluation. Many teachers dread a lesson observation, though not everybody. Lesson observations can take very different forms both in their duration and their purpose.

Formal graded observation

There are the formal lesson observations that will last for a whole lesson or a significant proportion of the lesson. Current guidance is that individual lessons should not necessarily be judged according to Ofsted grades; instead it is the quality of teaching and learning over time that should be used for performance management/appraisal purposes or for a whole school's evidence on the quality of teaching and learning. There has been a significant debate on the use of such grades for lesson observation with different schools and teachers taking very different stances. If you are asked to complete such an observation, you need to make sure that you are properly trained on lesson grading and such training should always include joint observations with a senior leader to help moderate your judgements. In fact, if you are asked to conduct a round of observations on your staff, the best advice would be to complete the entire first round with a senior leader.

Formal ungraded observation

There are also formal lesson observations but where a judgement is not made. Instead, the emphasis is on the feedback that you will give the teacher on the strengths and areas for development of the lesson. Such lesson observations were a mainstay of the performance management process and often the observer's feedback would be linked to an area of practice that the teacher would be seeking to improve on, in one of their performance management targets. You may feel less need for training on this type of observation. The most important thing is to balance your feedback. You are always looking for some things that the teacher is doing well and, even in the worst lesson, you need to limit your areas for development – some people may say that four is the maximum you should use; others would say never have more areas for development than strengths. When you come to deliver your feedback, make sure that you have time and space to do this. Some people would say always go to the teacher's classroom where they will feel most confident. Try not to say things like, 'I would have done it like this' or 'I would have used these resources'. The feedback is not about your teaching, it is about what you have observed.

Blink review

Many schools also use shorter lesson observations often known as 'learning walks' or 'blink reviews'. This is where the observer spends a lesson moving between classrooms and spending about ten minutes in each class. This can be an ideal opportunity to get to know your team as it is a lot less threatening than a formal lesson observation. You could just sit with the children and work with them for this time and not make any notes – all that time you are gaining important information about your team. You will see ideas of good practice that you may decide to ask your colleagues to share, and you will observe areas that look like they need improving on and again you could tackle this as a team. You could make a few notes after you've been in the classroom so you do not forget what you have seen.

Drop-in

Don't forget about all those informal observation moments, e.g. when you collect some resources from the classroom, deliver a message or walk past the classroom door. Try and get into the habit of looking at what your colleagues are doing and having discussions about this.

Peer and coaching observations are also types of observation but these are not generally about self-evaluation and so these are covered in Chapter 19 which looks at CPD.

Type of observation	**Benefit**	**Disadvantage**
Formal graded observation	• Formal judgement on the quality of teaching and learning is made • School has evidence for quality assurance documents • Gives you the opportunity to find out more about your teacher's teaching	• Concerns about grading a teacher on just one lesson/part of a lesson • Consistency of judgement is difficult • Teachers focus on the grade and not how they can improve • Can damage a teacher's confidence
Formal ungraded observation	• Teachers can receive good feedback on how to improve practice • Gives you the opportunity to find out more about your teacher's teaching	• There is no formal evidence for school quality assurance and appraisal • Teachers may want to know how the performance would be judged if Ofsted observed • Teachers can have more observations if senior leaders want to make judgements

Type of observation	Benefit	Disadvantage
Blink review	• You can see more teachers in a shorter time • Teachers can feel less threatened • You can gain useful snippets of information • You can look at a certain aspect of the lesson or a particular pupil group • It's a good way to get to know your staff and pupils	• Some teachers can 'turn it on' for ten minutes and this may be very different from normal practice • The issues you notice in those ten minutes may be dealt with elsewhere in the lesson but you don't see that
Drop-in	• It's a good way to get to know your staff and pupils • Promotes an open door policy for your staff	• Information cannot really be used for evaluation purposes • Can distract teachers from their teaching

Fig. 20 Benefits and disadvantages of different types of observation for a middle leader

Work scrutiny

Work scrutiny is an aspect of self-evaluation that is often delegated to middle leaders. Part of the reason for doing this, is that it should be something that is done reasonably regularly. Work scrutiny does not have to be something that you do on your own; instead it can be a task that you work on together in a team meeting. This gives your colleagues a good opportunity to share good practice.

Work scrutiny normally focuses on two aspects:

- **The actual work that the pupils are completing**
  At a whole school level it can be interesting to look at the quality of work that pupils produce in different subject areas. If you are a pastoral leader this could be the type of work scrutiny that you are involved in. Currently though in schools it is much rarer for pastoral leaders to have this involvement.
- **The feedback that the pupils receive from the teacher**
  It was not that long ago that work scrutiny was as simple as just checking that there was red ink in the books! The acceptance of assessment for learning as standard practice meant that feedback became much more focused on what the pupils needed to do to improve and how they could do this. Latterly, this has now moved on to the conversation that the pupil should be having with the teacher following assessment – which is expected to be evidenced in their books.

	X or ✓
Marking is up-to-date in exercise books.	
Comments made praise positives.	
Comments made also show pupils how to develop.	
Assessment is mostly clearly linked to assessment criteria (i.e. with levels or grades).	
Feedback is linked to learning objectives (i.e. the comments relate specifically to the skills taught or tested in the assessed task).	
There is evidence that pupils have had the time and opportunity to respond to the teacher's comments, e.g. by writing, 'Yes, I will try and use commas next time'.	
There is evidence that pupils have adjusted, repeated or improved skills or knowledge as a result of the teacher's feedback (e.g. a piece of work that has been redone scores a higher level, a redone question is better answered, additional notes have been added to the exercise book by the student).	
A photo has been taken by the observer of a pupil's work which may be used to share as good practice.	

Fig. 21 Work scrutiny template

Pupil focus groups

The final tool of self-evaluation tends to be a method of collecting the views of the pupils. This can be done using questionnaires, but this can prove time-consuming. The more usual method is a pupil focus group. A pupil focus group tends to consist of between six and eight pupils and you would have prepared a set of questions to ask the pupils their views on.

A pupil focus group could look at any topic from the standard of school food to how well bullying is being dealt with. A pastoral leader could use pupil focus groups to look at a range of welfare issues.

The focus of this chapter though has been on self-evaluation, focusing on issues around teaching and learning. A pastoral leader could use a pupil focus group to look at how pupils are managing with a range of subjects, whereas a curriculum leader could look at just their own area.

As with all types of self-evaluation, it is important to triangulate any comments that the pupils make with other evidence that you may have.

- Which lessons do you feel you are making the most progress in? How do you know this?
- Which lessons do you feel you are making least progress in? How do you know this?
- In which lessons is your work regularly assessed? Does the feedback help you progress?
- In which lessons is your work not regularly assessed?
- In which lessons do you feel you learn most effectively?
- Which lessons are the most interesting?
- In which lesson do you receive homework according to the timetable? Does the homework help you progress?

Fig. 22 Example pupil focus group questions looking at the effectiveness of teaching across the curriculum

- Do you feel you are making progress in [subject]? How do you know this?
- Is your work regularly assessed? Does the feedback help you progress?
- Do you feel you can learn effectively? Why?
- Are the lessons interesting?
- Do you receive homework according to the timetable? Does the homework help you progress?

Fig. 23 Example pupil focus group questions looking at the effectiveness of teaching in one subject

An alternative is to use pupil questionnaires. These are done less frequently at subject or pastoral middle leadership level but can give useful information. Your school may also use a questionnaire operated by a commercial company. Why not ask if you could have a look at some of the findings?

Working with your team on self-evaluation

It is worth highlighting that as a middle leader you do not have to conduct self-evaluation on your own. You could be working with senior leaders, other middle leaders or members of your team. You also need to continually consider how self-evaluation findings will enable your team to be more effective.

In terms of lesson observations, encourage your staff to observe each others' lessons, including yours. This could be ten minutes spent in someone else's classroom and then a discussion as to what they have learnt. You could conduct joint lesson observations and the three of you could sit down and discuss the learning.

Work scrutiny can easily be completed during a meeting. Each teacher gives their books to another colleague to look at and then give feedback. You could each take it in turns to highlight something that you have learnt from looking at another colleague's books.

For pupil focus groups, you could take it in turns to lead. In a curriculum area, different members of staff could have the responsibility for differing year groups.

Final thoughts

There are many different types of self-evaluation that will enable you to assess the strengths and areas for development for your area. It is important to try and use a range of tools and then to compare the findings from each of them and look for trends and similarities. It is important to remember that colleagues may be nervous of self-evaluation as they might see it as an opportunity for you to try and catch them out. Instead you need to try and use self-evaluation to help build your team, and one way of doing this is to work together as a team. Finally, remember it is not the self-evaluation findings that really matter, it's what you then do with them.

TO DO LIST:

- ❑ Reflect on your experiences of receiving observations.
- ❑ Reflect on being coached and coaching a colleague.
- ❑ Check out Mike Cladingbowl's tweets at @mcladingbowl (see Takeaway box).
- ❑ Read *Developing a Self-evaluating School* by Paul K. Ainsworth (see Takeaway box).

Chapter 12 takeaway

Teaching tip

What is your view on observation?

You will be aware that the issue of observation is always controversial for teachers. Some of your colleagues will find observation one of their most stressful moments of the year. Think about the observations you have received. Which of them did you find the most useful? What was it about them that made them valuable? If they were a negative experience, why was this? What can you summarise which would make the observations you take more productive for your team?

Pass it on

Coaching observation

If you have never done so, why not arrange a coaching observation with a colleague. Firstly meet to have a discussion about what you both intend to teach in a future lesson. Give each other advice. Observe each other teaching the lesson. Finally after the observation, have a second meeting when you discuss each other's lesson.

CPD book club recommendation

Paul K. Ainsworth, *Developing a Self-evaluating School*
(see Bibliography and further reading)

Tweeter's corner

Mike Cladingbowl is the former Ofsted National Director for Schools and is a currently an Executive Principal. You can follow him on Twitter: @mcladingbowl

13 Appraising and line managing your staff

Appraisal and line management are two of the more formal aspects of leadership which you will complete as a middle leader. Appraisal is the formal process of setting targets and monitoring them. Line management means the regular meetings that some leaders will have with their colleagues to help them stay on track and increase their effectiveness.

The basics

Middle leadership is about trying to ensure that your staff work towards certain targets and also improve their practice. This is sometimes called, 'holding people to account'. As a middle leader it is likely that a senior leader will be holding you to account over your results and the results that you are predicting. Those who are responsible for maths or English in both primary and secondary schools are likely to feel this pressure most acutely. Pastoral leaders of Year 6 or Year 11 may also feel under similar scrutiny.

Appraisal and line management are the two formal processes that senior leaders will use with you and then you will need to use with your staff.

- **Appraisal and performance management:** previously performance management may have been an event that only occurred once during the academic year when a meeting was held to review last year's targets and set new targets – which often nobody looked at for the rest of the year! 'Appraisal' is the name that many schools have now adopted for performance management, following the implementation of a new set of regulations including appraisal being linked to the pay progression of staff. There is an expectation that appraisal is now an on-going process with meetings occurring throughout the school year. Alongside this, the new forensic-style analysis of pupil targets, tracking and results means that staff at all levels of the organisation are regularly being held to account.
- **Line management:** Line management could be described as any meeting that you have with your staff where you ask somebody to do something. In the past middle leaders may have found that they did not do huge amounts of line management of individual staff. Instead, any instructions given would have occurred during team meetings. For many middle leaders such decisions may have been reached via discussion and consensus rather than them feeling like orders.

You may find that a senior leader has regular line management meetings with you and then a specific appraisal meeting with you once a term. You may decide that you want to mirror this process with your staff and this chapter will give you some ideas on how you can do this. It may be that you just use this chapter to help you with appraisal, e.g. setting and reviewing targets and then monitoring them during the year.

Basic questions

- How does your line manager organise meetings with you?
- What does this show you about the ethos of line management in your school?
- Have you had an appraisal meeting that you can use as a format for those that you will run?
- Have you read the appraisal policy?
- What do the previous targets for your staff look like?

The detail

The following sections will take you through the appraisal process. However, it is important to read this alongside your school's appraisal policy as there may be differences. Finally there will be suggestions on how you can develop a line management structure.

Appraisal

If you start your new role in September, it is likely that one of your first formal leadership tasks will be running the appraisal process for your staff. It is not uncommon for middle leaders who may be second in command in a curriculum area or who have responsibility for an aspect of a curriculum area to have a number of staff to appraise. This is because otherwise curriculum leaders can have too many to do. Also schools want to make it clear that all middle leaders really do lead people and one way of making this explicit is to make sure all middle leaders conduct appraisals. If you are a pastoral leader, you may find that you are not an appraiser as this role falls to curriculum middle leaders. In some schools staff may have an appraisal target though which links to their tutor group/teaching class responsibility and you may be asked to contribute towards this.

It can be useful to have your appraisal meeting first with your line manager so that you have the process modelled for you and you understand the culture of the targets that are set. However, sometimes the process is planned so that during the training days the middle leaders appraise their staff and then senior leaders complete their appraisal of middle leaders in the first few weeks of term.

Appraisal meetings

Your first task is likely to be reviewing each of your colleague's targets from the previous year and then setting their targets for the year ahead. This should be a scheduled meeting when you both have time to complete these two tasks. You need to meet in a location where you will not be disturbed. Remember that some colleagues may feel nervous about this meeting and this could also be your first formal individual meeting with them too – hence you will want to make a good impression.

You need to make sure that you have:

- the correct data to check the targets – in some schools you will be expected to provide this, as the appraiser, or it may be an expectation that the appraisee brings it with them
- additional documents such as evidence of the appraisal lesson observations that should have taken place during the year
- last year's targets and the documents which the school uses for review.

Reviewing targets

This should be a conversation between you and the appraisee, where you take each target one at a time and see whether your colleague has reached their targets. The most important target is often the one focusing on pupil progress. Remember that all targets should have previously been signed off by a more senior member of staff who will have also moderated them against whole school targets.

If your colleague has reached their targets it should be a simple process of signing to approve that they have done so. Do take your time to discuss what they did to reach the targets. Did they use specific techniques or intervention strategies which you can learn from or share with other colleagues?

If the appraisee did not reach their targets it may have an impact upon their pay progression. If the colleague is close to target, you could say that they are working towards them. If the colleague is not close to the target, then they have not made their target. In terms of your first round of appraisal it may be worth checking this process with a more senior member of staff before you undertake the interview.

Setting targets

Usually, before you set any targets, your school will give you some advice as to what they expect. In many schools a classroom teacher will have three targets. One related to pupil progress, one related to the quality of teaching and learning and one wider target.

Appraisal targets should be SMART: Specific, Measurable, Achievable, Realistic and Time dependent. Try to ensure that targets have a certain percentage allocated against them and do not refer to 'some' or 'most'. In terms of realistic this will always be a moot point. However in many schools, individual targets are linked to whole school measures. So it might be that a certain proportion of students should make expected progress. Whether the colleague feels that is realistic is then a matter with senior leadership rather than you. The target which is linked to the quality of teaching and learning will often be the one that teaching over time is at least 'good'.

The final target is the one that offers the most opportunities for flexibility. However, be careful that what appears realistic for a colleague may not be seen in this way by the school, especially if it requires expensive or time-consuming CPD.

Monitoring targets

It is important that over the course of the year you monitor your colleagues' targets. It may be that your school has a cycle of meetings which you are reminded about. You may even have meeting time allocated over the course of the year to do this.

What you are trying to avoid is that if a colleague does not meet their targets it is not a surprise for the school, and that the colleague cannot claim they haven't been supported. In terms of pupil progress, you will be looking at data and comparing the pupils' progress against targets. In terms of quality of teaching judgement, you should receive the outcomes of quality assurance, if you do not do it yourself.

You may be able to give the colleague some support yourself or you make seek advice from other more senior colleagues as to whether they can help.

In some circumstances if the colleague is a long way off achieving their targets, the conversation with more senior colleagues may be around more specific help and could result in an informal support plan. It is important that you do not let things drift along if they are not going to plan. You need to discuss it openly and honestly with the colleague you are appraising and the person who line manages you.

Line management

Appraisal meetings are unlikely to occur more than once a term, however you need to keep in touch with your allocated colleagues' progress, making sure that pupils in their classes are progressing and any other projects they are working on are also moving forwards.

The most effective leaders will have regular line management meetings with their colleagues to check progress. The first stage is to timetable the meetings so they become a regular slot. You are looking for occasions when your PPA time matches your colleagues'. Some senior leaders will conduct line management meetings once a week as they have far more leadership time.

You could divide the line management meetings in to three sections. Firstly you could look at pupil progress, then schemes of work for the next period of time and finally look at other projects they are working upon.

In a primary school you could work in parallel with the other curriculum co-ordinators so that you each conduct a line management meeting with a different member of staff each week. The following table gives a plan for this.

Week	Literacy	Numeracy	Science	Topic
1	No line management meetings as appraisal meetings are occurring			
2	Teacher A Teacher B	Teacher C Teacher D	Teacher E Teacher F	Teacher G Teacher H
3	Teacher G Teacher H	Teacher A Teacher B	Teacher C Teacher D	Teacher E Teacher F
4	Teacher E Teacher F	Teacher G Teacher H	Teacher A Teacher B	Teacher C Teacher D
5	Teacher C Teacher D	Teacher E Teacher F	Teacher G Teacher H	Teacher A Teacher B
6	No line management meetings as teacher completing data trackers			

Fig. 24 Example primary line management timetable sorted by key curriculum areas

As a curriculum leader in a secondary school you may decide to have line management meetings with each of your colleagues every fortnight and these may only last for half a lesson. Each fortnight you could look at the progress of a different age group of pupils. The following table gives a suggestion as to how line management meetings could be organised in an eight week half term in the Autumn. As the year rolls on you may need to readjust this in the light of shorter half terms.

Week	Teacher A	Teacher B	Teacher C	Teacher D	Teacher E	Teacher F
1	No line management meetings as appraisal meetings are occurring					
2	Yr 11	Yr 11	Yr 11			
3				Yr 11	Yr 11	Yr 11
4	Year 9 & 10	Year 9 & 10	Year 9 & 10			
5				Year 9 & 10	Year 9 & 10	Year 9 & 10
6	Yr 7 & Yr 8	Yr 7 & Yr 8	Yr 7 & Yr 8			
7				Yr 7 & Yr 8	Yr 7 & Yr 8	Yr 7 & Yr 8
8	No line management meetings as teacher completing data trackers					

Fig. 25 Example secondary line management timetable sorted by key curriculum areas

Final thoughts

Appraisal is one of the key tasks that marks you as a leader. Too many people have paid lip service to performance management in the past but it is a very powerful tool for raising the performance of your teams. Your staff deserve for it to be carried out properly and not to rush it or skim over it. This is your opportunity to give support to those staff who are struggling before it becomes a formal problem and it is also the time to celebrate the success of those who are performing well whilst also learning from them.

To do list:

- ❑ Reflect on your experiences of line management.
- ❑ Reflect on your school's appraisal process.
- ❑ Draw up a plan for your line management meetings with colleagues.
- ❑ Check out Action Jackson's tweets @ActionJackson (see Takeaway box).
- ❑ Read one of the books recommended (see Takeaway box).

Chapter 13 takeaway

Teaching tip

How are you line managed?

Spend some time thinking about the line management that you have received. This could be in your teaching career or from other experiences. What were the features of line management that encouraged and motivated you to work to the best of your ability? Which comments reduced your motivation? Then consider how you can use these experiences when you are in the role of a line manager yourself.

Pass it on

Get advice from others

Have a discussion with a senior colleague about their views on appraisal. Ask them how they go about setting targets and how individual's appraisal targets link in to subject area or whole school targets. Ask them to briefly talk you through your school's appraisal policy.

CPD book club recommendation

Ken Blanchard and Spencer Johnson, *The New One Minute Manager*
Josephine Smith, *Performance Management: Making Appraisal Work for Your School*
(see Bibliography and further reading)

Tweeter's corner

Action Jackson is a tweeter of continual positivity. Follow him on Twitter: @ActionJackson

14 Running effective meetings

When you are rushing from lesson to lesson trying to deliver the very best teaching you possibly can, you may begin to wonder when you are going to have the time to do the leadership that is in your job title as middle leader. As you become more experienced you will start to use all those little conversations with your colleagues as opportunities for leadership. These are the moments when you will try to gently coach an improvement in teaching and learning in your area. There are also the more formal occasions such as when you observe a lesson and then give feedback.

However, the most frequent opportunities for leading your curriculum area or year group are the meetings that will be timetabled on your school's 1265 programme (1265 is the number of hours that teachers are contracted to work during a school year). This can include after school meetings and INSET days. In some schools, meeting time is timetabled in the school day.

The basics

The main types of meeting that you will lead or participate in are team meetings (or sub sets of your team) and also one-to-one meetings.

Team meetings

In many schools there will be an afternoon when meetings are scheduled to take place, and these will be a mixture of whole staff, middle leaders, CPD and then your own curriculum or pastoral team meetings.

One-to-one meetings

Some schools have also begun to implement progress meetings in which a team leader will discuss the progress of students with individual classroom teachers. You will use similar skills for leading this meeting as you would with your whole team. Some middle leaders will find one-to-one meetings easier than team meetings and vice versa. The difficulty of one-to-one meetings will depend on the outlook of that member of staff, whereas team meetings can be a pressure cooker of a range of emotions of different colleagues.

It is likely that you will have already led one team meeting at the beginning of term (as discussed in Chapter 8). The aim of this chapter is to build on that chapter in a little bit more detail to give you more confidence in leading effective team meetings over the course of the year.

Basic questions

- How often are your team meetings?
- How much time do you have for each meeting?
- Which members of staff attend the meetings?
- Are there whole school set agenda items which need to be included?
- Are there any minutes from previous meetings that you need to look at?

The detail

There are three components to running effective meetings:

- **Planning the meeting** – this includes writing the agenda, the conventions that you set and the people who are invited.
- **Meeting tactics** – what you do during the meeting, including the tactics you can use to stop the meetings turning into frustrating cul-de-sacs.
- **Following up the meeting** – your actions after the meeting so that the discussions from the meetings are as productive as possible.

Planning the meeting

Just as you would not begin a lesson without some planning, the same will be true of a meeting. You need to carefully plan:

- what you are going to discuss
- how long the items will take
- what order to put them in
- and also have some view of what the outcomes should be.

Items for the agenda

It is likely that you will know the dates of team meetings in advance, so in the weeks leading up to the meeting, why not keep an ongoing list of possible agenda items that you would like to discuss. You may divide the items into three categories:

1. those which are sharing information
2. items for discussion which need something deciding
3. the sharing of good practice.

It is also likely that some of these items will be things that you or a member of your team may have highlighted or there could be some area that your line manager or another member of the senior leadership team has said that you must discuss. In addition, there may be tasks that teams have been directed to do, such as a quality assurance exercise, e.g. work scrutiny. It is worth keeping a list running in your lesson planner of issues that you feel need discussing. If there is a month between team meetings, you can easily forget items that you thought of soon after the last meeting. You could also find that time in your meetings gets taken up addressing urgent items that have occurred in the days leading up to the meeting rather than some of the more long-term strategic items. The same is true of issues that are raised by senior leaders in middle leadership meetings or in your line management meeting.

Any other business (AOB)

One of the easiest ways for a well-planned meeting to be derailed is by your colleagues raising 'any other business' items (AOBs) at the end of your meeting. These might be for well-intentioned reasons, but beware of those colleagues who may have more malevolent intentions. AOBs can catch you unaware, unplanned and can easily make meetings overrun. The best strategy is to have a rule that AOBs need raising in advance with a couple of brief notes about the discussion. One suggestion can be to share a draft agenda with your team a couple of days before the meeting and then ask for any other 'possible' items for discussion a day before the meeting. Just because an item is suggested does not mean you have to discuss it as you may not have enough time to include all these items. If you decide not to include items you should explain this to your colleague and offer them an individual occasion with you to discuss the issue so that you can keep it on your list for future meetings.

Keeping to time

It is quite likely that you will often have too many items on your agenda but you must be realistic as no one likes it if projected one hour meetings turn into 90 minutes or two hours, even if this is the result of their discussion.

One way of shortening the meeting can be to put information to share on a briefing sheet before the meeting along with your agenda and ask people to read this in advance and then bring queries they may have to the meeting.

Focusing on teaching and learning

To focus your meeting on teaching and learning, many middle leaders may ask a member of their team to describe a lesson or an activity that has gone well recently. A similar technique can be to host each meeting in a different teacher's classroom and ask them to describe how their displays support their teaching or how they have been developed. Both these methods can take the pressure off you to be the 'expert' and allow your team to feel more valued.

Ordering the agenda

Following this, it is important to consider the order of other agenda items, particularly those that could be controversial and cause lengthy discussion. Some people will put these last on the agenda so that they know they can get through all the other items and the end of the day will help form a guillotine on this item. You may not want to put it towards the end of the agenda as you believe it may cause some ill-feeling and sour any other points discussed after this. However, other leaders will put such items in the middle of the agenda so later points can bring the team back together. You might also find that your colleagues don't want to discuss the item at the end, and this may feel positive as there are no resulting disagreements. However, you run the risk of it being discussed at other points and more often, in the following meeting, instead.

In your agenda you could even write the type of outcome that is required so that your colleagues recognise the necessity of the agenda. This could include understanding an issue, sharing information/practice, collecting ideas or deciding on a way forwards.

Poor agenda	Good agenda
Department meeting- Monday M1 Students Exam marking Yr 9 scheme of work Department Social	English Progress Meeting Monday M1 - 3.45- 4.45 pm Intervention students in Years 9 and 11. Progress review. (JA). 10mins Standardising exercise - yr. 10 literature Assessment (see below) (JA) 30mins Yr 9 scheme of work - thoughts on first draft (EC) 10mins End of term celebration. Where? When? Who? Suggested date 20/07/12 (all) 5mins Minute taker: ST Please prepare for the meeting by: • Reading the attached draft of the Year 9 Non fiction writing Scheme of Work • Collating data on your identified intervention students and bringing to meeting • Bringing along your copy of the mark scheme found in your OCR syllabus www.ocr.org/engassesscriteria

Fig. 26 Examples of poor and good meeting agendas

The previous agendas are used in the training plans in Part 2 to help you develop your skills in leading effective meetings.

Over time you will begin to recognise the best way of structuring your agendas so that there is a balance of good discussion whilst ensuring that your meeting finishes as close to time as possible.

Meeting tactics

Just as with teaching a class there are two extremes that you should avoid: the meeting does not make the headway you wanted due to too much conversation (either positive or negative); there is little participation in the meeting from some of your colleagues.

Here are some tactics to explore:

Tactic 1: Planning your agenda

This has already been discussed above. Plan your agenda carefully and consider the points at which certain items are discussed.

Tactic 2: Direct questions to your team – ask for their opinion

Just as you could bounce a question around your classroom, try to do this with your team. This can both stimulate discussion and avoid the same person dominating the conversation. This may not happen instantly and it is something that you may have to work on over a period of time, especially if the previous ethos was one of being instructed by the chair of the meeting.

Tactic 3: Avoid conversational tennis

If someone makes a point, don't feel that you need to immediately answer it as this can turn meetings into conversational tennis where your team is on one side of the net and you are on the other. Instead, try and give someone else the opportunity to make a point or even answer the previous one by asking for opinions on this point or if there are any other views. You can then make quick notes on each of the points and give a longer answer trying to draw a number of points together.

Tactic 4: Meeting poker

You may decide to try and reduce your interventions which can stifle discussion by using the idea of 'meeting poker'. If you think of the game of poker you only have so many 'chips' that you can gamble with during each hand. Once you have placed all your 'chips' you can no longer participate. Using the tactic of meeting poker you may only allow yourself so many interjections per discussion point or even during the whole meeting. This then forces you to ensure that each point you raise has more value. Obviously it does not count if you are introducing the issue or asking for someone's point of view.

Tactic 5: Summarising

An important skill during a meeting is to summarise the points that have been agreed during a discussion. If this is not done, you can often have very fruitful conversations but it does not help move your team forwards. Try and get into the habit of listing a few bullet points from the discussion after each item on the agenda has been discussed, and just as important, listing what the next actions should be. If you can reach an agreement on who will be tackling those next actions then even better. A longer-term strategy is to ask one of your team members to voice these for you. It could be the person who raised the agenda item, the person who has responsibility for the issue or the member of the team who has raised the most points during the discussion.

Minutes

This leads onto who is taking minutes of the meeting. It is often tempting for you to feel that you need to take the minutes as well as leading the meeting, but this can be difficult to do. Instead, good practice can be for your colleagues to take the minutes on rotation. If you still feel that you wish to take the minutes yourself, just record the agreed action points and who is going to be responsible for completing them.

Following up the meeting

It is important that once the meeting has occurred you ensure it is followed up efficiently. Try and make some notes of your own of what you think has been agreed and any items that need placing on the next meeting agenda. You may decide to make some personal reflections about what went well and what you felt you could have done better for next time. Encourage the minute taker to send them to each person as quickly as possible. You may decide to just photocopy/scan handwritten notes so this is done more speedily. If there are actions that individuals have agreed to take on, don't just wait until the next meeting to see whether they have been done, instead have regular conversations to discover what progress they are making.

Final thoughts

Just like great lessons, the most effective meetings do not occur by accident. They are the result of careful planning, experience and reflection. You will also find that some meetings will run away from you no matter how much preparation you do. Try not to worry about this for too long. You cannot control the emotions and feeling that people will bring to the meeting, and sometimes your most loyal colleagues can accidentally derail a meeting due to an incident that has occurred that day. What you can always control is your efficiency in communicating both the agenda and the agreed action points.

To do list:

- [ ] Reflect on how other leaders use meeting tactics.
- [ ] Reflect on your discussion on dealing with difficult characters.
- [ ] Check out Kenny Frederick's blog posts on leadership (see Takeaway box).
- [ ] Read *Multipliers* by Liz Wiseman and Greg McKeown (see Takeaway box).

Chapter 14 takeaway

Teaching tip

Watching meeting tactics

The next time you attend a meeting which you are not chairing, try and observe the tactics that the headteacher or other senior leader uses to keep control of the meeting. You could see it as a little bit like observing a lesson with a focus on behavioural management and the strategies which a teacher uses to develop a positive working atmosphere.

Pass it on

Share your ideas – meeting tactics

Have a discussion with a colleague about meetings that they have attended. Was there a member of staff in the meeting who was difficult and attempted to derail a meeting? How did the chair of the meeting deal with this colleague? If you both chair meetings, you could do some peer coaching observations of each other's meetings. Have a discussion before the meeting about where you think the issues will be and how you've structured the meeting to avoid these. Observe each other's meetings. Then have a second discussion about how the meetings went and what advice you could give each other for the future.

CPD book club recommendation

Liz Wiseman and Greg McKeown, *Multipliers*
(see Bibliography and further reading)

Bloggers' corner

Kenny Frederick is an inspirational, former headteacher. Blog: blogsfromtheisland.wordpress.com or follow her on Twitter: @KennyGFrederick

15 Finding a balance between your teaching and leadership

Many teachers are constantly on the look out for anything that can magically create some more time amidst the hurly-burly of term time. You may look at our friends who work outside education who seem to have opportunities for a rich social life in the evening or at the weekend when we are often marking yet another set of exercise books, planning lessons, reading and writing papers or attending a governors' meeting.

You may feel this even more acutely when you become a middle leader. You may have thought that the additional non-contact time would you give you more time, but that can quickly be up swallowed by the additional tasks you have to do. In addition, you will want your lessons to be as high-quality as possible and on top of that, you always need to be prepared for the unexpected, such as one of your colleagues being ill and you needing to set work for their classes.

The basics

I have always found balancing my teaching and leadership roles a challenge, and during my teaching career I have read many time management books looking for a magical solution to pursue my role more effectively, complete tasks more quickly and save more time. It has always been a disappointment to me that I have considered this aspect of my professional life a weakness. It is also one that is always altering due to changing job descriptions, roles and family circumstances. You may find that this is the same and finding this balance becomes your own search for the holy grail.

You may look around the staffroom and think that all your fellow middle leaders and senior leaders are far more efficient than you and seem more organised. Yet often these colleagues are like swans gliding across the surface but paddling like crazy underneath. You may find that their work space at school or at home has an embarrassing pile of papers that are falling onto the floor or someone else's desk. You also cannot see their email inbox – this could be overflowing with unread emails. However, what they may have is some kind of system so that they are not falling into the trap of only completing school paperwork after it was requested a second time.

Basic questions

- Have you got a system to help you manage your time?
- Is your system effective?
- What do you feel is not working well?
- Can you identify what takes up most of your time?

The detail

The following sections will provide a range of different solutions that have helped others keep on top of their role and can do the same for you. At the heart of them are two aspects: identifying the key tasks and then deciding when to do them.

Getting organised

The starting point for many people's time management is often looking at their work space and comparing it to other's. If you feel that you are one of the people with the untidiest classroom or perhaps office, you may conclude that this problem could be your starting point. It is true that it is difficult to finely manage your time if you are always looking for things.

Paperwork sort out

You could begin by having a good sort out of your paperwork, or more likely your email inbox. If it is on paper you could order it all, resulting in a big pile of tasks to do. If it's electronic, you could read everything and then tag all the emails which require actions as tasks so you have an electronic list.

You could then make it your mission to work through them during odd free lessons in between a full teaching load and leading your team faculty. You may find that this begins to work for you. However, for many colleagues, by the end of the first few weeks you may feel that that you have worked even harder than usual, not really got anywhere, the piles on your desk are back out of control again, your email inbox has fifty unread emails and perhaps you need to go back to the drawing board.

Realistic aims

The standard next step is to decide that realistic aims are the answer. Think of all the tasks that you need to do on a weekly basis such as, mark books, plan lessons, attend regular meetings and sort emails. You could design your own timetable of what needs to be completed each day in a notebook, diary or planner. This can work to a certain extent but you may find that any type of incident or additional task can completely throw the system. You may even find that the notebook quickly becomes scruffy before itself gets lost under the paper mountain. The conclusion could be that a more sophisticated system is needed. Perhaps this is the time when you buy that leather Filofax that you've often thought of. You may decide that this is the time to buy a tablet or upgrade your smartphone to be able to synch with your email system and electronic calendar.

Transcribe your timetable and meetings into the diary pages or use the power of the electronic calendar system to ensure that they are all routine appointments. At the same time, ensure that you have an accurate to do list written. You could then begin to prioritise tasks according to their urgency using a numbered system whether in paper or electronic form. This could be the method that works for you. Certainly many people find this works for them.

There is often one key fault with this system that you will probably not find for a few weeks. The standard difficulty for people who use this system is that they notice the same things are always on their to do list and never move. These are often tasks that are not time dependent, which stay unmoved and undone, such as observing your team, rewriting schemes of work and any other project that you have conceived but not yet implemented. The following system aims to address this.

Vision and values

As a middle leader you will have a greater number of strategic tasks than a teacher. Therefore you are more likely to have a greater number of tasks that are not so immediately time dependent, hence the prioritisation skills in the previous section may have served you well as a teacher but do not have quite the same effectiveness for you as a middle leader.

We need to begin to look at our tasks in a different way to ensure that they are completed. Most tasks can be analysed according to their importance and urgency.

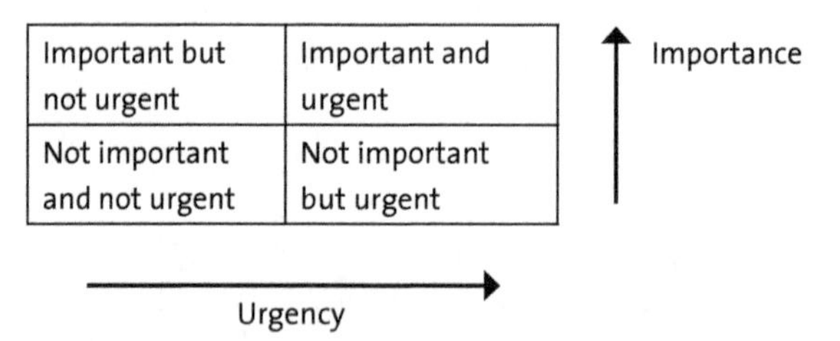

Fig. 27 Important/urgent

Important and urgent

We know what the important and urgent tasks are and it is human nature that we prioritise those. They could include the upset child, the next lesson we are about to teach or a request from the headteacher. However, where people do sometimes come unstuck with these tasks are the ones that take a considerable amount of time to complete. A good example here would be writing a set of reports to a deadline. We understand the importance and urgency of this task, but we can sometimes misjudge how long they can take to complete; this is especially the case in a new school. Further examples are:

- Setting lessons for absent colleagues.
- Dealing with a parental complaint about a colleague.
- Ensuring option book information is completed to deadline.
- Completing examination entry details.

Not important but urgent

We can easily get sucked into spending a considerable amount of time on things that are urgent but yet, if we think about them carefully in the grand scheme of things, they are not important. In teaching, these tend to be a lot of the conversations that we may have with some of our staff. If you are in the middle of setting lessons for an absent colleague, the team member who sees you writing on the board and pops in to talk to you is not your main priority but because of the timing it can feel urgent. It is important to build relationships and this does take an investment of time, however, there is also the scenario of those middle leaders who arrive in school early to complete a certain task and then find they get wrapped up in a number of conversations which means that they don't achieve what they intended to! In the worse case scenario you may find that you end up with more work to do.

Some middle leaders develop clever tactics to avoid this happening. The most obvious is to quickly explain that you need to focus on what you are doing at the moment. The second is to say, 'I can give you five minutes at the end of break or I can give you half an hour on Wednesday next week'. However, always make sure you have somewhere else to go to, such as a lesson to teach so that again the short meeting doesn't take up any more time. Some colleagues are in school but seem to hide so you never quite know where they are. Other colleagues may arrive in school and go straight to their classrooms and make a start on being organised for the day.

What you are trying to avoid being is the member of staff who arrives early and leaves late but spends most of this time in the staffroom and is always involved in a conversation but finds it difficult to get started on tasks. It is often pastoral leaders who this can be the most challenging for as so many teachers will want to have a conversation with them about a recalcitrant or troubled child.

Not important and not urgent

It can be difficult to dispassionately decide which of the things we fill our time with fall into this box as we always like to believe that everything we do is important at some level. We all need to switch off sometimes by doing a bit of internet surfing and this can be a therapy to sorting through junk mail. However, when it can become a problem is when these become a work avoidance tactic that we use rather than starting on something that is more important, especially when time is limited.

Important but not urgent

As has already been suggested, the tasks in this category are often the strategic tasks that we need to be completing as a middle leader. These are the development tasks such as planning for the future and researching new ideas. Then there are the more concrete tasks of beginning their implementation so that they turn into a reality. In a new school or a new role, it could also be the time it takes to build relationships with other colleagues that can easily be forgotten if we just focus on those things which have a definitive deadline.

Using vision and values to focus on the 'important but not urgent tasks'

One system that people use to try and ensure that these tasks are completed is to think about their vision and your values. The challenge that so many of us have is that we have lots of roles for which we may be working towards different goals. You could be a spouse, a parent, a carer, a volunteer in an organisation as well as being a teacher and a middle leader. Therefore, what you could try and consider is what is your vision for each of these roles. Then, to work towards this long-term goal try, at the start of each week, to identify one task from the important but not urgent list, timetable and record when you are going to do it and ensure you complete it. Hopefully, you may find this link to your vision and values will give you impetus to fulfil these defined tasks.

Teaching and leadership

One of the difficulties for many middle leaders is trying to maintain the balance between their teaching and their leadership tasks. You may find that the strategy of trying to consider what is your teaching goal for the year alongside your middle leader goal is a useful one.

It is impossible to put the same focus on your teaching as you did before you were a middle leader. This means that your planning must be more efficient than it used to be and you need to be looking at time-efficient ways of managing teaching processes such as your marking.

Some middle leaders will set themselves the teaching goal of trying to develop one new outstanding lesson a week, or one innovative lesson per class, per week. They may decide that if they ensure all their other lessons are good, the pupils are receiving a good deal.

What you must ensure is that you do not tilt the balance too far so that you are solely focusing on either your teaching role or middle leadership role. So even if you do not go as far as determining your vision for each role, you still try and allocate blocks of time to each of them.

Life after getting organised or vision and values

You may find after trying basic time management to get organised or the more sophisticated ideas in vision and values that actually you do not have a huge issue with getting your work done; instead the issue you have comes down to needing to be organised but being swamped with the number of things that you have to do. When this happens you can find that you keep looking at the same task or action many, many times without actually completing it. In this situation you need to have a system whereby you only look at a task twice at the most. The two-minute rule is a system that may help you with this.

The two-minute rule

If you are starting work and you are looking at stuff whether it is paper-based or electronic, think firstly: is it a task? If it isn't you have two choices: file it for reading or bin it. Do not be afraid of being ruthless. If it is an email, begin to create your own filing system so that your inbox is not always full.

If you have decided it is a task, then quickly determine whether it will take less than two minutes. If this is the case, do it now so you can tick it off. If it will take more than two minutes, decide whether you need to do it or if you can delegate it. If it is something that you need to do, plan when you are going to do it and calendar the task with a rough idea of how long you think it will take you. You could do this electronically or in your diary.

Sometimes the task may look really massive and you can feel overwhelmed by it. Rather than just timetabling it for the future, instead spend the two minutes deciding what the next action is and record this in your timetabling. When this comes up in your calendar you can focus on completing the next action rather than looking at the project in its entirety.

Final thoughts

You are likely to find that throughout your career balancing different elements of your job is always a challenge. You may be one of those people who keeps carefully honing their organisational techniques and at the same time finds speedier ways of getting the tasks done.

You may find that you are always looking for new time management approaches and find the novelty gives you the energy to use them. It could be a new system, new piece of hardware or a new app. If this is you, then don't worry about whether you will still be using it in a year's time as the invigoration of a new method will have made you more effective. The important thing then is to try different systems, read a new book, buy another piece of kit and not to worry if you don't stick with them. Instead, the enthusiasm in finding another approach can increase work rate and efficiency.

TO DO LIST:

- ❑ Reflect on how you can tackle the important but not urgent tasks.
- ❑ Reflect on how others manage their time.
- ❑ Check out Jim Smith's website on being a lazy teacher (see Takeaway box).
- ❑ Read one of the book club recommended titles (see Takeaway box).

Chapter 15 takeaway

Teaching tip

What is important but not urgent?

Most colleagues have a to do list. If you haven't, sit down and spend 30 minutes writing down all the tasks that you think you need to do. Try and classify your list into the four quadrants. It is unlikely you will write down many 'not important-urgent' or 'not important-not urgent' tasks. So think about what else has taken up your time in the last week and write it down under those headings. Think about how you can avoid these activities and these situations. Then have a look at the 'important-not urgent' task and make a commitment to tackle one of these this week. Allocate a time to do it and collect the resources along the way to do so.

Pass it on

Book group

Talk to a close colleague about how they manage their time. What tactics do they use? If they find time management difficult too, why not choose a book about time management from the list below, read it together and then support each other in trying the techniques listed. Time management can be a little like dieting; it is much easier if you have the support of someone else working on it at the same time.

CPD book club recommendations

David Allen, *Getting Things Done: The Art of Stress-free Productivity*.
Stephen Covey, Roger Merrill and Rebecca Merrill, *First Things First*.
Julie Morgenstern, *Time Management*.
(see Bibliography and further reading)

Bloggers' corner

Jim Smith describes himself as 'the laziest (but professional) teacher in town'. Look at his website at www.lazyteacher.co.uk or follow him on Twitter: @thelazyteacher

STAGE 5: ENJOYING MIDDLE LEADERSHIP

16 Improvement planning

One of your key tasks as a middle leader will be to continue to develop and improve the work of the area you lead. We accept that the best pieces of work are those which are planned in a written form. Hence, in your role as a middle leader you should write an improvement or development plan. Even if your school does not ask for this, you should be planning the actions that you intend to take over the year.

The basics

All schools should have an overall improvement or development plan and in most schools, middle leaders will be expected to prepare an improvement plan for the area they lead. In some schools these two processes will be dovetailed together and there will be a strong link between the two documents. In fact, the improvement plans from curriculum areas may be the appendices to the whole school improvement plan. You may also find that targets from the school improvement plan become targets for the improvement plan that you write. In the best schools, there will also be a clear link between improvement planning and the performance management cycle (see Chapter 13). In schools with the most effective improvement plans you would be able to walk into any classroom and see elements of the school improvement plan in action. This really would be the holy grail of improvement planning.

In some schools, improvement plans may be a three-year process for the whole school and individual areas but in other schools, middle leaders may be expected to write a new improvement plan each year. If you have started work at the beginning of the new academic year you may not need to write a new improvement plan until the summer term. You do, however, need to look at the improvement plan that the previous postholder wrote, as it is likely that senior leaders will expect you to be working towards it. This will especially be the case if there is a very systematic approach to improvement planning across the school.

Basic questions

- Is there an improvement plan already in existence for your area?
- What is the duration of the improvement plan? Annual or longer?
- When do you have to begin writing a new improvement plan?
- Do you write the plan within an overall school plan?

The detail

This following sections will help you with the process of developing a new improvement plan and consider what elements are likely to be in such a plan. Every school will have a different format but it is likely there will be similar sections. The key to a successful improvement plan is having very clear targets with an understandable, and hopefully succinct action plan, which you then work towards.

How to begin

The first stage is to gather copies of previous improvement plans for your area and consider them carefully:

- What previous improvement priorities have there been?
- How effectively have these been tackled?
- What format have these plans been presented in?

You may find that senior leaders decide that a new format will be more useful. Whatever format your school decides upon, most would consider that improvement plans should be written and presented as specific, measurable, achievable, realistic and time related (SMART) targets. However, schools often develop very specific improvement planning techniques.

The next stage is to look at your quality assurance or self-evaluation to consider what you feel needs improving within your area. Senior leaders may have done this for you, but if they haven't or if they have a meeting planned with you, why not consider some of the following questions.

	Question	**Notes**
1	Looking at the achievement data is there anything that concerns us?	See in-school data
2	Are there any differences between our subject data and the school's?	See in-school data
3	Are there any differences between our subject data and similar curriculum areas?	See in-school data
4	Are there any differences between our subject data and national figures?	See RAISE online (www.raiseonline.org)
5	In which areas of the curriculum are the children performing well?	Strengths
6	In which areas of the curriculum are the children performing less well?	Weaknesses

Fig. 28 Quality assurance questions for improvement planning

When discussing all of these questions you need to be asking yourself: why is this the case, and what can we do to improve the situation?

How to create a plan

You may find that your senior leadership team sets very specific goals that are similar to those used in performance management. Such targets could be based upon progress, e.g. 80% of pupils make expected progress, or they may be based upon teaching and learning, e.g. 80% of observed lessons are 'good'. What you then have to do is look at quality assurance questions and consider how far away you are from meeting these targets and what strategies or actions you think would make the difference.

You may decide that this is a conversation that you need to have with all of your team, or you may decide that at this beginning stage you only need to discuss the issue with fellow middle leaders in your area or your line manager. You may also find it useful to ask other middle leaders in your school how they are writing their improvement plans and what strategies they are considering implementing.

You may decide that these conversations are best supported by looking at the format of the current improvement plan to help give you ideas. However, some people may find that such documents initially stifle their creativity. If no new format is available, the following questions may help you.

	Questions for initial improvement planning
1	What is the goal?
2	What is the performance target?
3	Is this broken down into a series of focuses?
4	What individual strategies or actions will be implemented?
5	What indicators of success will you see?
6	How will these be monitored and evaluated?
7	When will these be done by? (time lines)
8	Who will have the responsibility?
9	Are there any financial costs?

Fig. 29 Questions for initial improvement planning

How to write the improvement plan

After all the talk, debate and planning there comes a point when all the discussion needs translating into a manageable and clear written document. This is best done by one person who collates all the thinking that has gone on during discussions, and formulates the plan into one document. Alternatively, if you are part of a large team or lead a large team such as a faculty with a number of middle leaders then once you have agreed, or been given a clear page structure, you could share out the burden of the task.

The example below shows how a department in a secondary school has the goal of developing teaching and learning but is focusing on improving the quality of assessment and feedback.

One of the difficulties with improvement planning is trying to ensure that your team have the opportunity to give some input. Discussing elements of it in a team meeting is one way of doing this, but time is always limited. You could decide to have a meeting one lunchtime a week to look at a different goal each time and members of your team can choose to attend if they wish.

Focus	Actions	Dates	Lead Staff	Success criteria	Time / Resources	Monitoring and evaluation
Use high-quality marking and feedback to help students improve	Department: Work scrutiny of year 11 books to establish current picture	End of September	All dept	Work scrutiny completed	1 hour September INSET day	Scrutiny record discussed with line manager
	Review departmental marking policy	End of September	HOD/ 2nd	Policy reviewed	2 hours	Discuss in line management meeting
	Rewrite or amend policy	October half term	HOD/ 2nd	New policy written	3 hours	Copy of new policy shared with line manager
	Use departmental meeting to share current good practice	September or October	All dept	Practice shared	Slots in two department meetings	Year 7 SLT work scrutiny. Is there progress?
	Head of English to explain use of green pens for pupil recording of feedback	October	All dept	Green pen marking trialled	Slot in department meeting Class sets of green pens for each teacher	SLT learning walks

Focus	Actions	Dates	Lead Staff	Success criteria	Time / Resources	Monitoring and evaluation
	Produce marking templates for end of module assessments and my year 11 mocks	End of November	All dept	Templates available and used	1200 stickers / reprographic costs	
		End of term	All dept	Department – all marking to agreed policy		Year 11 SLT work scrutiny

Fig. 30 Extract of curriculum improvement plan on raising standard of teaching and learning, focusing on assessment and feedback

Goal: Raise the standards of teaching and learning in the faculty so that most teaching is good.

Performance target: 80% of observed lessons are good by the end of the academic year.

Milestones

It is important to break down tasks into manageable sections. Some schools will do this by writing milestones. In the plan above, the milestones are based around which tasks will be completed at what time. So for example, the task of writing the new assessment policy will be completed by October half term.

A different approach is to consider the milestones in terms of performance and what this will look like at varying points of the year. The overall goal for the improvement plan above is that 80% of teaching will be graded as 'good' by the end of the year. The current figure could be 65% (good). So this could be broken down so that by the end of term 1 the figure will be 70% and by the end of term 2 it will be 75%. If the action is to improve assessment and marking this could be tracked through an SLT learning walk which focuses on this area with the aim that the marking and assessment will be graded as good for 70% of groups. As a middle leader this makes it very straightforward for you to measure where your team is against these targets.

Monitoring and evaluating

In many schools, your line manager or a senior leader should help you with the monitoring. It is important to try and ensure that monitoring and evaluation is not just about ticking off tasks, but that the tasks and activities are having a measurable impact on the children. The only way to do this is to make the link explicit between the improvement plan and the quality of teaching and learning or the quality of achievement. If these are not improving, the question could be asked: is there any point in the actions?

In the previous examples we have considered teaching and learning. In terms of achievement, many schools were looking at levels of progress, but with the changes in assessment and the withdrawal of National Curriculum levels, many schools are asking whether pupils are on target or not to reach either a set level of performance or to reach their target based on their prior attainment. Showing an improvement in these figures is likely to be something that senior leaders will want to monitor your improvement plan against.

Final thoughts

Improvement planning provides you with a good opportunity to evaluate the work of your team and to develop a plan to increase the effectiveness of your team. The process of clearly recording what you need to do and how you are going to do it, is extremely helpful for your own leadership and for sharing with your team.

You need to make sure that your improvement plan is a working document. You should be cross-referencing and recording how you are making progress with your plan over the year. In many ways this is your set of directions for the school year telling you your route.

The best improvement plans should then flow into performance management targets. So if you are writing this in the summer term, be thinking of how you could set individual targets for your staff which also work towards the goals in your improvement plan.

Your improvement plan now forms the script for the next academic years' work and the focus for your staff. If the actions of the plan are being carried out you can be sure that your area is moving forward in the direction you have agreed. It also acts as a reference guide. At busy times of year it is a useful document to refer to, to reassure yourself that area is moving in the right direction. At quieter times it is good to refer to it in order to check progress and monitor timescales. The improvement plan also provides a chart for agenda setting at some of your meetings.

To do list:

- ❑ Reflect on your experience in completing improvement plans.
- ❑ Reflect on the templates different schools have.
- ❑ Check out Heather Leatt's tweets @HeatherLeatt (see Takeaway box).
- ❑ Read *Good to Great* by Jim Collins (see Takeaway box).

Chapter 16 takeaway

Teaching tip

Writing an improvement plan

If you are not currently a middle leader and do not have to write your improvement plan, it's a good idea to have a practice. If you are running a project, then find a copy of your school's improvement planning template and think about how you would capture your project on this template. The biggest challenge is often the evaluation strand, so try and complete this section.

Pass it on

Share your ideas – improvement plans

Talk to a middle leader about their improvement plan. What do they find to be the most challenging aspect of writing it? How do they refer to it over the term? How do they share it with their team? Ask colleagues in different schools if they would be prepared to share their improvement templates with you and consider which template you like best.

CPD book club recommendation

Jim Collins, *From Good to Great*
(see Bibliography and further reading)

Tweeters' corner

Heather Leatt is an adviser and writes very useful analysis of changes in Ofsted structures. Follow her on Twitter: @Heatherleatt

17 Planning and leading an initiative

One of the most important aspects of being a middle leader or a potential leader is the ability to manage and lead initiatives which have a positive impact on the quality of teaching and learning in your area. From day one of your teaching career you will have been used to developing projects in your own classroom with the pupils you work with to improve their learning, but the difference here is that you will be aiming to implement initiatives that help pupils to progress in classrooms beyond your own. You will be working with and leading other school staff to turn your ideas into a reality.

The basics

You may be reading this chapter as preparation to becoming a middle leader. Leading a project can be an ideal experience to draw upon during an interview. You may also be a more experienced middle leader and have just written your improvement plan and be looking for some fresh ideas to turn that vision into a reality.

There are many suggestions for how to lead a project. The one area that they will agree on is that you have to break the project down into achievable chunks and this will vary according to how big the project is and how many people are involved.

This chapter will focus on smaller projects that you can lead within your curriculum area or your age phase rather than whole school projects, as they are more the reserve of a senior leader though the principles are still similar.

Basic questions

- Have you led any initiatives in the past?
- What went well and what could you improve upon?
- Do you know what project you want to develop?
- Which members of staff will be involved?
- What is the intended impact upon the students?

The detail

The following sections will look at implementing a project by considering starting out, working with staff, planning the project, keeping pace and measuring outcomes.

Starting out

When you have a good idea, the temptation is to tell anybody who might be involved and rush to enact it in your enthusiasm. This is fine when you are working on your own as this gives you the energy to get the project moving and if something does not quite work out you can alter it yourself and make it work. As soon as you are leading something with other staff this strategy is not usually as effective. If you discuss an idea with your team without showing them the detailed plan they may focus on the reasons why they think the plan won't work and the project can start off on a negative footing. When you return with the detailed plan their original negativity can be hard to shift. If they start the project and find faults, they may be more likely to abandon it rather than trying to troubleshoot themselves.

This is one of the differences of working in a more formal leadership role and unfortunately you cannot expect everybody to share your enthusiasm. If your previous experience of leading a project was working with a friend or a couple of friends, they may have been swept along in your positivity and helped you through the initial unplanned stages and not minded if everything was not tied down at the beginning.

Working with staff

One of the key elements of planning a project is the motivation behind it. It is this motivation that will make staff more prepared to work with you. Often the strongest driver is that known as the 'Burning platform' situation.

Burning platform

A burning platform is a situation that highlights immediate and radical change is required due to a dire circumstance. The term originates from a story about a man on an oil platform. One night he is awakened by an explosion and resulting fire on the platform. Striving to escape the impending flames, he is able to find his way though the chaos to the edge of the platform.

As the fire gets closer he has to make an immediate life or death decision. His only option is to jump more than 100 feet from the fire-ridden platform into the freezing North Atlantic waters. The likelihood is that if the jump doesn't kill him he will surely die from exposure within minutes if not rescued. With no other rational alternative, he jumped! Fortunately the man did survive the jump from the platform and was rescued by boat shortly thereafter. His philosophy had been 'Better probable death than certain death'.

The idea that the burning platform theory represents is that people are much more likely to accept change if there is a strong need required for this. What you need to do is look for this reason.

The starting place is often data, especially when it directly relates to the specific pupil groups. So it might be that when you are analysing data you see a certain group of students are not performing as well as they could be and your project will improve the outcomes for this group of students.

The project could also be to improve another measurable outcome such as behaviour or attendance. It may be that a certain group of students is struggling and you feel that a specific intervention can improve this.

The project could be a wider issue such as developing an aspect of teaching and learning. This will have a longer-term impact on pupil outcomes but it might have a quicker impact on the quality assurance of teaching and learning in your area.

When you are explaining the project to other colleagues you need to be careful with how much emphasis you place purely on numerical data. The eyes of some staff will glaze over with too much talk of data, so if you can also highlight specific pupils whom you think it will make a difference to this is worth explaining as it helps to place the whole idea in a real context.

Planning the project

The planning of any project is always key to its success. You need to be able to break it down into actions. If these are made time specific this will be really helpful. If you can construct a plan with certain actions in certain weeks this will make the project easier to manage and staff will be far clearer on when things need to happen. Some staff like to use action plans with milestones in to do this. There will be other staff that use spreadsheets or project management tools like Gantt charts. However you need to be careful that you don't spend ages creating a beautiful plan, causing you to get behind with your everyday work, or that there is not time to do the project as the plan has taken so long!

When you are doing this you can also keep an eye on other school initiatives that are happening that week. It is probably true that there is always something happening in schools and also if you require meeting time to work on the project, you will have little say on when this can happen. However, at the same time be aware of 'possible own goals' such as asking a group of staff to do a big piece of work in the week they are marking their mocks!

Keeping the pace

One of the challenges in leading a project is keeping it moving forwards. It may not seem it at the time but the easy part is launching the project; the hard point is ensuring it stays on track. This is where actions plans can be helpful, but you need to keep it as a live document. Annotate it or colour code when actions have been completed. Hold regular meetings with your staff to share the progress. If you can keep your team aware of the bigger picture they are likely to be more supportive of the project. One way of doing this is if somebody within the team will take responsibility for updating the action plans. Also be aware if some aspects of the projects are not working as well as you would have hoped. Sometimes as a leader you have to hold your nerve as you believe that patience will see progress but equally there are times when you have to have a rethink. Your trusted colleagues will often give you good feedback on this.

Measuring the outcomes

It is vital that you have a way of measuring the outcomes. This could be in terms of improvements in pupil attainment or progress. It could be a reduction in behaviour incidents or an increase in attendance. It could be that there is demonstrable improvement in the quality of teaching and learning. It could be less data driven and be a case study of certain pupils and the impact the project had on them.

Don't forget to celebrate the small gains. This can be whilst the project is occurring and you can observe positive outcomes, share them with staff and pupils. Again at the end of the project if things have worked well then celebrate it. It can be an opportunity for your team to showcase their skills.

Measuring outcomes can be very important to career progression too. If you are asked questions in an interview about a project that you have led and you can describe the improvement it has brought about, this is an important skill to have. Equally, if you can communicate the success of the project to senior leaders in your school in this way, this could help your career development

Final thoughts

As a leader you need to improve the outcomes of the students in your care. Implementing a project is often an ideal way of working towards this in a manageable fashion. Leading a project will give you a good opportunity to develop the key elements of leadership skills and if you can do it in a reflective framework, you will learn even more.

TO DO LIST:

- ❑ Reflect on all planning initiatives.
- ❑ Reflect with a colleague on initiatives that you have led.
- ❑ Check out Stephen Fuller's tweets @toffler73 (see Takeaway box).
- ❑ Read *The Multiplier Effect* by Liz Wiseman, Lois Allen and Elise Foster (see Takeaway box).

Chapter 16 takeaway

Teaching tip

Planning a project

If you are an aspiring middle leader, now is the time to find an opportunity to lead an initiative, if you haven't already done so. It could be offering to take on something in a subject area, such as rewrite part of a scheme of work. Plan out the project and then introduce it to the relevant teachers. Once it is up and running monitor its progress. Best of all is to have measurable outcomes.

Pass it on

Share your ideas – reviewing recent projects

Discuss recent projects that have been implemented with a colleague. What have been the difficulties? How did you measure outcomes? Were the outcomes positive and raised standards? If not, how could you have improved the project so it did make a difference?

CPD book club recommendation

Liz Wiseman, Lois Allen and Elise Foster, *The Multiplier Effect: Tapping the genius inside our schools*
(see Bibliography and further reading)

Tweeter's corner

Stephen Fuller is an assistant head in a rapidly improving school. Follow him on Twitter: @toffler73

18 Recruiting staff and succession planning

There will be some point during your middle leadership tenure when you need to recruit a new member of staff. This could be in your first few days in post or it could take much longer. The involvement you have in selecting a new member of the team will vary greatly according to your role and the type of school you are working in.

The basics

If you are a form tutor in a secondary school or a subject co-ordinator in a primary school you may have little involvement in new appointments. In a primary school, it is likely to be the headteacher and other senior leaders who will make the appointment. However, for your own future career development, you may ask if you can be involved in the process in some way.

In a secondary school, the curriculum leader is likely to have a lead role in selecting a new teacher. However, there will be times when you are working with a new teacher too, such as when a new senior leader has skills in your subject area. Finally, if you are a pastoral leader, you may have teachers allocated to your team or you may be able to influence which staff from within the school are allocated to your team but it is unlikely you will be involved in appointing new staff.

This chapter will look at the three main steps in building your team:

1. **Analysing your team:** The first step is to look at the current people in your team and the skills they possess – are there any gaps to be filled or lots of duplication? Answering these questions will then help you decide what skills you need to add to your team, and also from a CPD perspective what you may need to develop.
2. **Running a recruitment process:** The main element of this chapter is helping you run a recruitment process. Each school will differ in how much autonomy they give you on this element. However, senior leaders are usually grateful if a middle leader can make suggestions on how the process might run – especially if you also show an understanding of the wider running of the school. Remember, an interview day may be the most important task of the year to you but senior leaders will be balancing many other issues at the same time.
3. **Succession planning:** The final section of this chapter is considering succession planning. The best middle leaders will always be thinking ahead as to what might happen. They will be building networks and retaining contacts with colleagues so that if a member of staff leaves at short notice or is absent for a long-term illness they will already have some leads they can explore.

Whilst this chapter is more aimed at curriculum leaders, it is hoped that pastoral leaders will still find it of interest.

Basic questions

- Do you know what the strengths and weaknesses of your team are?
- Have you taken part in a recruitment process to select a new member of staff?
- What do you think works well when helping choose a new member of staff?
- Are there areas of the selection process that you lack confidence in leading?
- Have you plans to cover unexpected absence or resignations?

The detail

Over the following sections you will look at how to analyse your team, how to run a recruitment process and then how to develop succession planning.

Analysing your team

We often know what the headline strengths in our team are, but we rarely subjectively dig a little deeper. You probably know which members of your team are more skilled at behaviour management as you will have dealt with issues with those who struggle with this. You are also likely to know who is perceived to be the better teacher or delivers higher achievement (and the other extreme) from the results of self-evaluation. However the best middle leaders will also know information about members of their team's skills that are not in their current day-to-day practice. For example, as well as looking at the elements of the curriculum their colleagues are seen to be strong in delivering. A curriculum middle leader in an 11–18 secondary school might also ask what else their colleagues have delivered in previous schools or enjoyed studying themselves.

When you are looking at your team it is useful to analyse their strengths and weaknesses. The following table has been constructed by a head of maths and looks at teachers' enjoyment of working with certain ability groups and delivering certain courses and the grade their teaching has received, if available. If a teacher does not have a number against them, this is because the quality of their teaching in their area has not been assessed because they have not taught this area before.

Age/ability range	Head of department	2nd in department	Teacher A	Teacher B	Teacher C	Teacher D
KS3 low	☺ 2	☹ 2	☺ 2	☺ 3	☺ 2	☹ 3
KS3 middle	☺ 2	☹ 2	☺ 2	☺ 2	☺ 1	☹ 3
KS3 high	☺ 1	☹ 2	☺ 2	☺ 2	☺ 2	☹ 2
KS4 low	☺ 2	☹ 2	☺ 2	☹ 3	☺ 2	☹ 3
KS4 middle	☺ 2	☺ 1	☺ 2	☺ 2	☺ 1	☹ 2
KS4 high	☺ 1	☺ 1	☺ 3	☺ 3	☺ 2	☺ 1
A Level:						
C1	☺ 1	☺ 1	☺ 3	☹	☺ 2	☺ 2
C2	☺ 1	☺ 1	☺	☹	☺ 3	☺ 2
C3	☺ 2	☺ 1	☹	☹	☹	☺ 1
C4	☺ 2	☺ 1	☹	☹	☹	☺ 1
S1	☹ 2	☹	☺ 3	☹	☺ 2	☹
S2	☹	☹	☺ 3	☹	☺ 3	☹
M1	☺ 1	☺ 1	☹	☹	☹	☺ 2
M2	☺ 1	☺ 1	☹	☹	☹	☺ 1
D1	☹	☹	☺ 3	☹	☺	☹
D2	☹	☹	☺ 3	☹	☺	☹
FP1	☹	☺ 1	☹	☹	☹	☺ 1
FP2	☹	☺ 2	☹	☹	☹	☺ 1

Fig. 31 Table to show teachers' enjoyment and strengths in delivering elements of the maths curriculum in a secondary school

As a middle leader you would obviously look to see the gaps in the table either in terms of strengths or experience. It is easy to note in the example above, for example, that there is no outstanding teaching of low ability Key Stage 3 pupils, so this may be an area that needs developing or, when appointing staff, you may look for someone skilled in this. It is also noticeable that there is only one member of staff with both experience of and an inclination to deliver D1 and D2 A Level modules but that colleague does not deliver good lessons. There is also limited capacity for the S2 module. If certain colleagues leave there are also specialist skills that need to be replaced. (For non-mathematician; C represents A-level module in the Core, D represents A-level modules in Decision Making Maths, S represents A-level modules in Statistics, M is Mechanics and finally FP is Further Pure. All A-level subjects have a range of modules which can be selected by the teacher to deliver).

In a primary school, a PE coordinator for example, may conduct a similar activity to look at the skills in a small school. They may look at what skills their teachers have in Key Stage 1 and/or Key Stage 2 activities by producing a similar table to the one below.

Age/ability range	PE Co-ordinator	Headteacher	Teacher A	Teacher B	Teacher C	Teacher D
KS1						
Gymnastics	☺ 2	☹ 2	☺ 2	☺ 2	☹ 2	☹ 3
Multi-skills	☺ 1	☺ 2	☺ 2	☺ 2	☹ 2	☹ 2
Dance	☺ 2	☹ 2	☺ 1	☹ 3	☹ 2	☹ 3
KS2						
Gymnastics	☺ 2	☹ 2	☺ 2	☺ 2	☺ 1	☺ 2
Dance	☺ 2	☹ 2	☺ 2	☹ 3	☺ 1	☹ 3
Football	☺ 1	☺ 2	☹ 3	☺ 3	☺ 2	☺ 1
Netball	☺ 2	☺ 1	☹ 2			
Tag Rugby	☺ 1	☺ 2	☹ 3	☹	☺ 2	☺ 2
Quick Cricket	☺ 1	☺ 2	☹	☹	☺ 3	☺ 2
Rounders	☺ 2	☺ 1	☹ 3	☹	☹ 2	☺ 1
Quick 6 Hockey	☺ 2	☺ 1	☹	☹	☹ 3	☺ 1
Swimming	☺ 2	☹	☹	☹	☹	☹
Athletics	☺ 2	☹ 2	☺ 2	☹	☺ 3	☹

Fig. 32 Table to show teachers' enjoyment and strengths in delivering PE in a primary school

If the school was recruiting a new member of staff they could look to see if they had any applicants who had the missing skills or experience. An alternative would be to ask candidates during the process if they would be prepared to complete CPD in this area and then lead it with the children.

Running a recruitment process

The first thing you need to consider is how much are you required to do and how organised your school is in running appointment processes. In many schools, there will be a member of the SLT who works closely with the head's PA to make the process work and they may frown on your interfering, so instead you need to offer them your assistance. However, sometimes the senior leader will only be too happy for you to liaise with the head's PA directly as long as you keep them informed of what you are doing.

Placing the advert

Your school will have preferred locations to do this ranging from the *TES* to a website like www.eteach.co.uk to the local newspaper. There is also likely to be a standard advert template for you to tweak and add a sentence about your area. Most schools have generic job descriptions and profiles and these are written by senior leaders. When the advert is placed, you are likely to be asked to complete the details about your area for potential candidates. If there has been a similar process in a different area of your school recently, it is worth looking at their information as a guide; however the following list of points would also provide you with a scaffold:

- Overarching philosophy of the area
- Staffing of the area
- Accommodation of the area (e.g. a suite of classrooms)
- Resources of the area (ICT facilities, interactive whiteboards etc.)
- Results for the area
- Course offered and take-up
- Syllabus or long-term scheme of work
- Key resources

The key to this document is to give the information that the candidates need for their application whilst encouraging them to apply.

Planning the process

We all want the process to run as smoothly as possible, and there are no shortcuts to accurate planning. A timeline is required from placing the advertisement to the date of interview:

- What is the closing date for applications?
- When is shortlisting being carried out?
- When are you notifying candidates?
- When is the actual date for interview?

When putting my timeline together, I have always tended to work backwards from the interview date – usually determining this first by asking the headteacher for their availability, checking what is on in the school diary and checking there is an appropriate group for the candidates to teach. Schools will generally give two weeks from placing the advert to the closing date; traditionally these were on Fridays as that was when the *TES* was published. However most people now view adverts online. They will give three or four days for shortlisting, perhaps Friday afternoon to the following Tuesday/Wednesday. Candidates will then be notified with interviews occurring on a suitable day in the following week. Timescales may be shortened, the closer one gets to the resignation dates. Most schools will want to interview before May half term, February half term or October half term, so serving teachers can hand in their resignation and be available to begin work at the start of the new term.

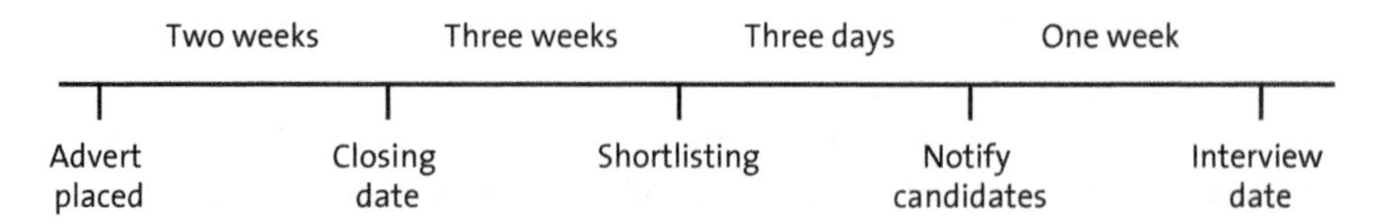

Fig. 33 Example timeline for the recruitment process

This leads onto the next section – the elements within the process.

The selection process

The first part of the selection process is shortlisting: deciding who to invite to interview. Unfortunately in some subjects and some parts of the country you may only have one or two to choose from. Yet in some primary schools and some subjects in secondary schools, you could have fifty applicants for the post.

There tends to be two extremes to shortlisting candidates. Some people will take a very scientific approach on scoring each candidate on each element of the job specification. Other leaders will read letters and have a gut instinct about who they wish to interview. The latter is something that is built up with experience so you would be far better scoring the candidates at this stage in your career. You may not choose to use the whole job specification; instead you could score candidates on a smaller number of factors, including:

- academic results
- teaching experience
- evidence of the quality of teaching
- personalisation of the letter on issues pertinent to your school
- wider experience.

Planning the interview day

Much of this is covered in chapter 6 of this book but from the candidate's perspective. Your role is to plan the schedule so that everything fits together on the day with the minimal amount of disruption to the rest of the school. You may feel that this is your most important day of the year as you are choosing a new member of your team, yet fellow middle leaders and teachers in other areas will be curious at best and may become quite agitated if your selection process affects their day. Most interview days will always have a formal interview, which is generally the last part of the process, and most schools will ask teachers to work with a class or a group of children so that the quality of their teaching can be gauged. You may choose to add other tasks to the day such as an in-tray exercise, a professional discussion or data task as described in chapter 6 but this is less likely for a main scale teaching post.

In chapter 6 the importance of teaching a lesson was highlighted for you as a candidate and it is likely that you will want to see a new member of your team teach a lesson, but at this point your thoughts need to be on how to make it as fair a test as possible to make comparison more straightforward. In a secondary school there are other complications such as a range of teaching sets for a particular year group in the core subjects. In non-core subjects due to options there may only be one class available at a time. Some schools will ask each candidate to teach the same group of children to make the test as fair as possible. I have never liked to do this and, in addition I have not liked to see candidates just teaching a single year group, e.g. only year 7 pupils. So for me, the result has tended to be a mixed ability preferably Year 9 lesson, but sometimes Year 8 depending on the timetable or the number of interviews that have recently taken place.

In a primary school where there are fewer groups, the candidates are likely to have to teach the same class or teach a small group from the class. The latter means each candidate can teach the same lesson but you don't see them with the whole class. You will need to decide with the headteacher which way you want to run it.

9:20	Candidates arrive. Identification and certificates checked (headteacher's PA)
9:30	Introduction to school (candidates/headteacher/you)
9:50	Teach lesson (candidates/headteacher/you/SLT)
10:40	Break time/coffee with the department (you/candidates/department)
11:00	Tour of the school by the school council (candidates) Lesson observation debrief (headteacher/you/SLT)
11:50	Shortlist candidates for formal interview (headteacher/you)
12:00	Lunch (candidates/you/SLT)
1:00	Formal Interviews (headteacher/you/governor)
	1:00 Candidate A
	1:45 Candidate B
	2:30 Candidate C
3:15	Deliberation (headteacher/you/governor)
5:00	Inform successful candidate and provide feedback to unsuccessful candidates (headteacher/you/candidates)

Fig. 34 Interview schedule

Interview day: introduction to school

It is usually a good idea to spend a few moments introducing the candidates to the school. Always remember that you still need to be selling the school to the candidates. Your headteacher may give the general introduction to the school with you then giving some detail on the area you lead. It is also important to try to put the candidates at ease; perhaps provide hot drinks and the toilets need to be signposted. Finally, this is the time to clarify any candidate's concerns about the interview lesson.

Interview lesson

This is a very different type of lesson observation than you may be used to. You need to make a decision as to whether you wish to see everyone teach and if you want to do a long observation of each candidate. Some people's preference is to have all the candidates teaching at the same time and have you and the same number of observers all spending short amounts of time watching each candidate. If you only have two candidates, they could teach back-to-back lessons and then you can watch both of them properly. Remember, as well as deciding who you think is the strongest teacher you also need to record areas of strength and those for development so you can give proper feedback to the candidates.

The interview

The first stage is to decide on the questions. Hopefully you will sit down with the headteacher prior to the interview day to decide on this aspect. The headteacher may give you a set of interview questions and ask if there is anything you wish to add. You should be thinking of a couple of subject-specific questions that you could ask. Prior to the interview the questions should be printed out for you in a format that you can annotate with your own notes about the answers. Remember, anything you write down will have to be stored by the school in case there is a complaint, so don't make personal notes about the candidates.

Some interviewers will score the quality of a candidate's answers. These can be totalled for a numerical measure of the interview. It is also good to make notes of the candidates' answers, again to help with feedback. The headteacher should chair the interview and the decision-making process afterwards.

Giving feedback

Nobody likes giving feedback to unsuccessful candidates and you may find the headteacher insists on doing this themselves, or they may ask you to help. In which case, have some concrete notes on a couple of things the candidate did well and some areas they need to improve upon. Always ask the unsuccessful candidate if they would like feedback. Some candidates will be angry or upset and will not like what you tell them, in which case stick to your script. There are also some candidates who really want to learn from the process and use it, even though painful, as a CPD opportunity.

Succession planning

In today's teaching world there can often be a shortage of potential candidates and I have seen too many middle leaders believe that placing an advertisement will be their panacea to finding a new member of staff. In certain subjects they can be sadly disappointed.

A good middle leader needs to be building up their network out of school for potential candidates. The traditional way is through hosting teaching practices for trainee teachers. Keep in contact with teaching students who have worked in your school, and when you have posts why not contact them and see if either they or their friends may be interested. Develop links with middle leaders in neighbouring schools and learn who their strong members of staff are, and if they have had good initial teacher training students who they have not been able to offer places to. If you receive a speculative letter, contact the colleague and say you don't have any posts at the moment but if they would like to do some work experience they are very welcome, and keep their contact details on file. The important thing is to remain open-minded and be constantly looking for good staff as you never know when you might need them!

Final thoughts

You may begin the recruitment process with a firm idea of the type of teacher you would like and end it by appointing a very different person. You need to keep an open mind and not be over hasty in making decisions.

You will also need to remember that it is unlikely that you are running the process and hence you need to be sensitive to those people in your school who are used to setting up the process and running it smoothly. You should be seeking to add value to the process by double-checking the process and suggesting ways in which it can be improved. Try and be as prepared as possible so that you are not running around at the last minute and hence could possibly panic. This will not help your decision-making processes.

To do list:

- [ ] Reflect on how to put candidates at ease during an interview process.
- [ ] Reflect on taking part or shadowing an interview process.
- [ ] Check out Nasima Riazat's tweets on @NSRiazat (see Takeaway box).
- [ ] Read *The Recruitment Handbook* by Josephine Smith (see Takeaway box).

Chapter 18 takeaway

Teaching tip

Interview: what works and what doesn't?

If you are a middle leader it will be likely that you have been interviewed twice, once for your main scale teaching job and once for your middle leadership role. Think about the processes you went through. What did the school do to make you feel comfortable? Which activities and tasks gave you the opportunity to display your skills and attributes? Vice versa: what made you feel uncomfortable and lacking in confidence? When you are involved in an interview process, remember these points and try and amend the process so that it is more effective.

Pass it on

Discuss your ideas - interviews

Ask senior leaders at your school as to whether there is the opportunity for you to help with an interview process to prepare you for when you need to interview for your area. This could be taking part in the shortlisting process, observing a lesson or even taking part in the interview.

CPD book club recommendation

Josephine Smith, *The School Recruitment Handbook*
(see Bibliography and further reading)

Tweeters' corner

Nasima Riazat is a regular tweeter on all kinds of school research. Follow her on Twitter: @NSRiazat

19 Managing your budget

In the current climate, budgets are very tight at all levels of school from the staffing budget (the largest element of any school's budget) down to capitation for a subject area. You need to know how to manage your budget so that the pupils you teach have the resources they require.

The basics

Most middle leaders will have some type of budget to support the area they lead. If you are a pastoral leader, you may find that this is a shared budget with other pastoral leaders. If you are a curriculum leader, it is likely that you will have sole responsibility for a budget.

For some colleagues, it can be a little scary having responsibility for public monies for the first time. In fact you may have read some of the current news stories about senior leaders who have spent money in a way that has brought themselves and their school into disrepute.

You should not worry about such things as all orders should go through the school's finance systems, and it is highly unlikely that as a middle leader you will be presented with a school credit card. My advice if you are, is to politely return it to the school to be held in the school safe!

It is more likely though, that you are given a budget from perhaps £500 to £10,000 and that your initial worry of spending the money incorrectly results in you not actually spending any at all!

Basic questions

- How much do you have in your budget for the year?
- When is the budget year end?
- Are there any records of last year's spending?
- How well resourced does your area appear to be?

The detail

The idea of the following sections is to give you the confidence to use your budget wisely; to plan out how to use it so you are not left short and also to give you some ideas on how to approach governors or senior leaders for further funds.

How much money do you have?

The first thing that you need to establish is how much there is in your budget. If you have taken over mid-year, then it is important that you quickly ask your finance department for a printout of the budget. Don't worry if you do not understand what is given to you. In many schools they are far more complicated than the average bank statement, and sums of money may appear twice. If you have moved from another school, you may also find that it looks very different! Ask for it to be explained. You need to know how much has been spent already, and remember to ask how much money has also already been committed – this is when orders have been placed or have been delivered but the bill for the items has not been paid. You need to be clear, as the budget cannot be overdrawn.

Once you have discovered how much is in the budget, you need to find out what the money is intended for.

Capitation

School leaders tend to set up capitation in two different ways. The first is where you are allocated two separate pots of money: one for running costs, the other for development costs. The second is where there is less flexibility and you will be given a sum of money which is the total amount of funds you have for the whole year and you have to carefully balance how much you need to spend on running costs and how much you need to spend on developing your area.

Running costs

These are standard areas of expense that are required every year without exception – the items that you need to allow the work of the curriculum area to go ahead. These are items such as exercise books, paper, other stationery and the replacement of single textbooks and resources that have become damaged. Altogether these may be called consumables. In some schools, photocopying or reprographics also have to be paid for out of this budget and this can be a large sum of money! I have worked in some schools that stop areas photocopying when the budget has been used. Something that can be of significant concern to your colleagues.

Development budget

This money is for when you wish to make an improvement to your area to make purchases that are not considered day-to-day running costs. For example, if you decide that you wish to purchase software for your scheme of work, this is a new development rather than ensuring there are enough exercise books for the pupils which is a running cost item. In some schools a proportion of the whole school budget is always allocated to the different areas. In other schools, as a middle leader you may have to bid for this pot of money via your improvement plan or via a separate bidding system.

Many new middle leaders make the mistake of constantly trying to scrimp and save to implement new projects. We are so used to hearing that there is no money in a school that we do our best to aid this situation. You may also hear your headteacher say that there is no money in the budget. In extreme cases that may be true, but it is said so often that it is not always the whole truth. In fact, new middle leaders will often hear this and so not put in any bids and then see other middle leaders receive funding for their area.

In some ways there is often a bit of a game to play – thinking what the headteacher is particularly interested in and seeing if you can link that to the improvements you are looking to make. One example is that a new head of maths wanted to purchase a new set of textbooks for Key Stage 3. The headteacher often commented on how he thought photocopying was a waste of money and he was sick of seeing scraps of paper in books. The middle leader explained to the head what they wanted to do and how it would raise achievement and was pleasantly surprised when the head funded the request. You might be able to think of initiatives that your head is often promoting and see if this can help your area.

To strengthen your bid further, it is often necessary to ensure it is included within your improvement/development planning for your area. This shows that it is not a whim but part of a longer-term plan. Again, if there is a clear link to overall school targets this will often help. You need to focus on how the spend will raise pupil achievement. Currently, in many schools it is important to link it to raising achievement for disadvantaged groups. Remember, schools receive pupil premium funding and are often looking for very practical strategies to narrow the gap. If you can think of a proposal that will do this in your area, you may find yourself in a strong position.

You may also be able to include it in your performance management targets. Perhaps your leadership target is to raise achievement in a certain part of your area and you can place the initiative as one of the strategies which will help this process.

Governor requests

In addition to the money that has been allocated to you and that you have secured from the whole school pot, there may be additional funds that you can bid for. These may be managed by the curriculum committee and allocated at the discretion of the governors and you may have to write a paper explaining why you require the funds and how it will raise achievement in your area. In some schools, you may even have to give a brief verbal presentation to a governors' committee for them to decide how they should distribute the funds they have.

One of the reasons for the involvement of the governors, is to give them greater involvement and knowledge in the improvement in teaching and learning. You will often find that governors wish to know how the funds will directly impact on pupils, and which pupils. It is often by marrying the ideas of improving achievement with thinking of specific pupils that you will find your proposal resonates best with the governors. You need to be able to show that the project will last over time and if you can show how you have run a trial and how successful it has been, they will have more confidence in it. Best of all, is if you can show some aspect of the pupils' work, how this will be improved and why the pupils themselves think it is important.

Multi-academy trusts

In some multi-academy trusts, you can find that the trusts may fund initiatives in certain areas and you may be lucky and find that you can use this. You may also be given a sum of money for a certain use. For example, one trust offered to pay for revision guides for Year 11 students in the core subjects as they wanted to raise results in this area and this was seen as a practical supportive action.

Bidding to other groups

Even though the economy is very tight at the moment, if you are imaginative and are prepared to put in some time, there are still grants that you can bid for. There are some subject bodies that will fund certain initiatives, for example if you are a science middle leader there are a number of bodies that will provide funding:

- The Institute of Physics has a 'Public engagement grant scheme' which provides up to £1,000 to individuals and organisations running physics-based events and activities in the UK and Ireland. (www.iop.org)
- The Science and Technology Facilities Council (STFC) has a small awards scheme for small, local or 'pilot' projects promoting STFC science and technology with awards up to £10,000. The expenditure can go towards materials, salaries and travel and subsistence. (www.stfc.ac.uk)
- The Royal Society runs a Partnership Grants scheme for teachers and scientists or engineers to work together on exciting investigations for 5-18 year olds. The maximum amount awarded is £3,000. You may find in your subject area there are similar opportunities. (royalsociety.org)

There are often local funding opportunities too, such as local newspapers, councils, shops and trusts which will all provide funding for activities. If you are a pastoral leader looking to run a project with a certain group of students, you may find that this would fit into these areas. Your school may subscribe to grants4schools (www.grants4schools.info/page/grantsschools/) which is a directory of a range of grants which schools can apply for.

For all types of bidding, the use of student pen portraits (see below) are always popular. They do not have to be real, but showing the link between the money and the actual impact on certain students is always very powerful.

Example of a pen portrait

The following pen portrait is for a bid for an online-revision tool.

Terry is in Year 11. He lives in a village which is seven miles from the schools and travels to school on a school bus. He has no other means of transport so has to leave school at the end of the school day and finds it difficult to access the after-school revision lessons. At lunch-time he enjoys playing sport and is regularly found on the rowing machine.

When he is at home he stays in contact with his friends via social media on his laptop and he also prefers to revise using ICT resources. The online-revision tool will give him the expert advice that he requires out of school. His class teacher will monitor the amount of revision he is doing. He will also gain school recognition on the completion of set hours of revision.

One word of caution though before you bid for any monies, is to share your proposal with senior leaders, just in case they either already have plans to bid to that fund or if they hadn't by highlighting it to them in case they may have an alternative proposal. This is obviously much less likely to happen with subject-specific funds. Senior leaders will often be very supportive of such proactive thinking and, if successful, will wish you to publicise your efforts. You may also find that this type of work marks you out for possible promotion.

Final thoughts

It is important to remember at all times, that you are dealing with public money and it is better to always err on the side of caution. You need to be using the monies at your disposal to raise achievement in your area.

There is a balance to be struck between the running of your area and developing it. You will not receive any plaudits if you run a project but run out of money for exercise books. It is also important to consider the needs of your staff. Different teachers will have different preferences over stationery. This may appear a small thing but life is much easier if you get this right.

You can use your funds to help raise the motivation of your teachers too. I worked with one middle leader who at examination time, would make sure she ordered some nice pens for her teachers to mark with or a new set of stamps. At other points in the year she may buy an education book for her colleagues. These were small costs with a big impact.

Remember to be imaginative when looking for funds. The starting point will be budgets in school and always link these to outcomes for specific children. At the moment pupil premium funding is good to tap into. Consider wider funding opportunities too, such as trusts, and if you are successful, publicise the project.

To do list:

- ❑ Reflect on the opportunities for writing a bid to run a project.
- ❑ Reflect on how other middle leaders manage their budget.
- ❑ Check out Micon Metcalfe's tweets on school finance (see Takeaway box).
- ❑ Read *A Practical Guide to Fund-Raising in Schools* by Paul Morris (see Takeaway box).

Chapter 19 takeaway

Teaching tip

Writing a grant application

Spend some time researching possible grants in your subject area; this could be both primary or secondary. Talk to a senior leader or school business manager about whether your school subscribes to www.grants4schools and this will reduce your research time. Then see if you could put together a bid for a project you'd like to run in school. If you can't find anything for your subject area what about working with another subject area? So for example if you lead literacy why not see if you could work with science to run a day's event which then could feed into a piece of writing and hence a funding bid could be written to one of STEM grant providers listed earlier in this chapter.

Pass it on

Share your ideas – managing budgets

Talk to other middle leaders about how they manage their budget. What system do they use? Do they keep their own spreadsheets or do they use those provided by the school? What advice can they give you? Are there any little school specific things you need to be aware of? Such as can unspent money be carried over to the next year? Is there a period of time when no orders are allowed at the end of the school's financial year?

CPD book club recommendation

Paul Morris, *A Practical Guide to Fund-Raising in School* (see Bibliography and further reading)

Tweeter's corner

Micon Metcalfe is a school finance director. Follow her on Twitter: @miconm

20 Taking control of CPD

By buying and reading this book you have already begun taking steps to take control of your own CPD and if you have done this for yourself, you are more likely to be open to developing the members of your team too.

The basics

Increasingly schools provide a wide range of in-house CPD opportunities for their staff, thereby reducing teacher's expectations that CPD is always a day-long course in one of the metropolitan cities. There is no doubt that in recent years, schools have become much more CPD savvy; the result being that individual teacher's training opportunities are increasingly closely linked to the school improvement plan. This may be good for making the best use of available finances, and with current budget pressures it is to be expected. However, the secondary impact is that there is far less latitude for teachers to gather wider personal development opportunities than there was in the past. Admittedly in the ten years I have been a teacher this has always been limited. It is greatly different from the world our more senior colleagues from the staffroom inhabited when they began their careers. They will remember halcyon days when it was possible to undertake a year's sabbatical to study for a master's degree on full pay. Some of them may have even taken the opportunity themselves.

Basic questions

- **What CPD opportunities have you taken?**
- **What is your school's approach to CPD?**
- **Are you aware which skills you would like to develop?**

The detail

The following sections look at approaches to widen your CPD horizons; what can you do to increase your skills and give your CV, and possibly your career, a boost too? With some imagination, determination and most importantly time, there are many projects that you could begin which would help your professional development.

Your CPD

Generally there are two major reasons why schools are reluctant to allow teachers on external courses: firstly of course is cost, but often the bigger barrier is staff being absent from school for a day, the cost of supply teachers and the inevitable disruption to pupils' learning. In the first part of this chapter, as well as highlighting more traditional CPD, it also presented a brief insight into some CPD examples that are available and take place outside of the school day, thereby removing the need to negotiate with the SLT for time out of lessons to attend. You may find that your school is prepared to subsidise some of the fees as a reward for your commitment.

Formal in-school CPD

The first thing to be aware of is that all of those after-school meetings where other colleagues are presenting, are in fact CPD opportunities. Best of all, these are bespoke CPD for your school and its context. Try not to see that hour after school as a waste of time which you would rather be spending marking or planning lessons, but instead aim to engage with it as much as you would any commercial CPD. Make it more real by keeping a record of it on your CV and if you are completing an application form, don't forget to include it too.

Informal school CPD

There are also a whole host of other opportunities for CPD in your school if you are imaginative and put your mind to it, for example:

- working with another colleague as a coaching pair – you could do this with one of your friends on the staff or somebody who is recognised to be a strong practitioner. Senior leaders may be prepared to cover you for occasional lessons to conduct coaching observations.
- working alongside middle leaders or senior leaders – you could arrange to conduct a joint observation, work scrutiny or data analysis.
- asking to support a colleague when they are investigating a serious incident or having a difficult conversation.
- offering to help implement a larger project.

It is a question of keeping your eyes open and being receptive to opportunities that can arise on a daily basis.

National professional qualification for middle leaders (NPQML)

This is the most well-known course for middle leaders. It is licensed and quality assured by the National College for School Leadership (NCSL). They do not run the course themselves, but across the country there are registered providers – often teaching alliances – who offer the course. In fact, your school may even be a member of such a teaching alliance. You have to apply for the course to such a provider and they can choose how they wish to structure the course.

The aim of the NPQML is to develop the skills, knowledge and confidence that you need to be able to lead a high-performing team in a school and to improve classroom practice. It is aimed at those who are already middle leaders in a school and who have the responsibility of leading a team.

National professional qualification for middle leaders

The NPQML is expected to take 12 months of study, but in reality it could take anywhere between six and 18 months. There are two essential modules, a further module of your choice and then a final assessment. The essential modules are:

- leading teaching
- managing systems and processes.

The three modules each require up to 50 hours of learning and, as with most NCSL courses, are based upon:

- practical learning in your school (estimate 20 hours)
- face-to-face peer and facilitated learning
- reading and reflection
- online learning.

In the leading teaching module you will learn how to develop and improve the teaching of your team and use strategies to help close gaps in attainment. In detail you should learn:

- the principles, models and practice of effective teaching and learning
- how to identify outstanding teaching and learning
- leadership strategies to influence and improve the quality of teaching
- leadership and management strategies for achieving high standards of pupil behaviour
- how to analyse and use performance data
- how to achieve and maintain high-quality subject specialisms within the team.

The managing systems and processes module will focus on how you can implement whole school policies with your team so that your team works systematically and is a consistent part of the whole school. In detail you should learn:

- the principles, theories and models of leadership
- effective management structures, systems and processes
- managing resources, including financial management
- how to manage teacher appraisals and staff performance
- behaviour management and pupil attendance
- health and safety legislation, including child protection.

You then choose an optional module which could fill a gap that you think you have, is closely related to your work or is a school priority. The optional modules are:

- effective leadership of special educational needs provision
- leading and developing staff
- leading an effective team
- leading change for improvement
- succeeding in middle leadership.

The final assessment is a task drawn from work on a school improvement priority where you lead at team level for an extended period. You'll need to show that you can make successful and sustainable improvement in your school and that you can use the NPQML experience to reflect upon and improve your own leadership skills.

This information has been taken from: www.gov.uk/guidance/national-professional-qualification-for-middle-leadership-npqml#whats-involved

Academic courses

As well as the NPQML there are also a range of academic courses that you can undertake during evenings, weekends, holidays and via distance learning.

If you search the internet, you will find that any higher education institution that offers a BEd or a PGCE will probably offer part-time courses which you could choose to study. One institution to look at is the Open University. This was the provider I chose when I was working in an independent school and I perceived reluctance by the school to allow staff to attend external courses. I wanted to keep my teaching fresh and have something extra on my CV. After I had proved my commitment with my first year's study, the school then part-funded my second year. The postgraduate qualifications offered by the Open University include: certificates, advanced diplomas and master's qualifications right through to doctorates with durations ranging from one year upwards. This type of qualification is a serious undertaking, both in time and financial commitment, but you may find other types of course which are shorter in duration and less costly.

Courses run by professional associations

Other avenues to explore are the courses offered by the professional bodies. You will find all the teaching unions provide courses, and subject associations will organise a variety of meetings and conferences.

The unions offer a wide variety of day courses, often free of charge, and sometimes you may find your travel costs are subsidised too. These may take place at the weekend so there would be no need to approach your school for time off to attend. A number of years ago I attended a course ran by the ATL which looked at career development and job search, the type of course a school would be very unlikely to fund but I found very useful.

There are also the different subject organisations that may run courses and also publish resources that are a valuable source of ideas. You might even decide to write up your own ideas and conduct some research with the aim of then publishing your work.

TeachMeets

TeachMeets have sprung up in recent years and are best described as 'pop-up' CPD events. A school or organisation hosts one in an evening for a couple of hours and anyone can sign up to present. The sessions are usually short and snappy, perhaps only four- or eight-minute slots. You can go along, they are usually free and you should get lots of ideas. You could even consider presenting yourself.

Read a book

Hopefully as you are finding, one of the most cost effective ways of giving yourself a boost or some fresh ideas is to browse through the education section in your local bookshop. You could find a subject-specific title or consider a book from a series like Teachers' Pocketbooks (www.teacherspocketbooks.co.uk). You could also consider generic management titles if you wish to improve your leadership, time management skills or even for job hunt ideas. I always found it surprising how reading such a title on a wet wintry Sunday afternoon would provide me with some optimism and zest to face the week ahead. I have included my favourite books in the CPD book club recommendation sections in the end of chapter takeaways throughout this book.

Social media

Many teachers now use social media as a virtual staffroom to build contacts and to swap ideas. Twitter is probably the leader in this field, but people do also use Facebook, LinkedIn or even Instagram. Over time you will build up a web of people to gain ideas or ask for advice. With all things though, the amount that you get out will reflect the time that you put in. There are also some people who just do not feel this is for them.

Extra-curricular interests

Lastly, do not forget courses that can develop your extra-curricular interests. These could range from refereeing to sports coaching to expedition leading. They should improve both your own personal skill level, and in addition could make you qualified to deliver sessions to your pupils, and because they are your leisure interest they will feel less onerous too.

Final thoughts

One of the crucial aspects of CPD for today's teachers is that you have to be prepared to take ownership. Your school will be interested in developing your skills to suit certain needs within the organisation. However you cannot expect the school to necessarily provide a wide breadth of opportunities. There are though many opportunities that you can take that will make you more proficient in your role, give you the edge at interview or just allow you to look at old problems with a fresh viewpoint. You may find that if you take the jump, make the commitment and then communicate your experiences to the school, they are prepared to support you with future endeavours. Hopefully the experience of learning something new or refining an existing skill will give you a boost to face Year 9 set 5 on a Monday, or just another morning at your current school.

As a middle leader you also have the responsibility to promote continuous learning and development for your team. So look for opportunities, share them and be positive about the CPD available within your school.

To do list:

- ☐ Reflect on the CPD you have received and further opportunities.
- ☐ Reflect on visiting a TeachMeet.
- ☐ Check out Stephen Logan's tweets on @Stephen_Logan (see Takeaway box).
- ☐ Read *Perfect Teacher-Led CPD* by Shaun Allison (see Takeaway box).

Chapter 20 takeaway

Teaching tip

Reviewing your CPD

Spend some time considering what CPD you have engaged in over the last few years. What has been the most valuable and what have you learnt? Research different CPD opportunities such as the NPQML or other middle leadership schemes that your school uses. Speak to a senior leader about whether there is the possibility of you taking one of these courses.

Pass it on

Go to a TeachMeet

Arrange with a colleague to go to a TeachMeet event. Look at TeachMeet.pbworks.com/w/page/19975349/FrontPage and see if there is one locally. Once you've attended a TeachMeet, consider whether there is something that you could present on at a future TeachMeet. This is a great way of gaining experience in delivering CPD.

CPD book club recommendation

Shaun Allison, *Perfect Teacher-Led CPD*
(see Bibliography and further reading)

Tweeters' corner

Stephen Logan leads a teaching school and organises TeachMeets. Follow him on Twitter: @Stephen_Logan

21 What next?

You may have fallen into being a middle leader, applied for it diligently or be one of the rare people in the teaching profession that have a carefully worked out career plan with a time frame of when you want to attain varying posts.

It is inevitable though that at some point in your middle leadership career you will begin to consider: what next?

The basics

Hopefully once you have sampled the excitement and invigoration of leadership this will have whetted your appetite to take on more responsibility. There are so many different types of leadership roles in school that you should always have an opportunity to find the role that suits your talents at that time.

If you are a second in department, it may be relatively straightforward to aim to be a head of department next. However, you may decide there are sideways moves or promotions if you move from a pastoral to a curriculum role. You may attain a promotion by taking on the same job but in a larger school, whether primary or secondary.

If you really want to focus on your leadership, then there is the potential to move to senior leadership as an assistant head or deputy head. There will always be some colleagues who call this 'moving to the dark side' yet for many of us these are some of the most challenging and rewarding roles in school. In the primary sector you may be able to move from being a middle leader to even becoming headteacher of a small school.

Hopefully you will not decide that middle leadership has put you off continuing to work in education. If so, this is really beyond the scope of this chapter apart from to say that there are various consultancy roles you may have the skills for.

Basic questions

- Are you happy in your current post?
- Would you like to work in a different type of school?
- Do you wish to widen your leadership experience with a different focus or would you like to retain your current focus?
- What are your aims for the future?

The detail

The following sections will take you through some of the different leadership roles available and also give you advice on career planning.

Different middle leadership role

There is a wide range of middle leadership roles and many teachers will have a number of middle leadership roles in their career. They may undertake curriculum roles such as being head of a department or a faculty and may also move to pastoral roles such as head of year. Once you have attained one middle leadership role you may find that it is straightforward to move to another middle leadership role, whether in your own school or a different one.

Why change to a new middle leadership role?

- It could be that you like your current role and would just like to change to a different school and gain a different experience building on the skills you currently have.
- It may be that you want to gain a little more responsibility or money but like your current role, in which case look for a similar type of role in a bigger school or perhaps a more challenging one.
- You may wish to widen your experience of middle leadership and swap from curriculum to pastoral or vice versa.

In the past, it was often said that you needed to have had a pastoral and curriculum responsibility before you became a senior leader. I don't think this is still the case, especially with pastoral leaders being more involved with achievement data now and curriculum leaders being expected to deal with pupil issues in their area.

Senior leadership

The next glass ceiling in terms of promotion is attaining a senior leadership role. In many schools there is a distinct division between senior leaders and other members of staff. Hence if you tell some of your colleagues you are thinking of this route you will inevitably receive comments about selling out or people telling you that you are not ready. Only you can answer that question.

The first obvious difference is that you will be on a different pay scale – the leadership scale. You will no longer get your upper pay spine payments and in some situations the pay for a senior leader in one school may be less than that for middle leaders elsewhere. The pay for senior leaders is determined from the headteacher's salary. The headteacher's salary is driven by the size of the school. The headteacher will be on a range and, if performance is good, the headteacher will move up this range. Other senior leaders will also have a range which must be less than the headteacher's. Again, following good performance the senior leader can move up the scale.

There is a big difference between a senior leader's contracted hours of work and that of a middle leader. In a state school, a middle leader is contracted to work 1,265 hours of directed time, whereas a senior leader does not have this: instead they are expected to work the reasonable instructions of their headteacher. The most obvious impact of this is that most schools have senior leadership team meetings. In some schools these will occur in the school day; however at others it could be before school, after school or in the evening. There is a mystique about SLT meetings at many schools as this is the meeting that often determines the development of the school and implementation of new initiatives.

Senior leaders are normally bound by a collective responsibility, so even if you have disputed a policy during a SLT meeting, if it has been agreed, you will be expected to put it into practice. There are some middle leaders who find this restrictive and hence do not wish to become a senior leader.

There is no doubt that many senior leaders will work longer hours than many other teachers as they will have their leadership tasks to complete and at the same time will teach a timetable and will be expected to be examples of good practice through their lessons and assessment procedures.

For many senior leaders, it is the opportunity to develop strategic leadership that gives them the real pleasure in their role – the chance to develop a project which impacts upon the whole school and involves many teachers is a real challenge. It is this skill that schools will be looking for from potential senior leaders and hence you will need to demonstrate it through your letter of application and the interview process.

Gaining a senior leadership post can be very competitive. In the current climate, many schools are reducing their SLT to save money. In addition, middle leaders from all specialities will apply for the same senior leadership post. Therefore there are likely to be far more people applying for an assistant headship than a curriculum leader post.

12 tips for aspiring senior leaders

Applying for posts

1. Think carefully about the location of the job and the impact that will have upon those you support and who will support you. If you are relocating, think about who will support your family, who will need help settling in, and about others who need you who would be a distance away. A major difference between senior leadership and middle management is loneliness as you have a smaller support network which mainly consists of other senior leaders.
2. Iron out your conditions of service before accepting the role. Do not take anything for granted. In your first weeks you do not want to be negotiating paternity or sick leave because a school is following the letter of law, granting the minimum requirements rather than the standard continual service you expected.
3. Carefully consider whether your personality fits in with the culture of the school. You may be more skilled than the other candidates and be flattered to be offered the post, but it may not be the right job for you. Being the most capable person for the post does not make you the best person for the school. If your motivation lies in managing change and seeking improvements, is an established school with a long serving staff the right environment for your talents?

Beginning the job

4. Don't take on additional tasks in your first month, even if you feel guilty that others are working harder than you. The initial weeks as a senior leader can be 'the phoney war' as you have a light teaching load and your leadership tasks may not have kicked in. When your responsibilities build you could reach overload. It is difficult to hand back those tasks without losing face or even being thought of as incompetent.
5. Make use of any available time in that first month to get to know the school and its culture. Effective school improvement can only be successfully implemented if you understand what is occurring in classrooms. In one school, it was suggested that I should not do classroom walkabouts, whereas in another the headteacher considered this an excellent use of time. I settled much more quickly into the second school even with initial wariness from the teaching staff after visiting classrooms unannounced.

6. Don't promote your subject area or Key Stage. Developing a whole school perspective can be one of the most challenging aspects of senior leadership, especially if you are heavily involved with a subject or section of the school. Putting forward your own area of the school can be very destructive to SLT coherence.
7. Learn the politics of the staffroom and dining hall for SLT. Teachers need space to let off steam and robustly debate any planned changes; however, if you don't visit these social areas, it is easy to become distant and not be able to develop alliances that can be vital. Visit the staffroom a certain number of times a week to provide opportunities for developing relationships without being overbearing.
8. Do not forget your own teaching. It could be impractical and place you under unnecessary pressure to make every lesson excellent, so instead develop strong structures ensuring good practice is used and pupils learn effectively. You will not then be embarrassed if a colleague responds to your observation feedback by saying, 'Do you do that?'
9. Set time aside to continue to develop your knowledge and keep up-to-date by attending INSET courses, network meetings or reading publications. It is impossible to move a school forward if you do not regularly discover what other effective schools are doing.
10. Ensure that you have some 'you' time. If you are continually at school late into the evening colleagues may rely on you to solve trivial but time-consuming problems. It is better for you to leave on the bell sometimes and work effectively throughout the term instead of becoming stressed and possibly burnt out.

Moving on

11. Don't stay in the post indefinitely if the job is just not for you. If you did not carefully consider the first three points this might even be in the first year. It is better for you to make this decision rather than be forced out, as has happened to two senior leaders I met. If you were good enough to get this job, you are more than capable of being appointed to another senior post.
12. Leave the job administratively well organised when you leave. However, be prepared for some criticism because whatever you

agreed with the headteacher may not be to the liking of your successor. There is little point in completing development tasks as others will have different priorities and it is likely they will not use your good intentioned efforts.

These twelve points are, by their very nature, headlines. There are plenty of books on the market which offer more detailed advice for senior leaders. These are personal views developed from my experiences both positive and negative; another senior leader may offer you very different advice. Whatever your ambitions, however, I wish you good luck for the future: senior leadership is always a privilege and a fascinating one at that.

Consultancy

There are many colleagues who do not work for a school full time but have set themselves up as consultants. It may be that they have a particular niche skill such as experience with a certain group of children or in a certain curriculum element. They will market themselves to schools and take on projects often training teachers in their specialist area.

There used to be many consultancy roles in Local Authorities but with the current academy programme, there are far fewer of these roles and instead consultants are usually self-employed.

If you feel that you want to work for yourself and would enjoy the challenge of marketing your skills and services and making new contacts, then this could be just the role for you. Many colleagues who follow this route may return to being employed directly by a school in the future.

Career planning

It is rare in schools, but some colleagues will roughly map out an idea of where they would like to be in their career after differing time periods. Some colleagues will even do this all the way through to headship, but other colleagues may just map out a plan to get to senior leadership.

A simple career plan with the aim of becoming a headteacher in seventeen years could look like this:

Number of years served	Role
0	NQT
3	Second in department
6	Head of department
10	Assistant head
14	Deputy head
17	Headteacher

Fig. 35 Career planner 1

It is important to remember that roles can look very different according to the size of the school. So a deputy head in a small school could be equivalent to a Head of Faculty or Key Stage Leader in a large school. The following career plan takes this into account:

Years	Small School	Medium School	Large school	What skills do I need to develop?
0	NQT	NQT	NQT	
3	Head of department	Second in department	Promoted post	
6	Pastoral leader	Head of department	Key Stage Co-ordinator	
10	Assistant head	Assistant head	Head of department	
13	Deputy head	Deputy head	Assistant head	
17	Headteacher	Headteacher	Deputy head	
21			Headteacher	
25	Second headship?	Second headship?		

Fig. 36 Career planner 2

There is also the challenge of trying to decide when is the right time to move school or even area if you are not being successful with your applications. It may be in that your first year of applying for roles you are only looking for post in your current school. If nothing appears in that year, you may widen your search and look for posts in your current school but also consider applying to posts with short commutes in a very particular types of school. Again, if you do not find anything suitable you may widen your search further. An example is given in the table below.

Year	Criteria
1	Promoted post in current school
2	Commute of 30 minutes to a Good/Outstanding school
3	Commute of up to 50 minutes to a Good/Outstanding school Commute of up to 30 minutes to a school that requires improvement
4	Relocate to a Good/Outstanding school Commute of up to 50 minutes to a school that requires improvement Consider schools that are in an Ofsted category (Either schools in special measures or serious weaknesses)

Fig. 37 Career planner 2

Final thoughts

One of my colleagues always said that she used to spend a year too long in each post and as result in her last year was bored by the post she was doing. I have another colleague who seemed to be able to move just at the right time for their career progression.

You can be very lucky and move schools just before the performance of your current schools dips. I can think of colleagues who moved in the summer and by the time their results came out the school had had a huge dip in results. A second moved at the end of the summer and then in October their school went from Good to Serious Weaknesses. If results dips or a school's Ofsted category worsens the demands can greatly change for leaders.

Sometimes people will look at the Ofsted status of applicants' current schools and unfairly consider that applicants working in an Outstanding school must be better than those in a 'Requires Improvement School'. You could be unlucky and keep going for interviews and not find your ideal post. I can think of a third colleague who was in this situation and then their school moved from Outstanding to Requires Improvement and suddenly they were no longer getting interviews!

You can only do what feels right for you at the time. It may be that your current school is the right one for you and you will see what opportunities arise. You may be very driven to being a headteacher in ten year's time and be prepared to move quickly from one challenging school to another to move your career forwards.

Whatever you decide, the third, fourth and fifth years of middle leadership may be the ones you look at wistfully later in your career: remembering how it felt to build your first team, the challenge of raising results across an area, spending time developing a colleague's teaching skills. Enjoy that time. Whatever your ambitions, however, I wish you good luck for the future: leadership at any level in a school is always a privilege and a fascinating one at that.

To do list:

- ❑ Reflect on constructing your own career plan.
- ❑ Reflect on the career pathways of other colleagues.
- ❑ Check out Rachel Jones blog posts on creativity in education (see Takeaway box).
- ❑ Read *The Reality of School Leadership* by Richard Parker (see Takeaway box).

Chapter 21 takeaway

Teaching tip

Write a career plan

Why not think about where you would like to be in your career at varying ages? Some people set themselves of becoming a headteacher by the time they are 45 for example and work back from there. Other people may say they want a specialist type of role such as being SENCO and then could work back and consider what skills they need to develop over a certain number of years.

Pass it on

Get career advice

Have a discussion with a senior colleague who you respect and enjoy talking too. Ask them how their career developed over time. What tips could they give and what things would they urge you to avoid? Did they have a specific career plan or goal or did their career evolve organically?

CPD book club recommendation

Richard Parker, *The Reality of School Leadership.*
(see Bibliography and further reading)

Bloggers' corner

Rachel Jones has a wide range of education interests. Read her blog at: createinnovateexplore.com or follow her on Twitter: @rlj1981

Part 2

Train others

1 Planning and preparing for your training

By this point you will have firmly established your career as a middle leader. You will have worked through the chapters in part 1 of this book, combining this self-study with other types of CPD to mould yourself into a successful middle leader and you may well now be looking forward to your next step up the career ladder.

Now is a great time to start thinking about how you can help others achieve what you have achieved. This part of the book provides advice on running CPD sessions and a set of training plans for you to use to help run sessions for other middle leaders in your school or those hoping to step up to middle leadership. First we will look at planning and preparing CPD and why it is a great idea to get your school involved in doing it yourself in-house.

The basics

There is no doubt that the most powerful CPD is that which is designed bespoke for your school. The best person to design and deliver such training is you! You know your school inside out. You know which are the most important issues within the staffroom and across the school. You know what has worked in the past and what has not. In many ways, if you bring in an external trainer it is a bit like teaching a class for the first time without having ever met them. That is not to say that external trainers are not an important part of the CPD on offer in your school, but they should be utilised in specific circumstances.

This aim of the chapter is to give you advice on how to plan a CPD programme so that you can ensure that your current middle leaders are as effective as possible and staff prepared to be the middle leaders of tomorrow. It will also look at who should deliver the training. It is likely that you will deliver some of the sessions yourself so there is advice on how to structure your own CPD session.

Basic questions

- Have you developed a training programme?
- How long will the sessions be and when will they occur?
- Who will deliver the training and who will receive it?
- Have you planned or delivered training to middle leaders?

The detail

If you are looking to develop the middle leaders at your school, the most likely time you will have available to do this will be in twilight training slots. You may be able to use some time during one of the INSET days at the beginning of term but it is probably unlikely you will have a whole day to deliver your training. Many schools will not have the capacity to take a group of middle leaders or those training to be middle leaders for a day. However it is still worth asking.

If your school still follows the guidance in the 'School teacher's pay and conditions document, also known as the 'burgundy book', all teachers who are not on the leadership spine are expected to work 1,265 hours of directed time per school year. Many schools will allocate one hour a week for meetings, which can be used for CPD. There are also five training days, which can be organised over the school year. Some schools will choose not to place each of these but instead disaggregate the time so that more time can be used after the school day for twilight training. This may mean that at points in the year you may have two hours to deliver training. Disaggregation of time to provide CPD at regular occasions across the school year is a very popular strategy with school leaders, but teachers and other colleagues do not always view it quite so favourably. You may also be able to have your trainees released for the last lesson of the day and tag this onto an hour-long meeting slot to give you a longer training session. A final alternative in a secondary school is to try and use some of the time gained after Years 11 and 13 have left to bring your middle leaders together.

After-school CPD

Many schools will describe CPD after the school day as 'twilight training sessions', which could be considered an unfortunate name.

Some schools never use the term twilight training. Instead, all after-school meetings are called 'improvement group meetings'. In some areas, 'twilight training' is the term used for any session that is longer than the standard one-hour meeting, commonly those that are at least two hours long. In such areas, many colleagues do not look on the term with any great affection!

You may decide to brand your after-school training sessions in a different way, such as a 'leadership development' slot. In addition, the use of one hour, ninety minute or two-hour meeting slots for training meant that the duration of the training could be chosen to suit the topic or issue.

The context of after-school training

You need to be aware of the context of the after-school training that you will provide. Ask yourself the following questions:

- Is it a programme of CPD training that will be delivered over the course of the year?
- Is it a one-off session?
- Is it compulsory for all middle leaders?
- Is it aimed at those who are new to middle leadership?
- Can more experienced middle leaders opt in to certain sessions?
- Will certain sessions be compulsory for all middle leaders?

There may be other contexts for middle leadership training, particularly if they are one-off sessions.

- Legal training sessions for all members of staff – e.g. the school nurse providing EpiPenTM training, an officer from the local authority delivering the regular update on child protection, or the local education business partnership explaining health and safety responsibilities for work experience visits.
- Training that has been highlighted as being of strategic importance; this could be as a result of an Ofsted action plan, suggestions from a school improvement partner or even due to an in-house audit on a certain issue, e.g. you may be working to improve your quality assurance at a middle leadership level.
- Specific training that teachers have asked for through their departmental meetings or middle leadership meetings, e.g. your middle leaders may say that they would like more training on holding appraisal interviews.

Planning after-school training

There are many factors that affect the effectiveness of twilight or after-school training and how the sessions are perceived by staff attending them. We all recognise the importance of our pupils approaching their lessons with a positive mental attitude and likewise one of our tasks in promoting twilight training is to consider similar issues with teachers attending these sessions and how to address this to increase staff positivity.

The five factors that could be considered are:

Fig. 38 The five key factors of effective CPD

1. The training environment

It is accepted by most educationalists that the environment in which learning occurs greatly affects its impact. I can still remember the first time I read *Accelerated Learning in the Classroom* by Alistair Smith, I particularly focussed on the section which considered the learning environment. When I returned to my classroom after the school holidays one of the tasks I set myself was to begin rearranging my classroom in line with Alistair Smith's suggestions.

However, at the same school only a year later I did not even consider doing the same with the room where after-school training was generally held! At that time, such training occurred in the staffroom. When all the staff were in that room it was packed and soon became very hot and stuffy. Many of the chairs in the staffroom were comfortable recliners with the addition of extra classroom chairs to create the required additional seating. The staffroom was also often untidy with magazines and newspapers covering the coffee tables. In training sessions in that room, it was often found that those on the comfy chairs would doze off – literally in some cases! – whereas those sitting on classroom chairs would fidget uncomfortably. If a teacher did want to make notes they would be trying to do so on their lap.

It's a good idea to have a room allocated to use for staff training. In many schools this may be the library or the school assembly hall. Why not have the room in a different arrangement for staff training so the room feels different and they do not feel like pupils? If you are using the school hall, could the school purchase a different set of furniture to be used for this purpose? In an ideal world, a school would have its own training suite or learning lab but even then it is perhaps unlikely that it would be large enough to contain all the staff.

If your middle leadership training is part of a programme, you could choose to host it in different classrooms but think about which classrooms could be pertinent to the training, for example:

- If you are doing training on leadership, could a business studies room be most appropriate?
- If you are doing training on data, do you have a 'war room' in the school where all the data is on the walls?
- If you are doing a session on outstanding learning, is there a classroom with excellent displays to support learning?

If you have links with neighbouring schools, what about seeing if they would lend you a room for an afternoon? This could be very cost-effective and means that you will have fewer disturbances. At one school I worked at, we used to have training at the headteacher's house as he lived just out of the catchment area!

It may appear flippant, but one easy way of making the staff look more positively upon the environment is to provide good quality refreshments before the event to try and prevent the 4:30pm sugar dip that many teachers feel. Why not ask the kitchen staff to provide freshly made coffee rather than more instant coffee so the area has a nice aroma – if it works for selling houses perhaps the same may be true for selling training! In addition, a buffet or cakes are a good idea, however as in all things, if it is a box of cheap biscuits it looks as though we don't value our staff! Some schools have the tradition of ordering in pizza for such training. Twilight training is often very cost effective so spending £50 on a buffet or cakes is a very cheap price for positive staff.

2. The timings of the training

There is no doubt that a twilight training session that starts at 4pm and finishes at 6pm in the first week of November after the clocks have changed is unlikely to be viewed favourably. It is easy for senior leaders to comment that it is part of their 1,265 hours and hence staff are contracted to do this, but if we wish to return to the ideas of Alistair Smith this is only going to be viewed via a reptilian mind set from our teachers. However, if you are delivering training for a specific group of staff you may have to expect that the whole staff events will have had first choice of dates and a slot like this might be your only option!

It is often a good idea to start the training as soon as the school day finishes but include 15 minutes at the start as staff comfort time to go to the toilet and get some refreshments, even if this means the training is 15 minutes shorter. If there is a member of staff on bus duty, why not ask a senior leader to do this shift for them so that the teachers can ensure they are more prompt for the training. Such an act may increase the positive thoughts. Even better can be if you can start the training in the last lesson of the day or straight after lunch. Your trainees will then feel that their training has more value. It can seem a good idea to start training at the beginning of lunchtime as then you can have a long chunk of time, however with the best intentions you may find that teachers are picking up issues at the start of this time and as a result the training can have a stop-start beginning.

Why not be flexible and have twilight training of different durations, some 60 minutes, others 90 minutes as well as two hours and try and select the time appropriately for the training. Many schools decide that they will have a two-hour twilight session, calendar it and then consider the most pressing issue and focus on that whether two hours is the appropriate duration or not.

It may not come as a surprise that the school I worked in with the most effective twilight training had a school day which finished at 2:55pm and as a result a two-hour training session still finished by 5pm and staff knew when they began their training that they would not be back too late, helping them with the logistics of everyday life.

3. The content of the training

The content for a two-hour training session must be chosen with great care. If there is a belief that the training is likely to be contentious, it may be better to split it over two one-hour slots rather than staff sitting and stewing for two hours. The best training for the two-hour slots is often that which the teachers believe in and hopefully will boost their self-esteem. This has even more value if it is something that has been suggested by the staff or if the staff have opted into the session. You will know your school and be able to identify how staff will view different topics.

One of most effective twilight training sessions I have attended was on pupil management. It had been requested by the staff and was delivered in such a way that it was impossible not to feel uplifted by the trainer. A twilight session which I delivered on coaching, on the other hand, would have been much more effective if it had been split into two separate one-hour sessions as that would have given me the opportunity to discuss them with other senior leaders rather than ploughing on with the training.

It could be considered that training content could be placed into two groups.

- **Information-giving** – this could be on a legal issue or setting the framework for future developments. At the end of a busy school day it is important to limit the length of time given to information-giving sessions as teachers can easily reach information overload. Keeping such sessions short and then moving onto another task can be an effective solution.
- **Developing skills** – you may find that developing middle leadership skills can often be more fruitfully delivered in a longer training slot giving teachers the opportunity to practise them after the training has been delivered. If training is delivered on a skills issue and there is no consolidation time, staff will forget the content. A good example would be if you are moving towards a new quality assurance system. The training could be delivered the week before you wish your middle leaders to run a work scrutiny so that any problems can be solved in advance.

It can be tempting to run a training session and then ask staff to use this information to begin planning how to implement it in their curriculum area. Most teachers would agree, however, that trying to be creative after a full day of teaching and even more so after another hour of training is nigh on impossible. In this situation it can be more effective to have the training input one week and return to the implementation the following week.

4. The leader of the training

Who you choose to run the training is likely to have an impact on the views of the participants. In my experience, middle leaders or classroom teachers have often delivered the best training. Their views often carry more weight with fellow classroom staff and it is an excellent career development opportunity. Senior leaders often have an important role in setting the scene before the training or in emphasising its importance at the end.

Advisors or school improvement partners can, on occasion, be very eager to deliver specific training. School leaders need to carefully consider, however, how this fits in with the school's strategic direction. Such colleagues may have a distinct message which they wish to communicate and it is likely that part of this will be that their topic is the most important thing for any teacher to be working on and it must come at the top of any teacher's priority list. As the person in charge of the training programme, when the deliverer is not present, it is your job to keep staff anxiety down and emphasise that this is one piece of development they are working on and should not take all their energies.

Sometimes the best leaders are those that the staff themselves may suggest. It could be someone they listened to at a conference, a consultant working at a local authority level or even a teacher from a neighbouring school. It is always much better to have a personal recommendation than to risk training by someone you just buy in from a training provider.

5. The structure of the training

Two-hour training sessions are often difficult to run effectively. It takes an exceptional training leader to keep staff interested and positive during the second hour of an after-school training session. Therefore, it can be good for the training to be divided so that the participants receive some input and then move them into different groups.

There are occasions when you may wish staff to work in pairs, perhaps if the training considers the specifics of an individual lesson. Lastly, you may wish staff to have some individual time to conduct some personal reflection or to practise a skill that is being developed. This is often the case if the training looked at an aspect of ICT and teachers need to have the opportunity to practice.

Final thoughts

In-school bespoke training can provide the flexibility to move our schools forwards when looking at certain issues. However, as all leaders recognise, a key role is to manage the well-being of our staff. If after-school training is to be truly effective, it needs to be used sensitively and at the right time so that our colleagues do not view it as another pressure.

2 Training plans

What follows is a training pack to help train aspiring middle leaders or to support the other middle leaders in your school in particular areas. There are eight training plans in total and they mirror the topics covered in the first half of the book. They are organised as a term's worth of twilight training sessions.

Your experience in the different areas will vary – you may feel confident to run some of the sessions on your own or you may need a more experienced member of staff, possibly a senior leader, to help you lead the session based on their experience.

Each training plan is organised in the following way:

Rationale

Reason for the training plan and who it is aimed at.

Length of session – *Recommended time slot you need for the session*

Training aims

The focus of the training

Training outcomes

What the trainees will get from the training

Links to school improvement plan

Will vary from school to school but this identifies where the training fits into the whole school CPD context.

Resources

What you'll need for each session

Training activities

The main part of the plan then describes step by step how to run the session, split into:

- Starter
- Tasks
- Plenary

What next?

What the trainees should do following the session.

Training plan 1: Leadership

If you are running a training programme which potential leaders and inexperienced leaders are participating in, one of the first sessions you might decide to lead, will be around 'What is leadership?'. Potential leaders or inexperienced leaders may well proved themselves to be very capable in their role as teacher. Yet this success will have been based on their own efforts. As a leader, you are looking for them to make that development to where they are gaining similar results from the colleagues that they lead. This training session will give the trainees the opportunity to explore ideas of leadership and then relate them to their current role or the one that they aspire to.

Rationale

This training session is designed to run as a twilight session and to be delivered to your new or potential leaders. They are likely to have varying levels of expertise and experience of school leadership, so this session will enable them to share their thoughts and ideas.

Leadership training plan

Length of session – two hours

Training aims

Participants consider their current leadership skills and explore ways to develop them.

Training outcomes

Staff will be able to:

- understand what leadership and management is
- have opportunities to develop their own leadership skills
- consider their leadership within the school's values.

Links to the school improvement plan

Leadership and management: Developing middle leaders.

Resources

- PowerPoint slide showing pictures of leaders
- PowerPoint slide showing school values
- Flip chart

Training activities

As staff enter the training venue, have a slide show of photos of leaders from literature, politics, history and the locality. Include everyone from Atticus Finch to Rupert Murdoch, from the Queen to your local mayor. Ask staff to have fun identifying the faces. If you wish, create prompt notes with a two-line biography of each leader under each one.

Starter

Duration: 5 minutes

1. Ask staff to select which of the people shown they admire the most and why, or to substitute these people with the suggested name of a leader they have admired. Ask them to turn and share that information with a neighbour or colleague of their choice.
2. Explain the aims of the session as laid out in the training plan.

Task 1: What is a good leader?

Duration: 30 minutes

1. Ask staff in small groups to make a list of what benefits and responsibilities leadership brings. Ask two volunteers from the session to be scribes and add the responses to two flip charts either side of the room. Hold a very brief discussion about which seems the more interesting list.

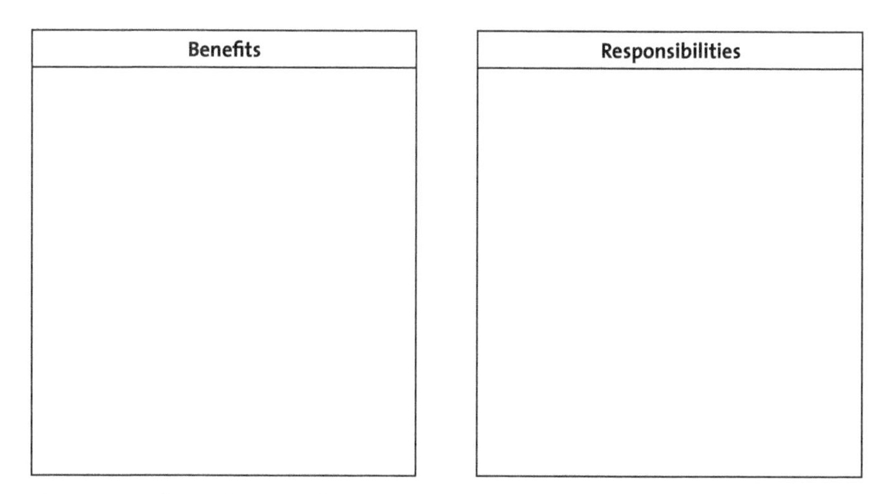

Fig. 39 Benefits and responsibilities

2. Next ask the same groups to consider what qualities a good leader needs. Share staff's suggestions too.

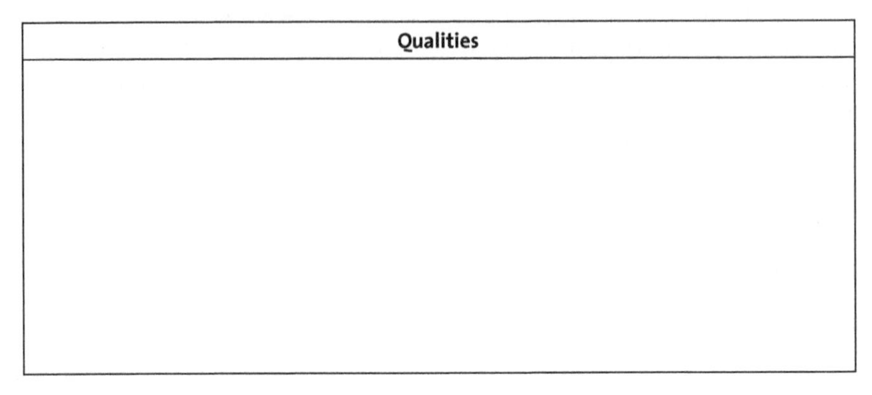

Fig. 40 Qualities

3. Flip the task on its head if you like at this stage. Ask: **What personality traits should a good leader never demonstrate, or work hard to eliminate?** You might discuss circumstances where national or international leaders have demonstrated these less positive traits resulting in lack of confidence in their leadership or even them resigning from their post. This should make for lively discussion! If this task is used you may like to lay down some ground rules of mutual respect at the start of the session in order to avoid any uncomfortable discussions between staff and the leadership team at the school!
4. Finally, ask the staff to try and define school leadership and discuss whether they have a separate definition for management

Task 2: What is school leadership?

Duration: 40 minutes

This task aims to develop the final section of the previous task by turning your trainees' attention to how people can lead others in a school environment.

1. Set up two discussion groups and invite staff to join whichever they feel most interested in or comfortable contributing to:
    - Group 1: considers the type of leadership issues and challenges that may face pastoral leaders.
    - Group 2: considers the type of leadership issues and challenges that may face curriculum leaders.
2. Ask each group to feed back to everyone on their ideas – again ask for two different scribes to record any ideas.

Task 3: Vision and values

Duration: 20 minutes

1. Use the same discussion groups as in the last task but divide them so that every group is four or less. Ask them to create their own vision for a curriculum area or pastoral grouping.
2. Then give them your school's values and ask them to consider how their vision supports that of the school's.

Task 4: Player manager

Duration: 20 minutes

1. Explain the idea of a player manager to the trainees and discuss the fact that people will be judging them on their teaching as well as their leadership.
2. Rearrange the groups from before so that curriculum and pastoral leaders are mixed and ask each group to discuss these questions:.
   - What judgements will staff make on them?
   - What are the biggest challenges in their role as a result?
   - How will they deal with these?
   - How will they prioritise tasks?

Plenary

Duration: 5 minutes

You could end the session with a chance for each member of staff (or student) to consider their own personal leadership style and/or areas for development.

What next?

To embed your trainees' learning:

- ask your trainees to keep a list of the leadership challenges that they face over the coming week.
- ask your trainees to watch the YouTube clip of Jim Collins discussing level 5 leadership (http://tinyurl.com/j5r8bql), and contrast this view of leadership with this training.

Download the PowerPoint slides that accompany this training plan: 'Training plan 1 What is Leadership?' from the online resources: www.bloomsbury.com/CPD-library-middle-leadership

Training plan 2: Accountability

A watchword in middle leadership is 'accountability' but what does this mean in practice and how can a school help its middle leaders develop the skills needed to be successfully accountable? This training session outlines 90 minutes of activities that give middle leaders an understanding of what is expected of them, and how they can determine whether they are fulfilling the expectations of the governing body in being accountable for results, pupil progress and the delivery of outstanding teaching and learning. It takes secondary school examples, but situations could easily be adapted for primary school use. It could be facilitated by you, a member of the SLT, or an objective 'outsider' (e.g. a school improvement partner).

Rationale

Experience suggests that:

- middle leaders are the key drivers for classroom improvement in a school
- the role of the middle leader has changed significantly in the past years from day-to-day management of a subject or pastoral area, to more strategic leadership of teaching and learning and the promotion of good practice
- for some middle leaders the dual role of supportive colleague/member of the team and challenging line manager can sometimes be hard to perform.

This training session is designed to take 90 minutes and be delivered to a group of middle leaders across all areas of the school and with varying levels of expertise and experience. The session focuses on what accountability means in practice and discusses typical circumstances when middle leaders will be expected to be proactive in their behaviour to secure the best possible progress for pupils.

Accountability training plan

Length of session – 90 minutes

Training aims

To gain a shared understanding amongst middle leaders of what accountability means in practice and how they can be more effective in delivering pupil progress.

Training outcomes:

Trainees will be able to:

- explain the key aspects of their role

- suggest which aspects are the most important in raising pupil progress
- consider how they can change their practice to become more efficient.

Links to the school improvement plan

Leadership and management: Developing middle leaders.

Resources

- Sticky notes
- Generic and actual middle leader job descriptions, plus a bank printout
- Support plan for an underperforming member of staff
- A support plan for a middle leader

Training activities

Starter

Duration: 10 minutes

1. Ask middle leaders as they enter the training room to write on a series of separate sticky notes what they feel they are accountable for in their role. Ask them to arrange these sticky notes on the desk in front of them for use in the next task.
2. Explain that the purpose of this training is threefold:
   - firstly to take some time to consider the key aspects of their role as middle leaders
   - secondly to consider which of the aspects of the role are the most important in assisting all students, current and future, to make the best progress possible
   - finally to consider whether they are meeting these priorities, what perhaps hampers them from doing so and what changes small or large, they might make to their day-to-day practice to address these priorities more efficiently. Suggest this training will ask them to reflect on their current practice and provide a focus for personal future professional development.

Task 1: What is the role of a middle leader?

Duration: 20 minutes

1. Give each trainee a copy of a blank generic middle leader's job description. You could use your own school's job description or use the one below. Working in pairs, ask them to spend 20 minutes writing their or their partner's equivalent job description imagining the role being performed by a highly effective and successful middle leader. You could ask different pairs to concentrate on a different heading.

TITLE AND GRADE OF POST	
JOB PURPOSE	
TO WHOM THE POSTHOLDER REPORTS TO	The postholder is responsible to the: • Headteacher in all matters. • •
THE PEOPLE LINE MANAGED BY THE POSTHOLDER	The postholder is responsible for: • • •
DUTIES AND RESPONSIBILITIES SPECIFIC TO THE POST	**Strategic direction:** • • • • • **Teaching and learning:** • • • • **Leading and managing staff:** • • • • • • **Resource management:** • •
GENERIC DUTIES AND RESPONSIBILITIES	To work within the framework of national legislation and in accordance with the provisions of the School Teachers' Pay and Conditions document. In addition the post is subject to compliance with: • • • • • **The duties and responsibilities detailed within this job description should be supplemented by those accountabilities, roles and responsibilities common to all classroom teachers, as set out within the School Teachers' Pay and Conditions document.**

Fig. 41 Blank job description

Task 2: The school's view on the role of the middle leader

Duration: 15 minutes

1. Now give out their actual job descriptions, one you have written or use the one below. Ask middle leaders to compare what they have written with your published or 'real' version and lead a discussion on key omissions/differences/surprises. A typical group will focus mostly on leading teaching and learning and perhaps resource management.

TITLE AND GRADE OF POST	CURRICULUM LEADER for ICT
JOB PURPOSE	• To act as an ambassador for the school by supporting our values and expectations of students and learning • To provide professional leadership and management for ICT to secure high-quality teaching, effective use of resources, effective coaching and mentoring and improved standards of learning and achievement for all pupils.
TO WHOM THE POSTHOLDER REPORTS TO	The postholder is responsible to: • The headteacher in all matters • Relevant members of the school leadership group in respect of curriculum and pastoral matters • Colleagues in terms of interacting on a professional level to promote a mutual understanding of the school curriculum with the aim of improving teaching and learning across the school/college.
THE PEOPLE LINE MANAGED BY THE POSTHOLDER	The postholder is responsible for: • The line management and supervision of all teaching staff within the faculty/department/curriculum area • Where appropriate, the supervision of support staff within the faculty/department/curriculum area • The coaching, mentoring and development of all staff within the faculty/department/curriculum area.
DUTIES AND RESPONSIBILITIES SPECIFIC TO THE POST	**Strategic direction:** • To promote the values, principles, policies, procedures, priorities and targets of the school • To develop and implement policies and practices for the curriculum area, which reflect the school's/college's commitment to high achievement and which are consistent with national and school/college strategies and policies • To establish short, medium and long-term plans for the development and resourcing of the curriculum area. • To monitor the progress made in achieving subject plans and targets, and evaluate the impact on teaching and learning • To manage the professional development of staff within the curriculum area and evaluate the impact on teaching and learning.

TITLE AND GRADE OF POST	CURRICULUM LEADER for ICT
	Teaching and learning: • To provide guidance on a choice of appropriate teaching and learning methods and coaching relating to the delivery of these methods • To develop and implement systems for recording individual pupils' progress • To ensure schemes of work are developed appropriately and evaluate their impact on teaching and learning • To evaluate the quality of teaching and standards of achievement/attainment, setting targets for quality-controlled improvement. **Leading and managing staff:** • To recruit and select teachers (and support staff where applicable) • To develop curriculum teams and individuals to enhance performance • To develop coaching and mentoring systems to ensure the support and development of all staff within the curriculum area • To plan, delegate and evaluate work carried out by team(s) and individuals • To promote a creative and collaborative working environment • To create, maintain and enhance effective relationships. **Resource management:** • To secure and allocate resources to support effective learning and teaching within the curriculum area • To monitor and control the use of these resources.
GENERIC DUTIES AND RESPONSIBILITIES	To work within the framework of national legislation and in accordance with the provisions of the School Teachers' Pay and Conditions document. In addition the post is subject to compliance with: • School policies and guidelines on the curriculum and school organisation • National standards for subject leaders • The Conditions of Service for school teachers in England and Wales and with locally agreed conditions of employment • Common core of skills and knowledge for the children's workforce • The National Standards for Teachers. **The duties and responsibilities detailed within this job description should be supplemented by those accountabilities, roles and responsibilities common to all classroom teachers, as set out within the School Teachers' Pay and Conditions document.**

Fig. 42 Job description for a curriculum leader for ICT

Task 3: What are the most challenging aspects of the role?

Duration: 10 minutes

1. Ask middle leaders to work with a different partner and using the job description, ask them to decide which are the most challenging parts of the role to perform.
2. Draw answers from each pair and look for common threads. Most middle leaders will talk about leading less willing members of their team and time management: tease these aspects out of the discussion if they aren't forthcoming.

Task 4: Challenging and supporting another colleague

Duration: 30 minutes

This section focuses on a middle leader's responsibility for challenging and supporting an underperforming colleague.

1. Present the short case study (below) of a fictional, ineffective main-scale teaching colleague.

A fictional pen portrait

Mrs Jones is an experienced teacher in your subject area who is having increasing difficulty in the classroom. Very low residual scores are documented for her GCSE and A level groups last year.

Concerns have been raised by a teaching assistant in her lessons, and as her head of department you too have concerns regarding health and safety and poor student behaviour. A formal observation judged her lesson to be level 3: 'requires improvement'.

She has had some extended time off already this year and has told you in the return to work conversation that she feels stressed when she thinks about schoolwork. She is keen to make progress and has expressed a wish since her targets were set to observe other teachers delivering good or outstanding lessons. Each week she sends a growing number of students to work with you. She works long hours at home as well as at school. Despite this, concerns were flagged in the whole school work scrutiny that, even though work was marked, comments made didn't really support students to make further progress.

> You have observed her once formally this term and senior staff have made two drop-in observations during an Ofsted preparation 'learning walk'. Two lessons were deemed 'requires improvement' and one 'good'.

2. Working in pairs, ask trainees to come up with an action plan or support plan intended to raise that member of staff's performance. Ask them to consider:
   - what needs to be done by them as line manager
   - what needs to be done by the member of staff concerned
   - who else might be involved (including SLT)
   - when events might happen and what outcomes would be wished for.
3. Present on screen a copy of a similar support plan (see below) and discuss the extent to which a middle leader can affect change before a senior leader may need to become involved and what support a middle leader might need from a more senior colleague.

Support plan

Overall target: to secure consistently good teaching every day

Key:

XX – middle leader

YY – member of staff needing support

HOD – head of department

AHT – assistant head teacher

SLE – Specialist Leader of Education

AA – outstanding teacher

Date	Action	Deadlines this week	Time needed	Monitoring	Monitoring record
Week 1	Meeting between XX and YY to discuss the support plan and how it will be delivered XX to informally observe YY during week 1 YY to liaise with behaviour SLE for support and record action points			XX to complete monitoring record and copy to HOD, YY and AHT	• Initial meeting before support plan begun that YY felt stressed about school. • YY feels that she works long hours but this is not making a difference. • Low-level disruption is a concern due to the number of pupils sent to HOD. • XX reassured YY that the support plan is to improve teaching and learning and to address CPD needs. • YY wants to deliver good lessons on a daily basis but acknowledges that this is difficult in some lessons.
Week 2	XX to informally observe YY XX to demonstrate mock marking template which can be placed in students' books YY to observe AA to identify how AA introduces a practical to ensure health and safety (YY to take notes)	Marking of mock exams		XX to complete monitoring record and copy to HOD, YY and AHT	

Date	Action	Deadlines this week	Time needed	Monitoring	Monitoring record
Week 3	XX and YY to observe AA with a tricky Y11 group in another subject area, time to be confirmed XX and YY to mark Year 9 books together (Wednesday 3:30pm) YY to plan lesson with behaviour SLE before being observed by XX and behaviour SLE (time to be confirmed)	Year 9 marking up-to-date		Work scrutiny of Year 10	
Week 4	Identify in lessons different strategies teachers use to tackle low-level disruption XX and YY to mark Year 10 books together. (Wednesday 3:30pm)	Year 10 marking up-to-date		Joint learning walk with behaviour SLE to observe good practice	
Week 5					
Week 6	Formal observation				

Fig. 43 Support plan for an underperforming member of staff

Plenary

Duration: 5 minutes

1. Ask your middle leaders to sum up what they feel is the difference between management and leadership of their department, and add to this what people feel they now understand by accountability.
2. Finally get each middle leader to write something positive about the way they feel another member of the group leads rather than manages. These can be given to the facilitator at the end who then circulates a summary of the training's discussion via email including the positive comments recorded.

What next?

To embed your trainees' learning:

- ask your trainees to keep a list of the leadership challenges that they face over the next week and discuss them with another trainee
- ask your trainees to consider what practical support they could give to a colleague they lead which could improve their performance.

Download the PowerPoint slides that accompany this training plan: 'Training plan 2 Accountability' from the online resources: www.bloomsbury.com/CPD-library-middle-leadership

Training plan 3: Understanding attainment and progress data

The previous training plan considered the concept of accountability for middle leaders and one of the items that middle leaders are most accountable for is attainment and progress data. This training session is designed to last 60 minutes and will give your middle leaders a fuller understanding of how attainment and progress data is used in your school. The trainees will have the opportunity to develop a shared understanding of the different types of attainment data and consider which is most appropriate for different purposes and for use by different individuals in the school. They will also be able to use some of the activities to increase the understanding of data within their team.

It is important to carefully consider who is the best person to present the training, as it may not be your data expert. Indeed, if you are on the data geek continuum you need to keep that thought in mind when you are delivering this training. You may decide that in such circumstances you are not the ideal person to deliver the training. Instead someone who is not renowned for talking about data may demystify the session.

Rationale

All schools are swimming in data. There is a huge range of different types and sources of data and as a result, new and aspirant middle leaders can feel mystified by which sources of data should be used for what purpose and why. There is currently a huge demand on our middle leaders to be able to understand data and for certain purposes you might decide to tweak this session to focus on a particular requirement.

If you feel that Ofsted is on the horizon, middle leaders will need to be able to explain the basic attainment measures that your school uses to measure progress. You may have moved to life after levels and wish to check that middle leaders are comfortable with this. Some schools use other types of data, including FFT, CATs data, MIDYIS or YELLIS data. In many ways it does not matter which type of data is used, as long as the middle leader can explain what it means to them and how it informs their practice.

It is also likely that middle leaders will use attainment and progress data to form some of the appraisal specific, measurable, achievable, realistic and time related (SMART) targets for your teachers so that they can show the progress they are making and hence have potential for movement up either the main pay scale or the upper pay scale.

Some parents and governors are becoming increasingly savvy in the use of attainment to understand the progress of their children or others in the school. It is equally likely, that the eyes of some parents and governors will glaze over when attainment data is discussed. It is therefore very important that middle leaders are careful in their discussions with parents about the data regarding their children so as not to give the wrong impression or cause worries. When governors are conducting their visits, there may be a brief discussion on data and again it is important to give the correct message.

If middle leaders are looking to further their career in your school or at another school, it is likely that a good knowledge of data will be required to help move a subject area forwards.

The likelihood is, for many teachers, if you mention attainment data they will immediately say they do not understand or are confused and this is likely to still be true if you are working with new or aspirant middle leaders. One of the reasons for this is that sources of data have changed over time, and just when teachers felt they understood something it is then taken away and a new version is introduced. Data is a minefield of acronyms and interpretation so it is important that new middle leaders have an agreed understanding of which types of attainment data should be used and also a shared understanding of what the different sorts of data mean. In any school there will be a few staff that are 'data geeks' (it might even be you) who produce booklets with pages and pages of coloured charts to pore over. However, this approach can often mean that nobody really knows what the data is telling them or how this knowledge should be used.

Understanding attainment and progress data training plan

Length of session – one hour

Training aims

To gain a shared understanding amongst middle leaders of how attainment and progress data is best used to inform pupil progress.

Training outcomes

Trainees will be able to:

- have a clearer understanding of how data can be used to inform their leadership
- see data use as a practical teaching tool rather than a science or an art.

Links to the school improvement plan:

- Leadership and management: Developing middle leaders
- Whole school improvement: Pupil progress, Teaching and learning, Target setting, Assessment and tracking

Resources

- Whole school data taken from www.education.gov.uk/schools/performance/?pid=pt2011_&cre=comparetoollink
- Class tracking data from a mixed ability, mixed gender optional subject (secondary) or mixed gender Year 6 class (primary)
- Flip chart paper
- Printouts (optional): Data sources and measures; Why do we need to use data?
- Sticky notes

Training activities

Starter

Duration: 10 minutes

1. Arrange the seats so that the trainees are in groups of four. Try to encourage staff not to sit in their subject groupings. There is currently a huge amount of data in the public domain about your school which parents and various

stakeholders can access. Print out the data about your school from the DfE website or the BBC website. Ask your staff if they are surprised about the data that is available. Which pieces of data particularly caught their interest?

2. Explain that the purpose of the training is to develop their confidence in using data. Explain that data can be as simple or as complicated as anybody wants to make it, but that middle leaders need to be able to understand data so that:

    - they can be sure that the pupils who they work with are making appropriate progress
    - they can hold members of staff to account whether this is through the formal appraisal process or during regular quality assurance meetings
    - they deal with concerns of governors and parents with confidence.

Task 1: What different types of data related to attainment and progress are there in your school?

Duration: 15 minutes

The information from the website will have highlighted some of the different types of data that is used nationally. In this activity you are beginning to focus on the specific data that is used in your school. As has already been suggested, some schools use a variety of commercially produced data to help analyse attainment.

1. You have already organised your trainees into groups. In this first activity, allocate half of the groups to look at progress and half to look at attainment. Give each group a piece of flip chart paper, which has been divided into three columns. Ask them to brainstorm the various data sources used in their school and list them in the first column; in the middle column the group should try and explain what the measure is; in the final column ask the teachers to indicate with a tick, question mark or cross how confident they are in using this measure.

Sources of data	What is it measuring?	How confident are you in using this measure?

Fig. 44 Data sources and measures

2. Ask each progress group to swap their paper with an attainment group. One member of each group goes with their piece of paper and explains what their group has filled in, highlighting the key data sets that are used in your school and reading their definitions. See if the other group can add any other data sets to the list.
3. Once this has been done, display every group's paper and invite trainees to spend a couple of minutes looking at what other groups have written.

Task 2: Why do we need to use data?

Duration: 15 minutes

This task will be most successful if your groups are in multiples of three.

1. Allocate each group one of the following three focuses: classroom teacher; middle leader or senior leader. Ask them to consider two questions:

- Why do they need to use attainment data in their role?
- Which types of data are most useful for these purposes?

One of the interesting things about this task is that you are asking the teachers to consider the use of data from different perspectives so this task will work best if the groups contain a hierarchical mixture of staff.

2. Have three flip charts on display, and collate each group's ideas on the flip chart.

Classroom teacher	**Middle leader**	**Senior leader**
Why do they need to use data in their role?	Why do they need to use data in their role?	Why do they need to use data in their role?
Which types of data are most useful for these purposes?	Which types of data are most useful for these purposes?	Which types of data are most useful for these purposes?

Fig. 45 Why do we need to use data?

Task 3: Tracking for middle leaders

Duration: 15 minutes

1. Most schools will have some sort of tracking system in their school with columns which relate to different data sources. Print out copies of the tracking information for a class in one particular subject and give each trainee a copy. This may be most effective if you select an option subject taught in a mixed ability group with a reasonable gender spread. It's worth asking the teacher's permission before you do this. Encourage the trainees to study the class data and ask them three questions:
   - What do you notice?
   - If you were taking over this class, how would the data inform your practice?
   - If you were a middle leader with responsibility for this subject what message would you be giving to the staff member?
2. Rather than taking group feedback on this task, ask one middle leader from each group to move to another group. The group then explains their findings to the middle leader.

Plenary

Duration: 5 minutes

Ask each trainee to write down on a sticky note a question they would like to ask about the use of data in the school. It could be highlighting a confusion that they have over a particular source of data or an action that they would like to perform better.

What next?

To embed your trainees' learning:

- Look at the sticky notes from the plenary and answer one question a day over the next week. Display the question and answer in the staffroom or email it to your middle leaders.
- Run a training session which specifically considers the data knowledge which your middle leaders need for an Ofsted inspection.
- Run a training session on setting SMART targets for appraisal and the data required.

Download the PowerPoint slides that accompany this training plan: 'Training plan 3 Understanding progress and attainment data' from the online resources: www.bloomsbury.com/CPD-library-middle-leadership

Training plan 4: Dealing with parental complaints

The previous training plan, considering data, commented that a middle leader might have to discuss data with parents. Unfortunately, such conversations are often based around a problem that a parent might have. It is a sad fact of current educational life that a considerable drain on leadership resources is dealing with an increasing number of parental complaints. One of the aspects of modern society is its increasingly litigious nature and whilst parents may rarely resort to the law, there can be an underlying feeling that any decision a school makes can be challenged and that their child is always in the right.

Rationale

All schools will have a complaints procedure which should be published on the school website, or within other school literature. Senior and middle leaders will often find that one result of a conversation with a parent where the outcome they desired has not been met, will be a request for further information on how they take their complaint to the next level. In the past it used to feel that unless there was an aspect of criminal law at stake or the parents were extremely challenging, a headteacher made a decision and that was the end of the discussion. Parents may have escalated the decision of a head of department or the head of year to the headteacher but then their decision was accepted. This is certainly no longer the case and even on some, what may seem relatively trivial issues, parents will challenge the headteacher's decision through a seemingly drawn-out process.

Some middle leaders may flippantly comment that senior leaders get paid to deal with such things and hence it is not their concern. Dealing with complaints has a parallel with managing pupil behaviour. Those colleagues who can deal with behavioural issues are often highly skilled in de-escalating the situation. Those who struggle with behavioural issues will either not tackle the incident at all or, at the other end of the continuum, will escalate it so that more senior leaders have to manage the situation. Managing parental complaints requires similar skills and senior leaders will be hoping that their middle leader will be able to prevent some issues growing so that they do not have to deal with them.

This session will give trainees the opportunity to consider their role in dealing with complaints and how this fits into whole school procedures. They will consider the range of complaints that can be met in a school and practise different strategies for dealing with them.

Dealing with parental complaints

Length of session – 75 minutes-90 minutes

Training aims

Trainees gain a shared understanding of how to deal with complaints.

Training outcomes:

Trainees will:

- have an awareness of the different complaints that are most common in school
- understand the complaints process and how it matches the current organisation
- consider how they could deal with different complaints.

Links to school improvement plan

Leadership and management: Developing middle leaders.

Resources

- A flow diagram for the complaints process which has been made into a card sort activity
- A set of cards with summaries of possible complaint scenarios
- Flip chart paper

Training activities

Starter

Duration: 10 minutes

1. Before the session, ask the headteacher, a head of year and a head of faculty for the five most common complaints they deal with from parents and place them in order of frequency.
2. With this information, play a game of family fortunes as a starter. Your group has to work out for each role holder what the five most frequent complaints are and place them in order of frequency.

3. Explain to the group that for all members of staff one of the most stressful issues for schools to deal with is around parental complaints. It does not matter if you are an NQT or an experienced headteacher: this is still true. In addition, in recent years there has been a considerable increase in their number. All schools will be looking for their leaders, at all levels in the organisation, to deal with complaints in the most skilful manner possible to reduce the negative impact on the school.

Task 1: The complaints process

Duration: 15 minutes

- Divide your trainees into groups with no more than six in a group. Explain to trainees that all schools will have a complaints process and within this there is often a flow diagram of how a complaint is handled, the stages involved and the time scale, which should be kept to.
- Create a card sort activity from this flow diagram by removing any numbers denoting the order and time scales. In addition blank out the person who deals with the issue. Each group then has to take the cards, arrange them in correct order, suggest what they feel the time scale should be for each stage and also decide who deals with the issue.
- New middle leaders may be surprised by how complicated the process is and the involvement of governors in it. Try to generate a conversation as to how middle leaders fit in the process.

Task 2: Who deals with the complaint?

Duration: 15-20 minutes

1. Create a list of common parental complaints or use the following.

Common parental complaints

- My child's English book has not been marked this term.
- My child has had no homework for the last month.
- My child is being persistently bullied.
- The teacher called my child an idiot in class yesterday.
- My son has long hair and was called a girl by a supply teacher.
- My child's maths teacher is frequently absent.
- My child sat an assessment last week and scored higher marks than many children in the set above but they have not been moved.
- My son was beaten up in school yesterday and nothing was done about it.
- Other girls from my daughter's year are harassing her on Facebook.

2. Ask staff, in pairs, to consider who should deal with each complaint. During this activity you are trying to highlight that senior leaders will want middle leaders to deal with complaints where they can, but at the same time where complaints could be issues of child protection or lead to potential staff disciplinary they should be dealt with by senior leaders. This is difficult to determine as all these things are on a continuum so one conclusion could be that when parental complaints are made, the middle leader should alert their line manager but they may still be asked to deal with the issue in the first instance.

Task 3: Dealing with a written complaint

Duration: 15-20 minutes

1. Ask each group to take one of the complaints from the previous task and write a brief email that they could imagine a parent would write when making the complaint.
2. Give the email to another group. The group has to write their actions and also their reply to their email.
3. Give this reply back to the first group. The first group then has to say how effective they find the reply.

Task 4: Dealing with telephone complaints or those made in person

Duration: 15-20minutes

There are two suggestions as to tasks you could use here.

Approach 1

As a group, brainstorm tactics and strategies which can be used when dealing with verbal complaints. Suggestions could include:

- Never have a meeting with a parent on your own.
- If you think a telephone conversation could be difficult ask someone else to listen in and make notes.
- Always plan an exit strategy for a phone conversation or a meeting such as a class to teach or another appointment.
- In a face-to-face meeting, always sit down before beginning the conversation.

Approach 2

1. Get trainees to role-play a parental complaint. This could be you and a colleague who is not a trainee or with a trainee.

2. Ask the group for feedback about what they felt were effective strategies and what they felt should be done differently. You should try and highlight some of the ideas noted in approach 1.

Plenary

Duration: 5 minutes

Finish the training session by asking the group to brainstorm the key points from each of the tasks. Each trainee can then record the points which they will try and implement during the coming weeks.

What next?

To embed your trainees' learning:

- Make a copy of the brainstorm which the group can stick in their planner as an aide memoire.
- Provide a case study on dealing with difficult people, which colleagues could read.
- If you have a potentially difficult meeting with a parent, invite a member of the group to sit in and take notes of the meeting and discuss it afterwards.

Download the PowerPoint slides that accompany this training plan: 'Training plan 4 Dealing with parental complaints' from the online resources: www.bloomsbury.com/CPD-library-middle-leadership

Training plan 5: Running pupil progress meetings

One of the key roles of middle leaders is to ensure the progress made by pupils is maximised for all the teachers that they lead. The Ofsted emphasis is increasingly on the progress that pupils make during their time in the school. This training plan is intended to give middle leaders the skills so that they can monitor progress and subsequently make relevant interventions to ensure progress matches pupils' identified potential.

Government sourced data, (like that provided in Raise Online, and Progress 8 measures) provides schools with progress data after pupils have completed Key stage 2 or GCSE study. Inspectors are however keen for schools to demonstrate that they are monitoring the progress of all pupils, at every stage of their careers at the school. During an inspection it is no longer enough to prove that pupils have made progress over time by the end of their studies at the school, or even indeed by the end of each Key stage. Now inspection teams are keen to see that every teacher is aware of the potential of each and every one of their pupils and that systematic processes are in place to challenge underperformance and celebrate success.

One of the impacts of this is that many schools now operate regular meetings between senior leaders and middle leaders and then middle leaders and classroom teachers to study pupils' progress. These meetings may have different names but in the training plan that follows they are referred to as pupil progress meetings.

Rationale

Different schools will have different tracking systems and routines in place to ensure that no child is left behind in any subject area or year group, and the most efficient systems will use clear and established methods for regularly monitoring progress above, below and on target. Given the revised National Curriculum at all Key stages and the Government's introduction of assessment without levels, schools have the opportunity to develop their own 'best fit' measurement of progress. Whilst the Government suggests this gives schools more independence and flexibility, there is also the resultant responsibility on every school to ensure that whatever replaces the monitoring of National Curriculum levels of progress is well-conceived, managed and sustainable.

This training plan allows for any individual school's system to be used, but at the same time prompts ways to ensure consistency within a school. This ensures that pupils and parents understand the way progress is measured and monitored, whilst classroom teachers and middle leaders understand the manner in which they are held accountable for their pupils' progress.

The session is designed to take 60 minutes and be delivered to middle leaders with responsibility for securing pupil progress in a particular subject area (e.g. a head or second in subject) or across subjects (e.g. a head of year or pupil progress co-ordinator) no matter what their previous experience is.

By running this training, the pupil progress meetings in your schools will not only address the issue of pupil progress over time, but you will also be promoting an expectation of consistency of pupil progress meetings across departments. Hence when Ofsted do visit your school, middle leaders should be able to talk consistently and confidently about the way progress is addressed for any child.

The session focuses on:

- the systems your school currently uses to track pupil attainment including the data that is generated by that tracking
- how that data might be used in pupil progress conversations or scheduled meetings
- how middle leaders should use such conversations to improve progress in their curriculum areas.

The training plan is equally relevant to primary and secondary schools. A prompt sheet is provided which can be adapted for use in your school. It can be used as a script in a pupil progress meeting between a middle leader and a class teacher.

No particular seating plan is required for participants but group discussion is required along with sight of a screen. Decide whether you want to divide your most outstanding middle leaders amongst participants or whether you want people to sit where they feel most comfortable. Either is fine for this session's activities. Discussion will work best in pairs or groups of three or four.

Running pupil progress check meetings training plan

Length of session – one hour

Training aims:

To gain a shared understanding of how to lead pupil progress meetings.

Training outcomes

Trainees will be able to:

- understand the systems your school currently uses to track pupil attainment including the data that is generated by that tracking
- recognise how that data might be used in pupil progress conversations or scheduled meetings
- use pupil progress meetings to improve progress in their curriculum areas.

Links to school improvement plan

Leadership and management: Developing middle leaders

Resources

- A3 paper
- Sticky notes
- Printouts (optional): A teacher's guide to pupil progress meetings; Pupil progress meeting form

Training activities

Starter

Duration: 10 minutes

1. Ask staff as they enter the session to do two things:
   - Jot down their response to the following question: 'If an Ofsted inspector were to ask you as a middle leader how you monitor the progress of pupils across your department/year group/area of responsibility, what would you say?'
   - Rate themselves as a middle leader on a scale of 1–4 overall after considering the following factors (1= outstanding, 4= inadequate): could you define 'expected pupil progress' in your area? Could you within ten

minutes describe the progress of any specified pupil in your area (whether they were in your class or not)? Could you describe the progress of specific pupil groups in your area, e.g. pupil premium, boys, low, middle and high prior attainment, more able? Could you describe the interventions that are currently in place for particular pupils who are not currently making expected progress?

2. Set the context for this session by clarifying the importance of pupil progress over attainment. You could use the following prompts on screen to guide your exposition.

Prompts

1. Pupil achievement is even more important than attainment.
2. 5A*- C measures at GCSE and levels at Key Stages 2 and 3 are being phased out in favour of a progress score for individuals at the end of Key Stages 2 and 4.
3. Data collection in school is used for multiple purposes (e.g. reporting to parents, informing pupils of their achievement) but most importantly for monitoring that teaching and learning is proving effective.
4. The Ofsted framework says that inspectors are looking for outstanding teaching and learning and will judge whether:
   - pupils' responses in lessons and over time, demonstrate sufficient gains in their knowledge, skills and understanding, including of English and mathematics
   - teachers monitor pupils' responses in lessons and adapt their approach accordingly; also, whether they monitor pupils' progress over time and use the information well to adapt their planning
   - teachers seek to assess the effectiveness of their own teaching and adapt the Framework, accordingly

(Inspection framework July 2014)

Task 1: Format for pupil progress data

Duration: 10 minutes

1. In whatever way suits you best, share the format in which pupil progress data is regularly collected in your school and talk middle leaders through it. You may, for example, do this by showing a screenshot of an Excel spreadsheet, paper copies of a student profile, or by other visual representations like student progress flight paths. In order to provide a context for the next part of the session, discuss the following:

- articulate how often you as a school collect information on pupil attainment and explain the choice of frequency
- remind staff what precise information you ask for from class teachers
- suggest how middle leaders have a responsibility to ensure the information their colleagues supply is accurate and up-to-date
- finally explain what conclusions data collection enables middle leaders and senior leaders to draw about pupils in their charge.

Whilst this task seems to state the obvious, it is important that middle leaders appreciate that the time and energy spent collecting data serves an important purpose and that the class teachers they line manage have a key role to play in using that data to inform their future planning.

Task 2: Running a pupil progress meeting/conversation

Duration: 20 minutes

The following guide may be used as a visual stimulus for the following discussion.

A teacher's guide to pupil progress meetings

What are pupil progress meetings?

- Five after-school meetings spread throughout the year.
- One hour total is allocated to be divided as seen fit by your subject leader/second in your subject (e.g. prioritising year groups to analyse, working with a particular member of staff, looking at specific groups of students such as SEN or pupil premium).

Why have these meetings?

- A chance for you to discuss the progress of students in your class(es).
- A chance to systematically identify students who are under-performing/performing well and direct resources (both time and effort) to ensure their progress.
- An opportunity to ensure your interventions are well-targeted.
- A chance to check that you are meeting the expectations set by your head of department.

How to go about them

You have limited time for quite analytical conversations, so you need to have prepared well for this meeting. The conversation needs to be focused, sharp and purposeful. Print out and fill in a pupil progress meeting form (use the one provided below, or create your own). Take this to your meeting to go through and make a copy to give your subject leader to keep.

Remember: Single person departments should work together to act as critical friends.

1. Explain what is meant by pupil progress meetings. (5 minutes)

   Present the logical suggestion that collected data needs analysing: not just collecting by senior and middle leaders but interrogating in a practical way by class teachers themselves who are best placed to use it to identify and reward successful pupils and to select under-performing ones. Regular time needs to be set aside to do this and the pupil progress conversations (you may decide to call them something else) need to become part of systematic school meeting structure with directed time allocated to them. Explain to colleagues where these meetings will fit on the school staff calendar.

2. Explain how you expect your colleagues to prepare for their conversation with you. (5 minutes)

   Use the Pupil progress meeting form below or an adaptation of it. You can elaborate, using your school data, how they would use the information at their disposal to prepare for the meeting.

Pupil progress meeting form

(To be completed by the class teacher prior to the meeting)

Subject..
Date..............................

Focus (e.g. year group/pupil group/class)..

Preparation:
Look at the data you have available on the group(s) of students you have been asked to analyse. Use the table below to record your responses to these questions. Use a separate page for each class/group you have been

asked to consider. Take two copies to the progress review meeting: one for you and one for your subject leader/second in department.

1. How many students are meeting expected progress grades?
2. How many aren't? Who are they? Why do you think they aren't meeting their expected progress grades? Please use the table below to document your conclusions.
3. Which students should be commended for performing at their target grade or above?
4. How are pupil premium/G&T students in your identified groups performing?

Student/group	Issue	What have you done so far?	Further action to be taken

Subject leader's notes

Planned actions at department level:

- What conclusions have you drawn?
- What are your resultant planned actions?

What?/How?	By when?	Who?

Fig. 46 Pupil progress meeting form

3. Running the conversation. (10 minutes)

   Now describe the conversation itself. Discuss with trainees whether they think it would be best to focus on a particular issue during the conversation (this would probably be dictated by departmental self-evaluation or the outcome of other analysis of department strengths or areas for development). This might be the progress of middle ability boys, pupil premium pupils or the more able, for example. Describe how the conversation should be focused and data driven but result in practical actions that should be recorded during the meeting. The Pupil progress meeting form (above) suggests what a record of the meeting might look like.

   Finally make it clear what is expected of middle leaders as a result of the conversations they have with their colleagues. What conclusions have they drawn about progress in their subject area? What actions do they plan to take as a result of the information gathered and the issues discussed? Again the pupil progress meeting form might help.

Task 3: Model a pupil progress meeting/conversation

Duration: 15 minutes

This can be conducted in one of two ways:

Method 1

1. As presenter you take on the role of middle leader. Prepare a colleague in advance to be your assistant in this task who will play the role of a class teacher. Share the data on the class you will use during the conversation with the rest of the participants. Now take 5–10 minutes to model a conversation. Use the prompts on the pupil progress meeting form to start your script off.
2. After you have role played a conversation, invite your assistant to share how s/he prepared for the conversation and how it felt to be questioned. As middle leader share how the conversation went from your point of view. Seek questions from the other participants.

Method 2

1. Invite all participants to role play a similar conversation to the one described in method 1 above in pairs. Provide the tracking data as it would appear in your school on a fictional class in a generic subject.
2. After they have role played for 10 minutes, invite participants to comment on their experience either from the point of view of a classroom teacher or as a middle leader leading the conversation.

Plenary

Duration: 5 minutes

After a session with lots of discussion a quick plenary is in order. Ask participants to look back at the way they assessed themselves at the start of the session. Invite them to consider whether the strategies discussed in the session will enable them to revise their judgement.

Don't forget to come back and review the effectiveness of this training session at a later date too. Perhaps you could do so after the first pupil progress conversations have taken place, or after a series of them have been completed. A middle leaders' meeting would be a good place to do this and using the 1–4 measuring system from the starter activity will hopefully enable you to evidence the positive impact of this training.

What next?

To embed your trainees' learning:

- Calendar the first pupil progress meetings immediately after this training session.
- Review effectiveness in a middle leaders' meeting by returning to the 1–4 measuring system from the start of this training.
- Middle leaders could write their own script for their meetings.

> Download the PowerPoint slides that accompany this training plan: 'Training plan 5 Running pupil progress meetings' from the online resources: www.bloomsbury.com/CPD-library-middle-leadership

Training plan 6: Leading effective meetings

The toughest thing for any member of staff to face after a day of teaching, is a long after-school meeting. If these meetings lack focus or purpose they can be an unwelcome extension to a busy week in school, with staff questioning whether their time would be better spent tackling their pile of marking or preparing the next day's lessons.

Despite this (and because of the increased accountability required of them) middle leaders often ask for more departmental meeting time rather than less of it. It is time that can be used to share good practice, move initiatives forward, cascade training, standardise work, coach staff and build a positive and supportive departmental ethos.

Rationale

Most middle leaders will probably have developed their own expertise in running meetings based on the good or bad practice they will have experienced themselves as more junior members of other teams. This training session gives them a chance to discuss and consider best practice and to leave the session feeling their good habits have been endorsed or they have some new practical strategies for making the very most of meeting time. The session focuses on the different elements of a good meeting and gives time to discuss:

- planning for a successful meeting
- composing an effective agenda
- running a purposeful meeting
- writing and sharing the minutes so they lead to positive actions.

This training session is designed to take 60 minutes and be delivered to a group of middle leaders across all areas of the school and with varying levels of expertise and experience. The session focuses on how to make meeting time purposeful and time-efficient. It also aims to help middle leaders consider ways to lead initiatives and promote departmental vision and values, whilst providing opportunities for other department members to take ownership of initiatives and feel they are a crucial part of the department's progress.

The training plan is equally relevant to primary and secondary schools. Even though the training is designed for middle leaders, the principles apply to any meeting, at any level in a school's organisation.

Leading effective meetings training plan

Length of session – one hour

Training aims

To give middle leaders the opportunity to share good practice on leading effective meetings.

Training outcomes:

Trainees will be able to:

- plan a successful meeting
- compose an effective agenda
- run a purposeful meeting
- write appropriate minutes.

Links to the school improvement plan:

Leadership and management: Developing middle leaders

Resources

- Sticky notes
- PowerPoint (optional)
- Flip chart/sugar paper
- Pens
- Printouts (optional): leading effective meetings agenda 1 poor; leading effective meetings agenda 2 good; Minutes template; Do and don't list
- Projector

Training activities

Starter

Duration: 10 minutes

You could use the starter as an opportunity to model an activity which could occur at the start of one of their meetings.

1. Give trainees sticky notes and ask them to stick them on the areas of the classroom that they feel best support learning, including a note of why?
2. Share your aims for the session using the training plan above to help you.
3. On PowerPoint or paper share two versions of an agenda for a typical department meeting. You could use this training session's agenda below as an

example. Demonstrate how an agenda is best if it follows the tenets of SMART target setting, i.e. that it is: specific; measurable (so that it is clear to see after discussion that a way forward has been decided); appropriate and attainable (discussing how to move from 45% to 89% in this summer's results might be a stretch too far); realistic; time-related (10 minutes will not be long enough to find a solution to a serious department issue).

Department meeting – Monday M1

Students
Exam marking
Year 9 scheme of work
Department social

Fig. 47 Leading effective meetings agenda 1: poor

English progress meeting
Monday M1: 3.45–4.45 pm

- Intervention students in Years 9 and 11. Progress review (JA) 10 minutes
- Standardising exercise – Year 10 literature assessment (see below) (JA) 30 minutes
- Year 9 scheme of work – thoughts on first draft (EC) 10 minutes
- End of term celebration. Where? When? Who? Suggested date 20/07/12 (all) 5 minutes

Minute taker: ST

Please prepare for the meeting by:

- Reading the attached draft of the Year 9 non-fiction writing scheme of work
- Collating data on your identified intervention students and bringing to meeting
- Bringing along your copy of the mark scheme found in your OCR syllabus (www.ocr.org/engassesscriteria)

Fig. 48 Leading effective meetings agenda 2: good

Task 1: Planning a meeting

Duration: 20 minutes

You can see from the above 'good' agenda that the middle leader has a clear idea of what they want to cover in the hour they have allocated. The department will be discussing a new scheme of work, standardising marking and reviewing a key student intervention initiative. The agenda instructs the team to bring certain things along to the meeting. There won't just be talk and discussion of a general nature, as the poor agenda would be likely to lead to, but instead a focused range of different tasks all with an allocated time and person leading on the discussion.

To prepare for this meeting, team members will have to do some reading, collecting of data and reflecting. They should come to the meeting with something concrete to discuss and personal opinions and thoughts. They will also be able to spend the meeting carrying out some professional assessment practice (the standardising task) whilst the head of department is there to monitor, support and intervene.

1. Talk trainees through the benefits of the good agenda. Ask them:
   - What does the middle leader need to do to plan for this meeting?
   - What will the team need to do?
2. Now ask them to construct their own four point agenda for their meeting next week along the same lines listed in the next table:
   - What needs to be brought to the meeting
   - What needs to be done by the attendees in advance of the meeting
   - Ensure they add staff initials to each point as well as an intended time for each agenda item.
3. Get them to share their agendas and any observations with another trainee.

Task 2: Setting the tone

Duration: 10 minutes

1. Ask trainees about the best and worst meetings they have attended. What was the mood or tone like? The likelihood is staff will talk about good humour, pace, professionalism and actions and outcomes as positive factors.
2. Ask them to work in groups of about four with two pieces of sugar paper. One should be used to record the features of negative meetings and one the features attributed to good ones. Give enough time for recording to be done and for five minutes of feedback to discuss attributes of good meetings.
3. Suggest to the trainees that if you do all the above in a professional, business-like manner, sticking to time, prepared in advance with the necessary resources and maybe even throw in a packet of biscuits as well then a positive team ethos will be built.

Task 3: Writing the minutes

Duration: 10 minutes

Everyone knows that after a meeting is over, opening the email attachment with the minutes in is sometimes a chore. Again, there are more pressing demands on time. Yet the minutes are an effective way of summarising the outcome of the meeting, recording next steps, clarifying decisions and the likelihood is they will be asked for by the SLT.

1. Use these 10 minutes to discuss and agree a common format for minutes across the school that:
   - requires minimum 'typing up'
   - focuses on action points rather than going over a whole discussion
   - are an 'at a glance' guide to the meeting
   - suggest you will trial them at the next middle leaders' meeting and views will be sought on their effectiveness. If you are a school that shares documents electronically via shared areas or in a drop box, post an example here as a template for future use. You might even agree to incorporate agenda items into the template for the minutes making the process even more streamlined. Use the table below as a suggested starting point. It is based on the good agenda above. One box has been completed as an example.
2. If you have more time, you could ask your trainees to design another minute-taking template which improves on this one and fits with the school's style.

Agenda item	Discussion points	Actions agreed	By when/by whom?
Intervention students in Years 9 and 11. Progress review (JA)	Booster sessions at lunchtime very effective and surprisingly popular. After-school sessions less so. Parental involvement suggested for 5 Year 11 students. Data collected.	JA to present findings to SLT at progress check meeting this week. All teachers of under- performers to contact parents. EC to compose letter to send out.	Letters to be sent next week. Further booster classes to run for next 3 weeks. Non-fiction writing the focus
Standardising exercise – Year 10 literature assessment (JA)			
Year 9 scheme of work - thoughts on first draft (EC)			
End of term celebration. Where? When? Who? Suggested date (all).			

Fig. 49 Minutes template

Plenary

Duration: 10 minutes

1. Share the following lists with trainees. In their groups ask them to add to the list.
2. Collect their ideas so that they can be typed up and shared following the training session.

DO	DON'T
• Allow time for planning the agenda • Keep the tone of the meeting positive throughout • Turn the discussion into action points • Give department members the opportunity to contribute by leading on agenda items or bringing examples to the meeting	• Try to fit too much into the meeting • Spend time on administration or information sharing that can be done outside the meeting by email or a memo • Use the meeting for moans

Fig. 50 Do and don't list

What next?

To embed your trainees' learning:

- Invite effective middle leaders to invite others to their next meeting and review any change in practice at the next middle leaders' meeting.
- Invite members of the SLT to attend and observe the next department meetings and provide feedback to middle leaders. This could form part of a departmental review or be part of your middle leader coaching programme.

Download the PowerPoint slides that accompany this training plan: 'Training plan 6 Leading effective meetings' from the online resources: www.bloomsbury.com/CPD-library-middle-leadership

Training plan 7: Setting consistent appraisal targets

In many schools one of the key ways of ensuring that middle leaders were conducting leadership was by them being responsible for the performance management or appraisal of staff. This would mean that a second in department in a small school would still have a member of staff to performance manage. In recent years, with the introduction of appraisal, one of the key changes has been the explicit link between meeting appraisal targets and pay progression. This means that whilst conducting appraisal for a small number of staff is an excellent introduction to leadership, it can mean that some new middle leaders can be quite nervous of the process, especially if this has not been well modelled to them in the past.

The foundation of successful appraisal is the setting of the targets. If this can be consistent across the school and the targets follow a SMART methodology (see below), the process of appraisal can be far more straightforward for the middle leader.

Rationale

This training session is designed to take two hours. It is designed to be delivered to a group of middle leaders. The session can be adapted for use with primary or secondary school colleagues. By the end of the training session, middle leaders should feel confident about their role in the appraisal process and the targets they should set.

Setting consistent appraisal targets training plan

Length of session – two hours

Training aims

To ensure middle leaders can confidently set targets.

Training outcomes

Trainees will be able to:

- understand the appraisal process
- understand SMART appraisal targets
- have practice at setting appraisal targets.

Links to school improvement plan:
Leadership and management: Developing middle leaders.

Resources
- Projector and PowerPoint
- Sticky notes
- Printouts (optional): Analysing targets using SMART methodology
- Example comments in target analysis
- School appraisal target pro formas

Training activities

Starter

Duration: 10 minutes

1. Ask trainees to think back to their appraisal over the years and to work in pairs or small groups to recall targets they have been set and discuss how they felt about those targets. Did they challenge/scare/depress/stimulate them?

   This task is simply designed to get middle leaders to reflect on their personal experience as candidates. By doing so they are putting themselves in an appraisee's shoes prior to understanding their role as interviewers. Share experiences as a group. Ground rules need to be carefully set for this task, that it will remain confidential.

2. Give a very brief introduction to the session, highlighting the aims and objectives.

Task 1: The appraisal process

Duration: 15 minutes

The starting point for this training session is ensuring that your trainees are clear on the appraisal process.

1. Ask your trainees to write down on a sticky note one issue that they would like clarifying about the appraisal process and to give this to a partner. Once they have done this, you need to give a short presentation on the appraisal process at your school. Elements, which you need to cover, include:
   - current appraisal regulations
   - the school policy
   - any additional rationale behind this

- the link between the appraisal and pay progression
- the process and its time line.

2. After you have given the presentation, partners try and answer the sticky note question from the information you give, which they then return to their partner.
3. Finally ask if there are any questions that have not been answered and then answer them.

Task 2: Analysing targets

Duration: 15 minutes

1. To begin this task you need to explain the SMART methodology: that all targets should be specific, measurable, achievable, relevant and timely.
2. Share the following targets:
   - Ask the trainees to use the following table (see below) to analyse the targets using SMART methodology
   - Improve some Ds to Cs in my Year 11 class
   - Ensure that 75% of my Year 11's predicted grades are C and above.

Target	S specific	M measurable	A achievable	R relevant	T timely	Comments
Improve some Ds to Cs in my Year 11 class						
Ensure that 75% of my Year 11's predicted grades are C and above						
All pupils to achieve their school targets						
100% of pupils achieve a GCSE grade C (top set)						
71% of pupils make expected progress in English (all KS2 level 3)						

Fig. 51 Analysing targets using SMART methodology

- All pupils to achieve their school targets
- 100% of pupils achieve a GCSE grade C (top set)
- 71% of pupils make expected progress in English (all KS2 level 3)

3. Discuss.

Target	S	M	A	R	T	Comments
Improve some Ds to Cs in my Year 11 class						No specific information about what the teacher will achieve
Ensure that 75% of my Year 11's predicted grades are C and above						Teacher has got confused over predicted grades and target grades
Ensure that all pupils achieve their targets						Is it better to list the number of grades this equates to and then if some pupils achieve above or below the target
100% of pupils achieve a GCSE grade C (top set)						Is this suitable for a top set?
71% of pupils make expected progress in English (all KS2 level 3)						Historically the national figure for this group has been a percentage in the 50s – has the teacher taken the department target in error?

Fig. 52 Example comments in target analysis

Task 3: The appraisal challenge

Duration: 25 minutes

1. It is important to give your trainees an opportunity to discuss the challenges they may face and how your school would support them. To try and depersonalise this, show the following pen portrait to the trainees. Ask your trainees to work in groups of four to identify the key challenges Mrs White faces.

Mrs White pen portrait: slide 1

Mrs White: long-serving head of science

- Good teacher
- Longstanding friendship with second in department. Good working relationship with department team.
- Rather 'battle weary'
- Keen to improve pupil attainment but not quite sure how to both challenge and support her team.

Mrs White pen portrait: slide 2

I've been a performance manager for years. I have always found it rather tokenistic. We have done work on SMART target setting but I have never really worked out what the senior team think the link is between performance management targets and our results at the end of the year. Because the whole process is confidential I have never really known what happens with staff in other departments. With this new rule about pay recommendations I feel I am being put in an awkward position with some of my colleagues who are also my friends!

2. Share the following possible answers.

Mrs White's key challenges: slide 3

- Using performance management process to challenge and support her team
- Fairness and transparency to all her team members
- Professionalism over friendship (or combined with?)
- Gaining the skills required to lead supportive but challenging conversations
- Taking the responsibility of pay recommendation seriously
- Knowing that she is operating in the same way and to the same standards as other appraisers.

3. Then explain to the trainees what you as a school would do to support 'Mrs White'. This could include the following points.

Action plan to support Mrs White: slide 4

- Setting the appropriate standard for Mrs White.
- Modelling or structuring a performance management review/ target setting conversation.
- Clarifying what appropriately challenging targets look like.
- Reassuring Mrs White that her judgements are recommendations and that the headteacher/governors will make the final call.
- Giving her the confidence to know her judgements are in line with others'.
- Creating documentation to support consistency and make the process suitably systematic.

Task 4: Setting targets

Duration: 40 minutes

Hopefully in task 1 you explained the different types of targets you set in your school. Many schools have 3 or 4 targets such as:

- Developing the quality of teaching and learning (professional practice)
- Improving pupils' progress (professional outcomes)
- Developing the quality of practice or improving progress across a curriculum area (leadership)
- Developing a specific element of practice (professional development)

1. Distribute the appraisal target pro formas that you use in your school. Working in the same groups, ask the trainees to set the appraisal targets for one of the following 'colleagues'.

Example colleague pen portraits:

Mrs Jones

- Experienced teacher and second in department in science.
- Having increasing difficulty in the classroom.
- Low residual scores for her GCSE groups last year.
- Concerns raised by teaching assistants in her lessons regarding health and safety.
- Poor student behaviour.

Ms Green

- In her fifth year of teaching science; in her third year at your school.
- Outstanding teacher.
- GCSE and A level scores last year significantly above school average.
- Acts as mentor outside the department.
- Disappointing attendance levels though.

Mr Smith

- In his second year of teaching science.
- Making steady progress and developing into a competent teacher.
- First set of GCSE scores last year were in line with school average.
- Some difficulties making accurate assessment.
- Great contributor to extra-curricular programme.

2. Either ask each group to swap targets and critique them, or ask colleagues from each group to pair up and role-play setting the targets.

Plenary

Duration: 15 minutes

Hold a question and answer session. Use the last 15 minutes of the session to allow your trainees to ask any burning questions they may have.

What next?

To embed your trainees' learning:

- Trainees take part in the appraisal process.

Download the PowerPoint slides that accompany this training plan: 'Training plan 7 Setting consistent appraisal targets' from the online resources: www.bloomsbury.com/CPD-library-middle-leadership

Training plan 8: Conducting successful interviews

Recruitment of good teachers is one of the key factors in a school's success. Middle leaders have an important role to play in the selection process and a senior leader who recruits a member of staff without involving the middle leader may soon live to regret it if the relationship between middle leader and the new colleague they have to line manage doesn't work. Recruitment therefore needs to be a collaborative process and a senior leader needs to rely on middle leaders to ascertain whether a candidate has good subject knowledge, can teach their subject well and will fit into the department. Middle leaders are unlikely to have received any formal training on recruitment unless they receive such training in post or have shadowed a colleague previously and are therefore likely to be as nervous as some of the candidates when it comes to the formal interview.

Rationale

This training session is designed to take 90 minutes and to be delivered to a group of middle leaders. The session can be adapted for use with primary or secondary school colleagues. By the end of the training session, middle leaders should:

- feel confident about their role in the interview process
- have a good idea of the kind of questions they would ask in order to elicit responses from candidates that would reveal both their strengths and gaps in their knowledge or skills
- understand how their role complements that of the senior colleague they might conduct the interview with.

Conducting successful interviews training plan

Length of session – 90 minutes

Training aims

To ensure middle leaders can participate confidently in an interview.

Training outcomes

Trainees will be able to:

- Consider appropriate interview questions
- Analyse the answers from interview candidates
- Develop appropriate non-verbal skills for interviewing.

Links to the school improvement plan:

Leadership and management: Developing middle leaders

Resources

- Projector and PowerPoint

Training activities

Starter

Duration: 20 minutes

1. Ask your middle leaders to think back to any interviews they attended as candidates. It doesn't matter whether this is for their most recent role or for a main scale teacher post in previous years. In pairs or small groups get them to recall any questions they were asked and discuss which they think were the best/worst/hardest/easiest/most probing/most inappropriate. This task is simply designed to get middle leaders to reflect on their personal experience as candidates. By doing so they are putting themselves in a candidate's shoes prior to understanding their role as interviewers. Share experiences as a group. There are likely to be some light-hearted anecdotes but try to tease out what middle leaders thought were the best questions and why.
2. Share the objectives of the session using those in the rationale above. Once you have done this explain that the training session is split into three sections:

- to reach a common understanding of what good practice in interviewing is, including how to frame questions which probe a candidate's full response
- how to judge the quality of responses and be able to compare responses from different candidates
- to understand the obligations and etiquette of a good interview.

Task 1: Asking the right questions

Duration: 30 minutes

This task is all about asking the right questions in the right way.

1. Explain and share some standardised questions you may already have for a main scale teacher in any subject (see box below for some examples). They should cover safer recruiting and good practice as well as school specific issues.

Standard questions for a main scale teacher interview

- Tell us about yourself and why you find yourself here.
- After spending a day in the school, why would you like to work here?
- Where do you feel is the place of modern foreign languages in a primary school?
- One of the areas that we are really seeking to develop is our mathematics provision especially in Key Stage 2: how could you help with this?
- Where do you see yourself in five years?
- How do you feel you could add to the extra-curricular provision at the school?
- Is there anything you'd like to ask us?
- Do you feel the process has been fair?

2. Next, ask middle leaders to work in pairs and take turns asking each other some of the questions. Ask them to consider how they got their partner to elaborate on short answers or develop good ideas. Discuss the language you could use to do this, e.g.
   - Ask questions to clarify unclear answers or probe for more, such as: What did you mean by...? Tell me more about...? How did you...?
   - Ask for evidence/examples to back up any answers they give. Don't take what they tell you at face value. For example, if you ask them about their ability to be flexible and adaptable to situations or use their initiative, ask them to give an example of a time when they had to display these characteristics.

3. Repeat the activity using a generic question such as, 'What was it about this post that attracted you to apply?' looking for ways to draw out deeper answers.
4. Ask the trainees to come up with four tips they would pass on to their colleagues on asking interview questions. You could share those below.

Tips on asking interview questions

- Avoid asking closed questions to which the candidate can answer only with a 'yes' or 'no' or another one word answer.
- Ask open questions, such as those starting with 'what', 'why', 'where', 'when' and 'how'.
- Avoid asking questions that give away the answer that you are looking for (leading question), e.g. 'I'm sure you like all aspects of working with children, don't you?'
- Ask one question at a time – asking multiple questions will confuse the candidate.

5. Ask the trainees to work alone for a few minutes to record some subject-specific questions that they would ask a candidate for a main scale job. Ask them to consider aspects of a role in their department that would be subject-specific, e.g. health and safety procedures in DT or science, differentiation in a mixed-ability English class. Ask them to draw up several questions bearing in mind the advice above.

Task 2: Ensuring interviews are fair

Duration: 20 minutes

This task is about making sure that candidates are treated equally and ensuring the middle leader will be able to make a fair comparison between them. It is recommended that interviewers apply a scoring system, similar to the one probably used when short-listing. Each interviewer can then complete a basic scoring sheet listing the criteria to be assessed and it becomes easier to give feedback to both successful and unsuccessful candidates.

1. Ask trainees to work in cross-subject groups to design a five-star scoring system for answers to interview questions. What kind of answer would get 0; what would get 5? The group could select one of the interview questions from task 1 and create five answers, one for each point in the scale.

2. Discuss
   You could use:
   0 = No answer or poor performance – an answer which is not relevant to the question or lacks any content
   1 = Answer is factually incorrect – incorrect or inadequate answer
   2 = Insufficient answer – a response has some relevance but was rather superficial and did not show any depth of understanding
   3 = Adequate answer – response was relevant to the question and demonstrated some understanding
   4 = Good answer – a response which demonstrated a good understanding and knowledge
   5 = Excellent answer – a full and detailed answer which demonstrates an in-depth knowledge and understanding of the subject.

Task 3: Presenting yourself as an interviewer

Duration: 10 minutes

This task discusses the demeanour you would encourage from a middle leader at interview.

1. Explain that a middle leader's role at interview is not to catch out, trick or eliminate candidates but to recruit for a reliable, inspirational colleague who will work with their line manager in the best interests of students. Discuss how body language, tone of voice and general demeanour can encourage rather than dissuade the best candidates.
2. Ask the trainees to discuss what kind of line manager they would hope to meet themselves as candidates. What traits would they deem to be professional and human? e.g.
   - Smartly but comfortably dressed
   - Warm and welcoming rather than austere and testing
   - Knowledgeable rather than vague or unsure
   - Well-prepared rather than disorganised
   - Friendly and inclusive rather than distant and hierarchical.

Plenary

Duration: 10 minutes

Finally, summarise your top tips for middle leaders in interviews. Ask your audience for suggestions and record them on a PowerPoint slide. You could include:

- prepare around five subject-specific questions in advance
- frame the questions in an open way and consider how you might prompt a more detailed response

- pick up on any subject-related issues raised by the candidate's application letter
- avoid leading questions or prompts
- make helpful notes that can provide feedback for unsuccessful candidates
- make sure demeanour is welcoming and professional.

What next?

To embed your trainees' learning:

- invite middle leaders to provide mock interviews for ITT students in your school
- build a bank of questions that middle leaders have used and share with other middle leaders when it is their time to participate in interviews for a post
- highlight blogs on interview process as wider reading.

Download the PowerPoint slides that accompany this training plan: 'Training plan 8 Conducting successful interviews' from the online resources: www.bloomsbury.com/CPD-library-middle-leadership

Bibliography and further reading

Ainsworth, P. K. (2010), *Developing a Self-evaluating School*. Continuum.

Ainsworth, P. K. (2012), *Get That Teaching Job!* Bloomsbury.

Allen, D, (2015), *Getting Things Done: The Art of Stress-free Productivity*. Piatkus.

Allison, S. (2014), *Perfect Teacher-Led CPD*. Crown House Publishing.

Bass, M. B. and Avolio, B. J. (1990a), 'The implications of transactional leadership and transformational leadership for individual, team and organisational development'. in *Organisational Change and Development* 4, 231–272.

Bennett, T. (2012), *Teacher*. Bloomsbury.

Blanchard, K. and Johnson, S. (2015), *The New One Minute Manager*. Thorsons Classics.

Collins, J. (2001), *From Good to Great*. Random House.

Covey, S., Merrill, A. R. and Merrill, R. (2015), *First Things First*. Franklin Covey.

Covey, S. (2004), *The 7 Habits of Highly Effective People*. Simon and Schuster.

Cowley, S. (2014), *Getting the Buggers to Behave*. Bloomsbury.

DfE (2015), 'School teachers' pay and conditions document 2015 and guidance on schoolteachers' pay and conditions'. Crown copyright.

Dunn, D. (2011), *How to be an Outstanding Primary School Teacher*. Bloomsbury.

Dweck, C. (2012), *Mindset: How You Can Fulfil Your Potential*. Ballantine Books.

Johnson, S. (1999), *Who Moved My Cheese? An Amazing Way to Deal With Change in Your Work and in Your Life*. Vermilion.

Lundin, S. C., Paul, H. and Christensen, J. (2000), *Fish: A Remarkable Way to Boost Morale and Improve Results*. Hyperion.

Morgenstern, J. (2004), *Time Management*. Owl Books.

Morris, P. (2000), *A Practical Guide to Fund-Raising in School*. Routledge.

Morrison McGill, R. (2015), *Teacher Toolkit: Helping You Survive Your First Five Years*. Bloomsbury.

Northouse, P. G. (2012), *Leadership: Theory and Practice*. SAGE Publications.

Parker, R. (2013), *The Reality of School Leadership: Coping with the Challenges; Reaping the Rewards*. Bloomsbury.

Smith, A. (1996), *Accelerated Learning in the Classroom*. Network Educational Press.

Smith, J. (2008), 'Leadership is a process, not a style'. *Secondary Headship*, Optimus Publications, Issue 69.

Smith, J. (2013), *Performance Management: Making Appraisal Work for Your School*. Optimus Education.

Smith, J. (2010), *The School Recruitment Handbook*. Optimus Education.

Stubbs, M. (2004), *Ahead of the Class*. John Murray.

Sutcliffe, J. (2013), *8 Qualities of Successful School Leaders*. Bloomsbury.

Syed, M. (2011), *Bounce: The Myth of Talent and the Power of Practice*. Fourth Estate.

Wallace, I and Kirkman, L. (2013), *Pimp Your Lesson!: Prepare, Innovate, Motivate, Perfect*. Bloomsbury.

Wiseman, L., Allen, L. and Foster, E. (2013), *The Multiplier Effect*. SAGE Publications.

Wiseman, L. and McKeown, G. (2015), *Multipliers: how the Best Leaders Make Everyone Smarter*. Harper Collins.

Yammarino, F. J. (1993), 'Transforming leadership studies: Bernard Bass' leadership and performance beyond expectations'. *Leadership Quarterly*, 10 (2), 285–305.

Index

Index